# Town and Country in the Middle East

# Town and Country in the Middle East

*Iran and Egypt in the Transition to Globalization, 1800-1970*

MOHAMMAD A. CHAICHIAN

LEXINGTON BOOKS

A division of
ROWMAN & LITTLEFIELD PUBLISHERS, INC.
*Lanham • Boulder • New York • Toronto • Plymouth, UK*

LEXINGTON BOOKS

A division of Rowman & Littlefield Publishers, Inc.
A wholly owned subsidiary of The Rowman & Littlefield Publishing Group, Inc.
4501 Forbes Boulevard, Suite 200
Lanham, MD 20706

Estover Road
Plymouth PL6 7PY
United Kingdom

British Library Cataloguing in Publication Information Available

**Library of Congress Cataloging-in-Publication Data**

Chaichian, Mohammad A.
  Town and country in the Middle East : Iran and Egypt in the transition to
globalization, 1800-1970 / Mohammad A. Chaichian.
      p. cm.
  Includes bibliographical references and index.
  ISBN-13: 978-0-7391-2677-6 (cloth : alk. paper)
  ISBN-10: 0-7391-2677-6 (cloth : alk. paper)
  ISBN-13: 978-0-7391-3220-3 (electronic : alk. paper)
  ISBN-10: 0-7391-3220-2 (electronic : alk. paper)
  1. Cities and towns--Iran--History. 2. Urbanization--Iran. 3. Cities and
towns--Egypt--History. 4. Urbanization--Egypt. 5. Globalization. I. Title.
  HT147.I6C45 2009
  307.760955--dc22                                                                2008032662

Printed in the United States of America

♾™ The paper used in this publication meets the minimum requirements of American
National Standard for Information Sciences—Permanence of Paper for Printed Library
Materials, ANSI/NISO Z39.48–1992.

# CONTENTS

## Part Three: Dependent Urbanization in Egypt

## Part Four: Divergent Paths of Dependent Urbanization in Iran and Egypt

# Preface

I became interested in the dynamics of spatial transformation and urbanization in Iran in the 1970s, when as a student I was working on my thesis at the University of Tehran's School of Architecture. This was a team project that I completed with my colleague and good friend Kamran Atai, who is currently the chief architect and urban planner in one of the leading architectural firms in Tehran, Iran. The project, a master plan for the city of Babol in the northern Iranian province of Mazandaran along the Caspian Sea took us on a three-year journey of numerous field trips and observations, countless hours of discussion, and a meticulous reading and reinterpretation of documents and field notes. The project included a comprehensive study of the city and its environs' demographics, patterns of rural-to-urban migration, and a detailed architectural plan for Babol's downtown revitalization. When in the late 1970s I was studying urban planning at the University of Michigan, I came to realize that there are stark differences, both historical and structural, between advanced industrialized societies and developing nations, in the ways city and countryside are interrelated as well as the processes of urban growth and urbanization. This theoretical awakening led to my defection to the field of urban sociology, particularly the critical sociological analysis of spatial transformations within a historical-comparative context.

This book addresses rural and urban transformation in two nations in southwest Asia and North Africa, namely, Iran and Egypt, related to their long-established economic and political dependency relations with Western colonial entities within the context of a global capitalist economy. It is a historical survey of the interface between town and country in the two nations spanning from the early-to-mid-19th century to the 1970s; a decade in which a new phase of globalization gradually altered dynamics of migration and urbanization particularly in developing countries. In the past three decades postmodern theories have celebrated a seemingly decentralized power relations at the global level, multiculturalism, and the dawn of "people's power" and "civil societies" specifically in developing countries. But in this book I will make the case that the post-1970s era has to be considered as yet another expansion phase of global capitalism that is geared toward facilitating economic and political control of developing nations by Western capitalist power houses, particularly the United States.

My historical analysis and documentation is based on the collective efforts of countless scholars and writers whose findings and intellectual contributions have been my guiding light. I am also indebted to my colleagues and friends Jo Dohoney for her encouragements and reading the original manuscript; Ayman Amer for reading the chapters on Egypt and providing me with up-to-date information and suggestions to refine my analysis; Masoud Kheirabadi for reviewing the final manuscript and his constructive recommendations; Linda Scarth and Marilyn Murphy for their kind support and spending countless hours to locate the hard-to-find documents and reformatting maps and images; and Kenneth Hall for his insightful suggestions to revise the book's title so that it is congruent with its contents. My special thanks also go to Patrick Dillon and Michael Sisskin, the Acquisitions Editors at Lexington Books for their support, patience, diligence, and constructive and thoughtful suggestions that greatly contributed to the book's quality and timely publication. Finally, I am grateful for the Production Department staff at Lexington Books, Michael Wiles in particular, who helped me in formatting the manuscript and finalizing maps and images for final production.

It goes without saying that I am solely responsible for the book's contents, both in terms of presentation and interpretation of data.

# Introduction

A systematic study of the historical roots of dependent urbanization in the Middle East in general, and in Iran and Egypt in particular has long been overdue. In this book I am particularly interested in the socio-spatial manifestations of dependent urbanization related to each nation's *incorporation* into the world capitalist economy before the age of globalization. Although globalization is not a new phenomenon, the new era of globalization can be defined as "[T]he closer integration of the countries and peoples of the world which has been brought about by the enormous reduction of costs of transportation and communication, and the breaking down of artificial barriers to the flows of goods, services, capital, knowledge, and (to a lesser extent) people across borders" (Stiglitz, 2002:9-10). In *The Conditions of Postmodernity* David Harvey (1990) also identifies two distinct historical periods of economic production and consumption modes, namely, the pre-1973 "Fordist-Keynsian" period and the "postmodern flexible production" period since 1973. Although Harvey does not consider the post-1973 period of flexible production as the new era of globalization, his critical analysis nonetheless provides a context in which all other theories of globalization can be comprehended. He considers the transition from first to second period as "a transition in the *regime of accumulation* and its associated *mode of social and political regulation.*" (121-124). The Fordist production was characterized by a rigid mass production, standardization, large inventories, vertical corporate structures, an increasingly deskilled labor force trained for performing single tasks but with collective bargaining power, and a regulating state that monitored fluctuations in production and consumption patterns via indirect income and price policies. In contrast, flexible production is based on "small batch" production with minimum to no inventories, a decentralized production process that relies on subcontracting and outsourcing, a two-tiered unskilled and skilled multi-tasking labor force with minimum collective bargaining power, and a deregulated economy under the auspices of an entrepreneurial state that intervenes directly when the capitalist economy is endangered due to a declining profit rate (Swyngedouw, cf. Harvey, 1990: 177-79).

Using David Harvey's two-stage global capitalist production model, I investigate the nature of the two nations' political economies and the extent to

1

which they were incorporated into the world capitalist economy from the 1880s to the 1970s (first stage). The process of *incorporation* during the first stage varies greatly from one peripheral nation to the next, as internal social forces such as class conflicts and struggle over the control of the state power have a decisive impact on the nature and degree of incorporation. Within this framework, I then set out to examine whether or not different *patterns of dependence* such as dependence on export of raw materials or agricultural products; associated *forward and backward linkages* between the major export items and the rest of the economy; and different *timing and modes of incorporation* have contributed to different patterns of rural-urban migration and "hyper-urbanization" in Iran and Egypt.[1] I consider the first stage of incorporation as integration of local production processes into a world-wide division of labor created out of the world capitalist system's need for expansion and capital accumulation. This is partly determined by the way capitalist expansion pursues particular ends such as 1) the immediate possession of important sources of production like land, minerals and other raw materials; 2) liberation of labor power from pre-capitalist agrarian economy and its coercion into the service of capital; 3) introduction of a commodity economy in pre-capitalist economies of peripheral countries; and 4) separation of trade from agriculture.

The rationale for selecting Iran and Egypt is rooted both in their similarities and differences in relation to their histories of involvement in international trade and eventual incorporation into the world capitalist system. In terms of similarities, both Iran and Egypt have a long history of what Childe (1964) calls "literate urban civilization." Second, at the present time the two nations are among the largest, most populated, and with a long history of urbanization in the Middle East. Third, although in different historical sequences, compared to pre-colonial urbanization both countries have experienced an over-concentration of population and its outcomes such as uneven economic and spatial development in a few metropolitan cities after their incorporation into the world capitalist system. For example, according to a United Nations report out of 16 cities of over one million inhabitants in the Middle East and North Africa regions only three cities had populations exceeding 5 million in 2000—Cairo, Tehran and Istanbul (UN-Habitat, 2004:1). Finally, at the present time both countries' economic organization is based on a combination of private and state capitalist development, which in turn has been shaped by the demands of an international market under the control of the multinational corporations. With regards to dissimilarities, the most fundamental is the two societies' incorporation into the world capitalist economy under different historical conditions: While Egypt became a British colony; Iran never lost her legal sovereignty and thus experienced a different type of dependency. Moreover, Iran's economic dependence was, and continues to be based on oil production, while that of Egypt was initiated by cultivation of long-staple cotton for the world markets that continued to be the dominant export commodity until the 1950s (Chaichian, 1988).

Related to hyper-urbanization, the field of comparative urban research has generally lacked a well developed theoretical framework within which to have a cross-cultural examination of the social, economic and political processes that accompany the rapid urban growth in major cities of the "Third World."[2] There are two discernible theoretical camps within the field of urban sociology. Modernization theorists attribute *hyper-urbanization* to unchecked population growth, rural-urban migration, and Third World countries' failure to conform to Western industrialization schemes. In criticizing these assumptions, Neo-Marxist political economists argue that the problem of hyper-urbanization is a symptom of "dependent" or "peripheral" capitalism.[3] But regardless of how one determines the causes, the consequences of hyper-urbanization can be identified as widespread poverty, proliferation of squatter settlements, low industrial wages, unemployment and underemployment, a bulging tertiary or service sector and the presence of a large informal sector in the economy of the cities.[4]

The book is organized into four parts. Part I is comprised of two chapters, and in chapter 1 I postulate that dependent urbanization is epitomized in hyper-urbanization which in turn is the spatial manifestation of a dependent capitalist economy. Using historical documentation and comparative analysis, in chapter 2 I identify three broad historical stages for the study of urbanization in the periphery: 1) pre-colonial political and economic developments (1800-1880s); 2) colonial penetration, organization and domination (1880s-1950s); and 3) neo-colonial domination through speculative investments and the control of import-substitution industrialization process by multinational corporations (1950s-1970s).

Parts II and III are devoted to a historical documentation and analysis of the socio-economic and spatial changes which have facilitated the process of dependent urbanization in the two countries. In particular, my focus is on "patterns of urbanization" created out of the interaction of spatial units such as cities and regions, and subsequent formation of spatial hierarchies. I also examine the political economy of dependent urbanization and petty commodity production in Iran and Egypt. By focusing on Tehran and Cairo as the two most important urban centers I examine the dynamics of uneven spatial development and its function for the maintenance of dependent capitalist economies in these two countries. Chapters 3-6 and 7-10 provide a systematic analysis of the socio-economic and spatial changes in Iran and Egypt from 1800 to the 1970s, respectively. In each part, I evaluate the relationship between town and country in pre-capitalist period and historical conditions which paved the way for dependent capitalist development and dependent urbanization in Iran and Egypt. Chapters 6 and 10 are devoted to a historical analysis of socioeconomic conditions that have contributed to the formation of "hyper-urbanized" metropolitan cities of Tehran and Cairo, respectively. In particular, I evaluate one important aspect of urban economy in the peripheries, namely, the employment structure of the petty commodity production sector for Tehran and Cairo. Since petty commodity producers are considered as a historical by-product of the process of dependent urbanization; I closely examine several occupational categories within this sector such as small scale industrial activities, self-employed artisans and service providers who facilitate distribution of consumer goods in the market place.

Finally, in Part IV (Chapter 11) I provide a comparative analysis of dependent urbanization in Iran and Egypt related to each country's unique history both in terms of internal and external processes of social change. The findings in this book indicate that different types of dependency have contributed to differences in timing of the two nations' first stage of incorporation into the world capitalist economy. In particular, there has been a significant time lapse between the origination of a dependent urbanization process in Iran and Egypt manifested in emergence of divergent patterns of urban hierarchy and urbanization as well as employment structures within each country's urban petty commodity sector. For instance, focusing on Tehran and Cairo as the two nations' capital cities I conclude that Tehran's sociospatial development in the post-1920s is comparable to that of Cairo in the aftermath of British occupation and colonization of Egypt in 1882.

The findings of this study indicate that by the mid-1970s Iran and Egypt were fully incorporated into the first stage of a global capitalist economy, to use Harvey's model (1990), but in various degrees have since resisted to accommodate the systemic demands of the post-Fordist globalization process (second stage). It is my contention that dependent urbanization in both countries has played a significant role in displacing rural population and inducing their migration to major urban centers, who in turn have challenged the ruling elites' efforts to complete the second stage of incorporation by demanding drastic social changes. Abrahamian (1982: 530–537) provides such analysis by examining the urban bases of the 1979 Iranian revolution, and Denoeux (1993, esp. pp. 154–156) examines the urban-based social and religious networks in Egypt and the role they play as formidable agents of social change and forces of resistance against globalization.

## Notes

1. In examining the effects of a particular industry on other activities, Hirschman (1958: 98–119) distinguishes between "backward linkage effects" and "forward linkage effects." The former arise from the input needed to supply production in a given industry; and the latter arise from the utilization of the output of the industry as inputs in new activities. See Chapter 1 for a detailed discussion of the concepts.

2. See Walton, 1976: 302; Safa, 1982: 3. The concept of "Third World" has long been refuted as an ahistorical and demeaning definition of all those countries which are caught in a cycle of dependent development under the auspices of an expanding world capitalist economy. As I will discuss later in Chapter 1, "Third World" nations are

identified as "peripheral" countries, in contrast to the capitalist countries that are controlling the world capitalist economy, or the "center."

3. See Castells, 1980; McGee, 1971; Mingione, 1981; Slater, 1978.   — !  all They based on 70's.

4. See Walters et al., 1980.

# PART 1

# Comparing Iran and Egypt: Theoretical and Methodological Considerations

# Chapter One

# Urban Political Economy and the Search for a Theory of Dependent Urbanization

The field of urban sociology witnessed the emergence of a new theoretical paradigm during the late 1960s. A proliferation of social anomalies and emergence of numerous urban crises across the globe challenged the dominant conservative theories and generated unanswered questions about "increasing class and racial inequalities rather than social integration, urban decay rather than ecological competition and succession, protest organization rather than anomic disorganization, and politics of domination rather than pluralism."[1] This new urban social science paradigm had diverse origins in theory and practice. But the works of writers such as Castells (1980, 1989), Lojkine (1976), Pickvance (1976), Harloe (1977), Harvey (1973, 1991, 2005), Hill (1977), Gordon (1971), and Tabb and Sawers (1978) had enough in common to constitute a general theoretical paradigm which might be called the "radical urban political economy."[2] Aiken and Castells (1977: 7) postulate that the new urban sociology focused on the urban socio-economic and political processes at a macro-level, used historical analysis in order to make sense of intricacies of urban problems, and emphasized the inevitability of the process of social change within urban systems. More specifically, the new urban sociology rejected the functionalist methods that isolated different parts of an urban entity and examined them as independent social units. Within this context, then, Castells (1978: 16-17) defines the political economy of urbanization in capitalist societies as the spatial manifestation of concentration and centralization of capital and "its constant battle against the tendency toward a lower rate of profit." This concentration and centralization as a part of capital accumulation takes place in a spatially organized environment. Based on the above assumption, in his study of urbanization in the United States, Hill (1977) further

9

defines a capitalist city as "a production site, a locale for the reproduction of the labor force, a market for the circulation of commodities and the realization of profit, and a control center for these complex relationships. Thus the capitalist city functions as a spatial generative center through which growing quantities of surplus product are extracted."

According to this line of analysis, urbanization in capitalist societies is an inseparable part of the general conditions of production, consumption and reproduction of social forces of production. Hence, peculiar forms of the capitalist city are considered as a direct outcome of the need to reduce indirect costs of production, circulation and consumption of commodities. Some consider the capitalist city as an efficient production site which will speed up the rate of rotation of capital, from investment to realization of profit and reinvestment, and reduce the period during which capital is not utilized productively (Lojkine, 1976: 122).

## Urban Political Economy and Dependent Urbanization[3]

The foregoing discussion represents the new field of urban political economy that is mostly concerned with urbanization in the core capitalist societies. Nonetheless, this has generated an impressive amount of research and propositions that distinguish between the nature of capitalist economic development in the *center/core* (developed nations) and *periphery* (developing nations) and their respective effects on urbanization. Studies of urbanization in the *periphery* are particularly exemplified in the works of Castells (1980, 1989), Gugler and Flanagan (1978, 1988, 2004), McGee (1971), Mingione (1980), Portes and Walton (1976), Roberts (1978) and Slater (1975 and 1978) that I collectively identify them as *theories of dependent urbanization*. The following discussion is an overview of the theoretical contributions related to dependent urbanization, which is of prime concern in this book.

In examining patterns of urbanization and industrialization in Latin America, Roberts (1978: 9) refers to urbanization in a classic demographic sense of the increase of "urban population as compared with the rural one," but as a direct consequence of "far-reaching economic transformations on the national and international plane." With both external and internal core-periphery relations being examined, Roberts stresses the "unevenness" of the pattern of "dependent development" and locates Third World cities in a worldwide system of capitalist production, consumption and accumulation (op. cit., 11-18). However, he considers an internal structure of class relations which functions to the economic advantage of the metropolis in the center and perpetuation of underdevelopment in the periphery. Related to urbanization, he puts emphasis on the importance of a class analysis and argues that while an analysis of the social structure of a city is based on its economic relations, one has to give equal weight to political structure as well. Finally, Roberts rejects the viewpoint that considers Third World urbanization as a problem of overpopulation in urban areas with high levels of unemployment or underemployment. It is not the lack of a stable, well paid industrial employment that causes overpopulation, he argues, but rather the contradictory process of capital accumulation in the Third World cities. That is, access to cheap and abundant labor not only powers the factories, but also provides complementary services and ancillary manufacturing for the benefit of the capitalist sector (Roberts, 1978: 6-7).

Similarly, Castells (1980) also asserts that the study of urbanization in developing countries must be integrated into an overall analysis of *underdevelopment* within a world capitalist system through understanding of the development-underdevelopment dialectic. In general, Castells identifies four significant characteristics of the urbanization process in the periphery as: 1) population concentration in large urban centers without integration into an urban network; 2) the absence of a continuum in the urban hierarchy; 3) socio-cultural distances between rural communities and urban areas; and 4) the ecological juxtaposition of the "native" and "Western" in societies that have experienced colonial rule (op. cit., 42-43). He further distinguishes three types of historical domination under which dependent urbanization reveals, in forms and rhythms, the articulation of economic and political relations of domination:

1. Colonial domination, with, as its essential objectives, the direct administration of an intensive exploitation of resources and the affirmation of political sovereignty.

2. Capitalist-commercial domination, through the terms of exchange, procuring for itself raw materials below their value and opening up new markets for manufactured products at prices higher than their value.

3. Imperialist-industrial and financial domination, through speculative investments and the creation of local industries which tend to control the movement of substitution of imports, following a strategy of profit adopted by the international thrusts throughout the world market (Castells, 1980: 44).

Among geographers who have criticized the inadequacies of development geography and have contributed to the political economy of dependent urbanization, Slater (1975, 1978) has a special place. Although his contribution does not exceed than few articles, some of his works should nonetheless be regarded as an introductory outline of the process of dependent urbanization in pre- and post-colonial periods. Following Bettelheim (1972), Slater adopts a structuralist position of the *modes of production* approach and attempts to formulate the historical specificity of peripheral capitalism. He identifies the growing international mobility of metropolitan (core or center) capital and further explains the main consequences of the capitalist penetration into the peripheries as: 1) the continuous extraction of the local surplus product; 2) the guaranteed self-expansion of foreign capital via the local state apparatus; 3) the non- antagonistic relations between the interests of the pre-capitalist social forces and those of the colonial capital which prevent the formation of a national bourgeoisie; and 4) the unequal nature of exchange between the core and periphery and the impossibility of an independent capital accumulation in the latter (Slater, 1978: 32-34). With regard to urbanization, Slater further identifies three phases of spatial structure under colonialism within a given colonized territory:

I. *Pre-colonial structure (before the 1880s)* which is characterized by the existence of the local and regional trading circuits, long-distance trading routes with a varying number of urban centers and in certain cases coastal trading posts.

II. *Colonial penetration, initial concentration, and the beginnings of internal expansion (1880s-1920s)*: the essential feature underlying this period, according to Slater, is the introduction of capitalism in the form of plantations, settler estates and mining centers into the pre-capitalist territories. In addition, the need for stable political conditions often led to the creation of a colonial state apparatus that could ensure the reproduction of a suitable environment for the functioning of capitalism. Finally, various types of urban centers (e.g., colonial capitals, administrative centers, strategic centers, local market towns, and mining towns) arose during this phase.

III. *Colonial organization and continued expansion (1920s-1960s)*: this period is marked by extensive agricultural and forestry concessions through further extension of transport networks, particularly railroads, and by development of one-line economies along the main arteries (Slater, 1975: 145). Furthermore, the urbanization process initiated in the second phase entered into a higher stage, that is, the development of an urban hierarchy in which the colonial capitals enjoyed the greatest concentration of industrial and commercial activities. Equally, colonial capitals and certain regional urban centers became pivotal points of centripetal transport networks. Despite rare attempts by peripheral states to initiate a decentralized national economy, the new colonial capitals were a clear evidence of an uneven development of the mainly externally oriented urban economies.

Slater sketched the preceding model in the 1970s, an era that David Harvey (1990) considered as the end of globalization's first phase.[4] My focus in this book is also on the three historical phases that are outlined by Slater. But at this juncture it is important to outline the main features of globalization from the 1970s to present time, or what Harvey identifies as the second stage of globalization based on a transition from *Fordism* to *flexible accumulation*.[5] The initial stage of this phase was marked by a diminished investment opportunities for multinational corporations followed by the Organization of Petroleum Exporting Countries' (OPEC) decision to raise oil prices in 1973, and increasing public discontent in the peripheries including Vietnam, Iran, Egypt and Nicaragua, to name a few. The economic recession in the 1970s unleashed more than two decades of intense economic restructuring in the center countries, particularly the United States.[6] This postmodern era of flexible accumulation is signified by creation of highly flexible labor markets at the global level; intensification of technological and organizational innovations in order to drastically reduce labor costs and increase rates of investment return; drastic expansion of the service sector and related economies; a 'time-space compression' process that uses satellite communication technology to speed-up the processes of decision-making, planning and production; and exerting more pressure on workers at all levels of production both in the *center* and *periphery* (Harvey, 1990:147-48).[7] As I will discuss in Chapter 11, the second phase of globalization has made its marks on dependent urbanization by drastically altering the center-periphery economic and political relations and imposing new financial rules on the governments in the peripheries via the IMF and the World Bank, as well as introducing new political players such as the non-government organizations (NGOs).

## Urbanization and Social Class Relations

The study of urbanization as a socio-economic process has to be based on a clear and unequivocal interpretation of spatial analysis, yet should not be regarded as a substitute for class analysis. Rather, as Soja (1980: 207) suggests, it can be an integral part of our understanding of the way various social classes resolve their conflicts and promote their economic and political interests. This necessitates a clear understanding of social class relations for both pre-capitalist and capitalist modes of production. Related to dependent urbanization in the periphery, colonial powers set out to undermine pre-capitalist social relations by separating the direct producers from their means of production in order to introduce capitalist relations of production. Historically, this has been achieved by a variety of mechanisms such as taxation, land reform, forced migration and settlement of tribal populations. In general, capitalist development in the periphery continues to be both "restricted" and "uneven" for two reasons. First, capitalist relations of production fail to establish their dominance in large sectors of economy such as agriculture, where economic relations remain mainly non-capitalist. Second, in cases where capitalist relations become dominant, they do not succeed in substantively bringing various labor processes under their control. For instance, while advanced industrial technologies are established in certain capitalist sectors such as extractive and import-substitution industries, production techniques in other sectors of the economy remain predominantly pre-capitalist. This is basically due to the lack of interest by colonial powers to invest and expand capitalist relations in sectors where capitalist development in the colonies might restrict the markets for commodities produced in the center (Taylor, 1979).

It is based on both the uneven and restricted nature of capitalist development in the periphery that we can define uneven geographical (spatial) development as well. Mandel (1968: 371-73) observes that regional underdevelopment is a universal phenomenon that manifests itself in unevenness of capitalist development in the industrialized center on the one hand and colonial/semi-colonial periphery on the other. In this process the industries of the former destroy the crafts and domestic production of the latter. As a result, a significant number of workers who are detached from pre-capitalist labor process cannot find employment in a nascent but growing dependent industrial sector. This leads to a chronic unemployment and an artificially induced over- population especially in urban areas. Based on the foregoing discussion and also theoretical contributions of Castells (1980), Gilbert and Gugler (1982) I identify four processes that delineate the dynamics of capitalist expansion and dependent urbanization in the peripheries.

First, disruption of pre-capitalist forms of agricultural production caused by a penetrating commercial agriculture and introduction of monetary taxes in rural areas induce rural-urban migration. As a consequence, urban and rural craft industries are undermined by the import of manufactured goods which in turn lead to a higher rate of unemployment among rural migrants and urban artisans. Second, surplus generated in the colonies, both monetary and in-kind, is usually extracted either by indigenous ruling classes whose interests in one way or another are in line with those of the capitalist interests in the center. Third, part of the rural work force and urban artisans in small towns who are detached from pre-capitalist forms of production gradually move to largest cities in search of employment. While a tiny portion of this migrant population is absorbed by the mostly capital-intensive urban industrial sector as wage-laborers, the bulk of the urban work force becomes involved in labor-intensive commodity production and service-related activities. Finally, the above processes are accompanied by an emerging centralized government bureaucracy in colonies, with the main objective of providing an adequate infrastructure for a dependent industrial development in the main urban centers.

## The Problematic of "Hyper-Urbanization" in Developing Countries

At the macro-level, the rapid rate of urbanization in developing countries during the post-World War II period led to the creation of a body of research on the so-called problem of *"over-urbanization."* By definition, over-urbanization meant a higher degree of urbanization (i.e percentage of population living in urban areas) as compared to the level of industrialization (i.e., percentage of non-agricultural labor force) in a given country. Based on the above definition, Davis and Golden (1954) took the percentage of economically active males not engaged in agriculture and the percentage of population in cities of 100,000 and more in a large sample of countries, and found a correlation coefficient (r) of 0.86 between the degree of industrialization and the degree of urbanization. Davis and Golden then presented the relationship between the two variables in a regression curve and found certain countries like Egypt, Greece, Korea and Lebanon to be significantly off the line (1954: 8). That is, related to their achieved level of industrialization their degree of urbanization was much higher than expected. Thus the above-mentioned countries were identified as over-urbanized with an "abnormal" urban growth.[8]

This cross-section analysis of urbanization was effectively criticized by Sovani (1954: 113-116) for ignoring qualitatively different stages of Industrialization. By separating the countries into two groups based on their level of industrial development, Sovani found the correlation coefficient (r) between urbanization and industrialization to be 0.39 for "developed" and 0.85 for the "underdeveloped" countries. Sovani concluded that "(T)he association between the two variables is much more closer in the underdeveloped countries than in the highly industrialized countries or, by implication, that the pace of urbanization in the underdeveloped countries is much more closely dependent on the pace of industrialization than in the highly industrialized areas."

Thus in the case of the developed countries, the correlation coefficient (r) became strong again when it was calculated for the year 1891 instead of 1950 (r = 0.84). Sovani also criticized another approach taken by UN/UNESCO (1957) that elevated in a quite ethnocentric way the course of urbanization and industrialization in four developed countries, namely, the United States, France, Germany, and Canada into a norm; and regarded the correlation between the two variables at different historical stages for these countries as a measure of normality. This led to the conclusion that Asian countries were over-urbanized because the four developed countries had a similar level of urbanization by the mid-19th century, but with a higher percentage of their labor force engaged in non-agricultural activities (UN/UNESCO, 1957: 133). Sovani called this formulation as "chimerical and so unusable" because of its implicit assumption that the course of industrialization and urbanization in all countries "should radiate more or less in close conformity to the path taken by them in the four countries mentioned, if it is not to be classed as abnormal" (1954: 117). Other critics like Brookfield (1973) and McGee (1971) also argued that even if it were valid to compare the present experience of the developing countries with those of the now developed nations in the past, no policy conclusion could be drawn from such comparisons (cf. Gilbert and Gugler, 1982: 163).

Much of the conventional studies of over-urbanization have also been concerned with city-size distributions in which the largest city (primate) is many times larger than the next city; with the primate city's alleged positive association with national development (Jefferson, 1939) or negative, parasitic relation to national economy (Hoselitz, 1955). In fact, in most cases over-concentration of population in the primate cities has been the sole factor for referring to a country as over-urbanized. But in the course of understanding the peculiarity of Third World urbanization the urban political economy paradigm offers an alternative analysis. For instance, Castells (1980: 41-42) acknowledges the significance of "primacy" and "over-urbanization" as a "point of departure" but looks for the theoretical means of posing the problem in non-tautological terms. Similar to Castells' historical-structuralist and socio-demographic analysis of dependent urbanization but with more emphasis on the issue of over-urbanization Mingione (1980) defines the "great urban areas of the Third World" as the administrative- commercial centers for import-export companies which function as the "bridgeheads of the penetration of capitalism into the rural periphery of underdeveloped regions" (Mingione, 1980: 134). In general, Mingione considers the rapid urban growth in the periphery as a "process of urbanization without industrialization and a conversion of rural over-population to urban over- population" (op. cit., 135). For him, an examination of over-urbanization (urban primacy) related to the underdevelopment cycle becomes the key issue in understanding dependent urbanization. He then conceptualizes three situations under which "over-urbanization" might occur in the "Third World." First, "over-urbanization and underdevelopment without any dependent industrialization" that is mainly based on the unequal exchange of exporting raw materials and importing manufactured goods. As a result, it is very difficult to increase employment capacity in the production sectors. Second, "over-urbanization and under-development with the addition of large and intermediate capital-intensive industries" that is dependent upon multinational corporations. In this case the capital-intensive plants consume a large part of local resources without creating enough jobs for the community, but they create a "politically important" yet "quantitatively limited" working class at the local level. Third, "over-urbanization" takes place due to export of valuable raw materials (particularly oil) some countries accumulate financial capacities, allowing the state to import whole processes or industries from advanced countries. Under this final stage of over-urbanization, Mingione concludes that the "Third World" countries are "unable to break the dependence and unequal exchange cycle" due to the capital- intensive nature of imported industries which are incapable of absorbing the surplus labor force; as well as the absence of producing-goods industries in the periphery that leads to further dependence upon core countries (Mingione, 1980: 138-144).[9]

Despite initial attempts by Marxist scholars to understand the process of dependent urbanization in the periphery, few studies have systematically tackled the process in which the emergence of one or two major cities retards the development of provincial centers and creates uneven urban growth in peripheral societies. Mingione's conceptualization of the problem should be considered as the first step toward a more detailed analysis of over-urbanization. The major problem with his analysis lies in the fact that there is no indication whatsoever of the processes which lead to over-concentration of population either in rural or urban centers in the periphery. Gilbert and Gugler (1982: 38-46) have tried to overcome this deficiency by providing a historical explanation of this process of urban and regional population concentration by identifying two historical phases: 1) the spatial changes associated with the export-oriented phase of the economy during colonial and early post-colonial phases; and 2) the spatial changes associated with the inward-oriented industrialization/modernization process in the post-colonial phase. During the first phase, the growth of major cities that leads to urban primacy is linked to the degree to which one or more urban centers control the flow of international trade and the generated profit. In most cases, concentration of the state bureaucracy and private interest groups in the capital are crucial factors in establishing the dominant status of this "primate city" over provincial urban centers. The second phase of spatial changes in the "Third World" was marked by the 1930s depression and the post-WWII process of import-substitution industrialization (ISI) in the peripheries. Since many of the new industrial enterprises were financed and/or controlled by multinational corporations, and because of the advantages and benefits of a central location, ISI has in most cases taken place in the largest cities with a tendency to "create a highly concentrated urban complex" containing "the bulk of the higher-income groups, the greater part of the social and economic infrastructure, the termini of the transport system, and the national government bureaucracy." Because of the uneven nature of dependent capitalism, the seamy side of hyper-urbanization is "widespread poverty, proliferation of squatter settlements, low industrial wages, unemployment and under-employment, a bulging tertiary or service sector, and the presence of a large informal sector in the economy" (Walters et al., 1980: 15).

## Dependent Urbanization and Petty Commodity Production

Many economists see the problem of development in the "Third World" as stemming from the division of the economy into dual sectors: a *modern* sector geared toward large-scale production for export, and a *traditional* sector geared toward small-scale peasant and artisan production for the domestic market (Safa, 1982: 5). The emphasis on the distinctiveness of each sector of the urban economy appeared first in the work of Geertz (1963) in Indonesia, who distinguished between the "bazaar economy" and the "firm economy." According to Geertz, the bazaar economy is made up of a large number of small enterprises. Being highly competitive, these enterprises rely on the intensive use of labor and seek to minimize risks rather than profit maximization. On the other hand, the firm economy is based on rationalization of production processes and capital accumulation for further investment and firm expansion. Geertz considered each sector as being antithetical to the other, that is, the existence of the bazaar economy limits capital accumulation and hinders the expansion of the firm economy, while the expansion of the firm economy gradually eliminates the bazaar economy. The dual economy assumption was further developed in the works of Chayanov (1966) and Franklin (1965, 1969), who identified two systems of peasant (informal) and capitalist (formal) production in the "Third World" countries. Friedman and Sullivan (1972) extended the concept by proposing a tri-sectoral model of urban economy comprised of a corporate production sector, a family enterprise sector, and individual operators. However, in all these studies, the informal economy was considered as an obstacle to the expansion of the firm economy.

The dual economy approach has been widely criticized for its mechanical view of segregation between the modern capitalist sector and subsistence activities of the poor. For instance, Santos (1977) emphasizes the dialectical relationship between these sectors in the form of two interacting and interlocking "upper" and "lower" circuits of urban economic activities having two distinct sets of characteristics. This type of exchange relations leads to a transformation of wealth which is directly beneficial to the functioning of the capitalist sector (see table 1.1). Studies by McGee in Southeast Asia (1971), Hart in Ghana (1973), and Souza and Tokman in Latin America (1976) also indicate that most of the urban poor work in small-scale enterprises which require a low level of skills and capital investment and often utilize the labor of unpaid family members to cut down on production costs. Some scholars of African urbanization have placed particular emphasis on the way in which pre-capitalist rural subsistence sectors subsidize the "formal" sectors and there-fore lower the production costs of labor in the cities (Meillasoux, 1980; Wolpe, 1980). Similarly, Roberts (1978) argues that the existence and growth in numbers of the poor in peripheral societies suggests that they function as a reserve army of labor for the growth and development of the modern sector of urban economy. He distinguishes between the "small-scale" and "large-scale" sectors, and defines the former to include all activities "which are associated with large-scale production such as craft workshops, repair shops, petty traders and self-employed artisans" (Roberts, 1978:114).

In another account of the relationship between the large-scale economy and small-scale enterprises in Peru, Scott (1978) argues that the independence of those working in the latter sector is largely illusory since in cities of the underdeveloped world, small-scale enterprises are often dependent on merchants and large-scale enterprises which provide capital and raw materials. Roberts (1978: 115) also points out that it is more profitable for large-scale firms to expand production by commissioning small-scale firms to undertake parts of their production. Furthermore, as the studies by Leeds (1971) for Brazil, Peattie (1968) for Venezuela, Hart (1973) for Ghana and Eckstein (1975) for Mexico clearly demonstrate, the small-scale economy is neither "traditional" in the techniques it uses nor in its types of activities. The coexistence and articulation of the large- and small-scale sector is an evident feature of cities in the peripheries. It is now also recognized that the informal economy does not develop simply in the interstices of the traditional activities deemed unprofitable by the modern sector. On the contrary, it is constantly reconstituting itself in response to changing conditions in the "modern sector" (Safa, 1982: 7).

In brief, the main criticisms of the "informal sector" concept may be outlined as follows. First, it has been argued that urban enterprises represent a continuum of scale and characteristics that do not fit in the two-division schema of the formal/informal economy (Missen and Logan, 1977). Similarly, small-scale enterprises reflect the fragmented nature of the entire labor market, rather than being an isolated economic sector (Breman, 1976). Second, the "informal sector" concept is problematic because of its inward-looking nature. That is, instead of emphasizing the integration of small-scale production into the totality of the production process, most studies have concentrated solely on the characteristics of "informal sector" enterprises (Breman, 1976; McGee, 1978). Third, the critics question the strong association of the "informal sector" concept with the conservative theory of modernization. For example, Moser (1978) argues that the utilization of the "informal sector" concept by economic planning agencies such as the International Labor Organization (ILO) has encouraged the view that the problems of unemployment, poverty and under-employment are the result of an imbalanced economic structure; and that a careful planning policy within the existing socioeconomic and political structure can solve the problem in less developed countries. Another critic asserts that because of the capital-intensive nature of capitalist production in "Third World"

**Table 1.1.  The Two Circuits of Economy in Underdeveloped Countries**

| | Upper Circuit | Lower Circuit |
|---|---|---|
| Technology | Capital-intensive | Labor-intensive |
| Organization | Bureaucratic | Primitive |
| Capital | Abundant | Scarce |
| Work | Limited | Abundant |
| Regular wages | Normal | Not required |
| Inventories | Large quantities, and/or high quality | Small quantities, poor quality |
| Prices | Generally fixed | Negotiable |
| Credit | From banks and other institutions | Personal, non-institutional |
| Relations with clientele | Impersonal and/or via documents | Direct, personal |
| Fixed costs | Important | Negligible |
| Publicity | Necessary | None |
| Re-use of goods | None, wasted | Frequent |
| Overhead capital | Indispensable | Not indispensable |
| Government aid | Important | None or almost none |
| Direct dependence on other nations | Great, outward-oriented activity | Small or none |

Source: Santos (1977:51)

cities the labor force detached from pre-capitalist forms of production could not be fully utilized. Thus, alongside an industrial work force a "semi-proletariat" emerges which is "sporadically employed in the state sector, the service sector, or in sectors dependent upon foreign consumption" (Taylor, 1979: 231).

In a similar analysis, Gugler (1982: 173-179) further identifies three types of "semi-proletariat" which he prefers to call "surplus labor in disguise." First, the *unemployed*, who, based on some regional estimates for 1975 comprised 6.9 percent of urban labor force in Asia (excluding China and other centrally planned economies), 10.8 percent in Africa and 6.5 percent in Latin America. Second, the *underemployed* or the underutilized portion of urban labor force that includes seasonal workers who depend on fluctuations in certain types of economic activity such as recreational services and construction; street vendors who give the semblance of fully employed individuals; and the artificially employed who are hired as members of a solidarity group (such as family enter-prises) even at times when there is insufficient work. Finally, the *misemployed*, who maybe employed full time but contribute little to social welfare. This is what may be called a lumpen-proletariat that embraces individuals like beggars who cannot be considered as productive workers within a capitalist economy. Castells (1980: 42) also considers the semi-proletariat as a "reserve army for a non-existing industry" in the periphery. Hence, a careful analysis of the "seamy side" of hyper-urbanization at the macro-level will help us to better understand the dynamics of dependent urbanization.

As an alternative to the dichotomous model of formal/informal sectors of the economy, a handful of scholars set forth the "petty commodity production" approach in order to analyze small-scale urban economic activities (Breman, 1976; Santos, 1976, 1979; Gerry, 1979 and Moser, 1978). The term "petty commodity" in this approach is utilized in the Marxist sense, that is, a product that has a use-value and yet it is produced for exchange in the market (Forbes, 1981: 117).[10] Others argue that a vast majority of small-scale enterprises within the informal sector fit into the category of "petty commodity production," a transitional sector that links pre-capitalist (feudal/agrarian) and capitalist economic sectors (Moser, 1978). For some, petty commodity production exists "at the margins of the capitalist mode of production but nevertheless integrated into it and subordinate to it" (Lebrun and Gerry, 1975:20). One important component of this integration is the transfer of value from the petty commodity to capitalist sector. To be more specific, the labor-time component of commodities produced in the petty commodity sector is exchanged for commodities produced by capitalists in the market which embody less labor-time, while in relative terms their prices do not reflect their greater efficiency of production (Santos, 1976). This results in a net transfer of value from petty producers to the wage-earners involved in capitalist production (Bienefeld, 1975). The unequal nature of exchange relations is inherent in the integration process, which leads to a transfer of wealth directly beneficial to the functioning of the capitalist sector. Petty commodity production therefore is not a static form of production in danger of extinction or elimination by capitalist production. In fact, some case studies indicate the opposite view, that petty commodity production is in a constant state of change with a tendency to convert pre-capitalist artisans into a wage-earning workforce and production based on capitalist relations (Bienefeld, 1975; Gerry, 1979).

The importance of petty commodity production for the maintenance of the capitalist sector is acknowledged by non-Marxist scholars as well. For instance, Hirschman (1958) distinguishes between "backward linkage effects" and "forward linkage effects" of a particular industry or economic activity on other economic activities. While the former arise from the input needed to supply production in a given industry; the latter originate from utilization of the output of the industry as inputs in new activities. Hirschman's analysis can be used as a conceptual tool in order to demonstrate the interaction between petty commodity and capitalist production in peripheral societies.

First, with regard to backward linkage effects, Gerry (cf. Moser, 1978: 1059) provides empirical evidence on the overwhelming degree of dependence of petty commodity producers upon capitalist industry in Dakar (capital city of the African nation of Senegal) for the provision of raw materials and basic technological equipment. Second, related to forward linkage effects, by citing several case studies Acharya (1983: 435) demonstrates how a large number of national and international capitalist enterprises sub-contract part of their production tasks to small-scale industrial units. The importance of petty commodity production sector for capitalist enterprises is best described by Roberts (1978: 17):

> Large-scale enterprises may be unprepared to risk expanding their fixed investments in the face of an uncertain market for their product and fluctuations in demand. It is more profitable to expand production, when necessary, by the out-work systems. . . . Since workers in these can be laid off with little or no cost when market demand drops.

Thus casual labor is employed by large factories and enterprises on a contractual basis with no commitments to provide medical benefits and pensions. Petty commodity production therefore becomes a convenient complement of the large-scale capitalist production due to the peculiar nature of market relations. Finally, in the realm of distribution, petty traders are utilized for marketing the commodities produced in the capitalist sector for a simple reason: to reduce distribution costs and accelerate the circulation of surplus value for its realization in the form of profit.

Based on the preceding discussion, I identify two levels of analysis for the study of dependent urbanization in Iran and Egypt: 1) the study of *patterns of urbanization* which focuses on the interaction of spatial units such as cities and regions, and formation of spatial hierarchies (see Hymer, 1971; and Cohen, 1981); and 2) the study of single *spatial units* such as a city or region with regard to the spatial requirements of pre-capitalist and capitalist modes of production. Related to the latter, I will compare and contrast processes of capital accumulation, production, and distribution of goods and commodities in the two hyper-urbanized cities of Tehran and Egypt.

## Notes

1. See Walton, 1981: 374.
2. See Walton, 1976.
3. Some scholars have deliberately chosen the terms "periphery" and "peripheral capitalism" for their specific meaning, instead of using "dependent" and "dependent capitalism." Slater (1978:29f) clearly points to the rationale behind this distinction:

> The concept of "dependent capitalism" is most clearly associated with Latin American literature on dependency and a weakness of much of the theory originating from this tradition is that the term "dependency" is too vague . . . as we can include Canada and Australia under such category. On the other hand, "peripheral capitalist" as used by both Amin and Sontag refers more specifically to those social formations that have originally been incorporated into the world capitalist economy as colonies and which continue to experience disarticulated forms of capitalist development.

However, "peripheral capitalism" as a concept tends to undermine indigenous social forces that affect the dynamic process of social planning and change in developing countries; and I prefer to use the terms "dependent capitalism" and "dependent urbanization" in my historical analysis.
4. See the Introduction for my discussion of Harvey's model.
5. On this issue see the Introduction.
6. "Economic restructuring" is defined as the shift from an economy featuring high-wage, unionized jobs to one in which corporations cut real wages, resist union organizing and shift production to low-wage sites overseas. For a classic discussion of historical origins and nature of economic restructuring see Bluestone and Harrison (1984).
7. For a discussion of 'time-space compression' and its contribution to a new regime of commodity production and flexible accumulation see Harvey (1990: 284-307).
8. In another attempt, Gibbs and Martin (1962) formulated a series of hypotheses on the dependence of the level of urbanization on industrial diversification (as an indication of division of labor), technological development, and the degree of a society's external exchanges. Based on the data for forty five countries, they then verified that the higher these variables, the higher the percentage of urban population.
9. "Producing goods industries" are simply based on the technology that enables core industrial countries to manufacture machines that produce machines that in turn

produce consumer goods.

10. According to Marx (1988: 46), "the utility of a thing makes it a use-value. But this utility is not a thing of air. Being limited by the physical properties of the commodity, it has no existence apart from that commodity. A commodity, such as iron, corn, or a diamond, is therefore, so far as it is a material thing, a use-value, something useful. This property of a commodity is independent of the amount of labor required to appropriate its useful qualities. . . . Use-values become a reality only by use or consumption: they also constitute the substance of all wealth, whatever may be the social form of that wealth." Based on this definition, items produced by the petty commodity sector enter capitalist relations when their "use value" is exchanged with money, equivalent to their "exchange value."

# Chapter Two

# Iran and Egypt: Comparing the Incomparable?

In his classic treatise *The Sociological Imagination,* C.Wright Mills *declares that* "all sociology worthy of the name is historical sociology" (Mills, 1959: 146). He further contends that a historical understanding of social, economic and political structures necessitates a comparative study of societies in different time periods:

> Comparative study and historical study are very deeply involved with each other. You cannot understand the underdeveloped, the communist, and the capitalist political economies as they exist in the world today by flat, timeless comparison. You must expand the temporal reach of your analysis. To understand and to explain the comparative facts as they lie before you today, you must know the historical phases and the historical reasons for varying rates and varying directions of development and lack of development (ibid., 151).

In this book I intend to examine comparatively how the two dependent economies of Iran and Egypt have variously interacted with an international political economy, and how the interaction between international and national socioeconomic forces has contributed to uneven urban development. In general, there are two approaches to the comparative method in the social sciences. The first approach aspires to the model of a controlled experiment whereby the cases selected for comparison have a great deal in common. The second approach maintains that vastly disparate societies may be studied on the assumption that certain "universal characteristics" may be discovered that hold across systems (Przeworsky and Tuene, 1970).

An alternative logic for comparison has been proposed by Lubeck and Walton (1979), who, in their comparative analysis of urban class conflict in Nigeria and Mexico go beyond a point-by-point comparison within a world systems perspective. For them, comparison is made not for its own sake; rather the goal is to achieve a full appreciation of both the similarities and differences.

25

This is done through a historical analysis of the circumstances under which different social entities have become incorporated into the world capitalist economy. Following Lubeck and Walton, I also consider Iran and Egypt as two "historically specific" entities that have to be understood in terms of their own social, economic, and political institutions during specific historical periods. Notwithstanding the importance of analyzing capitalism at the world level, it is my contention that the "national economy" has to remain the basic unit of analysis as a concrete, historically created social, economic and political entity (see Chinchilla and Dietz, 1981). This is particularly pertinent and applicable to Iran and Egypt prior to new phase of globalization process since the mid-1970s. I do not intend to uncover causal-deterministic core-periphery relationships that have affected socioeconomic and spatial developments in Egypt and Iran (e.g., Wallerstein, 1974, 1979). Rather, my analysis is based on an appreciation for the decisive role of internal forces such as class relations and state power that influence the course of events in interaction with colonial centers. Since the historical specificity of Iran and Egypt make point-by-point comparison impossible, and rather irrelevant, I identify four factors to examine dependent urbanization processes in each nation: 1) Differences in dependency relations; 2) different timing and modes of incorporation into the world economy; 3) patterns of rural-urban migration; and 4) the question of urban primacy. I will briefly sketch each of the four factors in the following section.

**Differences in Dependency Relations**

This refers to the types of economic relations in Iran and Egypt that have produced different forms of dependence after each nation's incorporation into the world capitalist economy. For instance, the discovery of oil and its production for the world market in Iran contributed to a specific type of dependence. First, excessive oil revenues enabled the government to import agricultural and industrial products and thus suppress and retard the development of primary and secondary sectors of Iranian economy. Second, the capital-intensive nature of oil production created no backward linkages since it did not rely on indigenous technology and support services and only employed a tiny labor force (Fesharaki, 1976; Girvan, 1976). Finally, Because of the oil industry's peculiar nature of extraction and exportation of oil, except for few localities in southern Iran it provided no considerable forward linkages within the national economy such as the development of petrochemical industries, or development of roads and highways and related industries such as automobiles and mass transit systems (Halliday, 1979).

Related to Egypt, the replacement of a subsistence agrarian economy with a mono-culture, export-oriented economy geared toward production of cotton for European markets set the country in a different path of dependent development.

First, unlike oil, agricultural production for export required an efficient infrastructure and transportation network and thus the need to invest a portion of the earned revenues in Egypt by the colonial administration (Crouchley, 1936; 1938). Second, unlike oil, agricultural production also provided a strong internal backward linkage, and due to its labor-intensive nature employed a considerable portion of the rural labor force while as an outcome of colonial policies the contribution of cotton cultivation to economic development and job creation in other sectors of the Egyptian economy remained minimal (Richards, 1982).

**Different Timing and Modes of Incorporation**

I postulate that the complimentary and sometimes contradictory patterns of interface between certain social classes who represent pre-capitalist and capitalist economic relations influence the structure and direction of development in Egypt and Iran (see Bettelheim, 1972; Balibar, 1970; Bradby, 1980). This leads us to the recognition of the role of the state and importance of "political-ideological" factors in reinforcing the economic and political power of certain social classes within each society (see for example, Poulantzas, 1973; Leys, 1977; and Munck, 1981). In general, two distinct possibilities regarding the penetration of capitalism in pre-capitalist societies can be perceived: 1) the "transitional period" in which the pre-capitalist and capitalist modes are both present, and state power is shared among representatives of dominant classes from each mode; and 2) the subsequent domination of class or classes representing one mode of production over other classes and the role of state as the sole political agent of the dominant economic forces.

Related to Iran and Egypt, we need to identify and define the prevalent pre-capitalist modes as well as the prerequisites for the introduction of capitalism into each of the two social entities. In general, at least two factors are needed as prerequisites for the presence and maintenance of a capitalist economy. First, monetary capital must be accumulated in the hands of a class which has effective control over the means of production. Second, direct producers in pre-capitalist economies must be effectively separated from their means of livelihood such as land and tools, so that they can function as wage-laborers in the newly introduced capitalist enterprises.

In order to understand the dynamics of the penetration of capitalist relations into pre-capitalist economies in the periphery and the historical outcome of such process I have identified three distinct historical periods:

1) Penetration of the periphery by European merchant capital (16th to mid-18th century); 2) penetration of the periphery under the dominance of competitive capital (roughly the 1750-1850 period); and 3) The colonial and neo-colonial stages (mid-19th century-present) during which pre-capitalist modes of

production in the periphery have been systematically undermined and in cases completely eliminated by an aggressive colonial strategy of introducing capitalist measures (see Lenin, 1968; Taylor, 1979; Hobsbawm, 1969; Castells, 1980).

**Patterns of Rural-Urban Migration**

In a study of migration patterns in Iran, Bharier (1972) argues that up until the 1930s there was no extensive rural-to-urban migration but movements of population "within" both rural and urban areas. On the contrary, rural-to-urban migration in Egypt started as early as mid 19th century, which in turn affected urbanization process (Richards, 1982). For instance, Egypt's agricultural production has always been contingent upon fluctuations of the aggregate demand in the world market. Hence, the socioeconomic structure of the rural communities and rural employment opportunities became contingent upon the ups and downs of the world capitalist economy. On the other hand, Iran for most of the 19th century remained a "semi-colonial" state that functioned as a buffer zone safeguarding British colonial interests in Asia from Russia's colonial interests and expansionist policies (Ashraf, 1971). In addition, production of oil for the world market had no direct effects either on rural or urban areas; since oil revenues functioned as a from of "collective economic rent" in the hands of the state functionaries that further made rural and urban development contingent upon state-sponsored planning (Fesharaki, 1976; Halliday, 1978). Therefore, urban and rural development in Iran always remained at the mercy of the ruling class and its state apparatus for planning and funding. This is an important issue that I will explore in the following chapters.

**The Question of Primacy**

As I discussed in Chapter 1, modernization theories in most instances have focused on city size distributions in which the largest city (primate) is many times larger than the next city. They have also emphasized the primate city's alleged positive association with national development, or its alleged negative and parasitic relation to the national economy (Jefferson, 1939; Hoselitz, 1955). In this book I am not interested in the question of primacy, but instead in "over-concentration of population in few cities," or "hyper-urbanization" (Abu-Lughod, 1965a; Mingione, 1980; Walters et al., 1980).

Over-concentration of population in few urban localities seems to be a universal phenomenon in peripheral countries. My focus in this book will be on two important processes, namely, uneven urban growth and concentration of economic activities in major urban localities, and the role of petty commodity production in the economies of Tehran and Cairo as the two "primate cities" in

Iran and Egypt. In terms of uneven urban growth and ensuing results, the 1930s depression and the effects of the Second World War led to the imposition of import-substitution industrialization (ISI) in peripheral countries as a universal colonial policy. Since many of the new industrial enterprises were financed and controlled by multinational corporations, ISI took place in the largest cities and accentuated the uneven growth and development of what is commonly known as "primate cities" due to the advantages of a central location for an effective control by the center (see Gilbert and Gugler, 1982). In Egypt's case, by 1965 almost 60 percent of trading firms, 72 percent of the brokerage firms, 52 percent of warehouse companies and 45 percent of the banking institutions were located in two hyper-urbanized cities of Cairo and Alexandria (Abu-Lughod, 1965a). These two cities also contributed close to 50 percent of the total value added by manufacturing and employed 45 percent of industrial workforce in 1976 (The World Bank Development Report, 1979). On the other hand, since the early 1960s modern industry in Iran was (and to great extent it still is) synonymous with Tehran, where about 40 percent of industrial workforce was concentrated; where there was a large and constantly growing service sector; and where all corporations had their headquarters (Kazemi, 1980; Looney, 1977).

## Issues Concerning Data Collection and Analysis

In this book I utilize several primary sources of data. The major primary sources for Egypt are: a) the population censuses for the years 1947, 1960, 1966, and 1976; and b) statistical indicators for the 1952-1979 period. All of the above sources were prepared by the Central Agency for Public Mobilization and Statistics (CAPMAS) that provide information about rural/urban population changes and rural-urban migration. As for Iran, the population censuses of 1956, 1966, and 1976 provide comprehensive data about population changes, migration patterns and employment conditions in urban areas. In particular, the 1976 Census investigates the patterns of rural-urban migration and identifies original places of emigration and final destinations, which are of great importance for the study of hyper-urbanization.

In addition to the primary sources, secondary sources are extensively consulted in this book as well. As for Iran, several studies investigate the historical roots of urbanization (e.g., Issawi, 1969; Banab, 1978 and Bahrambeygui, 1977). The rest of the studies may be categorized as 1) purely descriptive accounts of urbanization (Gaube, 1979; Boyne, 1961; Beckett, 1966; Bonine, 1979 and Kheirabadi, 2000); 2) modernization and developmentalist studies of urbanization (Clarke, 1966; Clarke and Costello, 1973; Costello, 1976; Danesh, 1987; English, 1966; Kazemi, 1980, Madanipour, 1998, and Paydarfar, 1974); and 3) demographic studies of urbanization which evaluate the extent of urbanization on the quantitative volume of population movement (Bharier, 1977; Paydarfar, 1967). As for Egypt, the works of Abdel Hakim and Abdel Hamid (1982) and Bonine (1997) provide a demographic analysis of urbanization. Of note is El-Shakhs and Shoshkes' study of globalization's effect on Cairo's growth (1998), and Ghannam's postmodern anlysis of urban space in Cairo (2002). But Abu-Lughod's "systemic-historical" approach to urbanization in Egypt is the most valuable source of information (1961, 1964, 1965a, 1965b, 1972, and 1989). Finally, several other studies have also tackled the problem of dependent urbanization although in passing and in general terms (e.g., Antoniou, 1979; Issawi, 1969).

The existing governmental data for Egypt and Iran are sometimes incomplete, or utilize generalized classifications and categorizations which do not fit the specific criteria being used in this book. But despite the absence of such data, this project aims at utilization and reinterpretation of existing data in order to initiate a debate and further research in the field. Several problems have made comparison between the two countries problematic. First, most of the statistics for the 19th century Iran and Egypt are at best "guess estimates," compiled based on the statements of travelers, military attaches, foreign advisors and traders. Thus utilizing the sketchy data to support an analysis always runs the risk of unwarranted errors. Second, there have been government-sponsored census enumerations in Egypt since 1882, but those of Iran started as late as 1956 with only semi-official statistics available for previous years. Also, the census years for Iran and Egypt are different, further complicating the matter. For example, for the third period (1950–1970) I had to utilize the Egyptian population censuses for 1947, 1960 and 1966, while relying on the 1956 and 1966 censuses for Iran. Although as I stated earlier the intention here is not to make point-by-point comparisons, the above shortcomings created difficulties in comparing even the processes of social change within each of the three historical periods. Third, there exists the problem of definition, both for historical accounts and statistical data such as variations in designating a settlement as a "town," a "city," or an "urban place" in the official and unofficial vocabulary of Iran and Egypt. For instance, for the 19th and early 20th century period one has to rely on casual observers and travelers who identified certain settlements as "rural" or "urban." Furthermore, there are no available data in the official censuses for the study of petty commodity sectors in Iran and Egypt. This made it necessary for me to reinterpret and create new relevant data, especially related to the Iranian situation.

In studying the role of petty commodity production in urban economies of Iran and Egypt, I had to scramble for limited information and insight in few studies and official statistics that pertain this important urban economic sector. In Iran's case, industrial censuses for 1963, 1964 and 1976 prepared by the Statistical Center of Iran are main sources of data. There is only one interpretive study of petty commodity production in Iran, and that is the "dualistic" approach of Amuzegar and Fekrat (1971) whereby they examine the coexistence of a large traditional (static) sector and an advanced (dynamic) export-oriented sector. Therefore, a careful analysis of the role of the informal economy (especially the small-scale industry) in Iran's socioeconomic activities has to be undertaken. As for Egypt, I have consulted several sources of primary data such as the annual labor force sample surveys for Egypt by CAPMAS, and the Egyptian Census of Industrial Production prepared by the Ministry of Finance. The works of Mabro and Radwan (1976), the World Bank's Survey of Small-Scale Industry in Egypt (1977), and particularly Abdel-Fadil's study of the informal sector employment in Egypt (1983) also provide valuable data about the role of petty commodity production in the Egyptian economy. A comparison between the "organized" component of petty commodity production in the two countries, namely, small-scale manufacturing sectors employing less than 10 workers, indicates the presence of divergent patterns. For instance, based on the 1973 data, while the small-scale industries accounted for 85 percent of Iran's industrial labor force and 43 percent of the value added, the corresponding figures for Egypt were 33 percent and 16 percent, respectively (Mabro, 1973; Mabro and Radwan, 1976). In his study of Egypt's informal economy, Abdel-Fadil (1983) estimates that 24 percent of Cairo's employment is provided by the small-scale manufacturing and handicraft activities. In Tehran's case, while no systematic research on the subject has been conducted as yet, the results of my analysis indicate a higher share of petty commodity production in its economy during the post-World War II period.

## Questions of Concern

Our historical journey in this book starts in the early 19th century, during which the pre-capitalist societies of Iran and Egypt were penetrated by European colonial powers that fiercely competed for the control of new markets and the supply of raw materials. Pertaining to urbanization process and changes in urban hierarchy and spatial structures, I have identified three specific historical phases (after Slater, 1978):

1) Pre-capitalist spatial structure prior to colonial penetration (before the 1880s); 2) Colonial penetration and the beginnings of internal process of economic and spatial expansion (1880s to 1920s) with a continued colonial organization and domination (1920s to 1950s); and 3) Neo-colonial process of economic and spatial concentration or *new dependence,* through speculative investment and control of the industrial development by multinational corporations in the peripheries (1950s to the late 1970s).

The exploratory questions in this study are formulated at two levels: 1) an examination of dependent urbanization in Iran and Egypt related to the dynamics of the world capitalist economic system; and 2) a focus on particular cities and their unique historical experience of spatial development. At the first level I will examine the overall patterns of dependent urbanization such as spatial hierarchy and historical specificity of rural-urban migration in different periods. At the second level, I will then analyze and compare the historical development of two cities of Tehran and Cairo in relation to their concrete positions both within the "national" and "world system" political and economic boundaries. By under-taking a comparative analysis of dependent urbanization in Iran and Egypt I intend to provide some answers to the following questions:

1. To what extent do different types of dependence and hence, different forward and backward economic linkages contribute to the development of different aspects of urbanization in Iran and Egypt such as urban hierarchy, uneven urban development, and communication and transportation networks?

2. What are the main areas of economic activity for the petty commodity sector in Tehran and Cairo; and to what degree have the petty commodity and capitalist sectors been articulated in the two cities?

Within above framework, I postulate two hypotheses. First, plantation systems and specialized export-oriented products contribute to the emergence of primate cities in the peripheries, and tend to restrict urban growth at the local levels. The uneven and enormous growth of a few Egyptian cities like Cairo and Alexandria since the mid-1800s, compared to a more "even" growth pattern of urban hierarchy and absence of a primate city in Iran up until the 1920s tend to support this hypothesis. Second, the differences in patterns of migration, rural-urban in particular, are related to differences in types of economic and political dependence.

# PART 2

# Dependent Urbanization in Iran

# Chapter Three
# Town and Country in Pre-capitalist Iran
# (1800-1880s)

*[handwritten marginalia: "not urban but local — in general?!"]*

Conventional historical accounts of pre-capitalist Iran by Iranian historians and authors are in general descriptive, in which historical developments and changes are understood through personal conflicts among the ruling kings and elites.[1] But few studies by both native and Western scholars have systematically analyzed pre-capitalist Iranian history which represents three distinct theoretical frameworks.[2] The first approach which has been developed and introduced recently, is an eclectic combination and theorization of Marx's concept of the "Asiatic mode of production;" Wittfogel's concept of "Oriental Despotism" (a la Marx) in the so-called "Hydraulic civilizations;" and Weber's "ideal type" of "Oriental Patrimonialism." In particular, this approach applies Marx's historical analysis of social change that characterizes inner dynamics of various *modes of production* and their *articulation,* and his labeling of many non-European pre-capitalist societies such as Arabia, Persia, India and Tartary as *"Asiatic,"* allegedly being qualitatively different socio-economic systems of production.[3] The fundamental principle of the Asiatic village community is that the individuals do not become independent of the community while these isolated communities are unified under the rule of a despot as the head of the central state. Hence the foundation of what Marx calls as "Oriental Despotism" becomes "(T)ribal or common property, in most cases created through a combination of manufacture and agriculture within the small community which thus becomes entirely self-sustaining and contains within itself all conditions of production and surplus production" (Marx, 1964: 70). Related to Iran, one scholar identifies the post-Safavid Iranian society from 16th century onward as an "Asiatic patrimonial despotic" entity (Ashraf, 1970: 313). By stressing the differences between the "urban structure of Iran and the West," or the persistent and important element of bureaucracy and the bureaucratic nature of land tenure in the former, Ashraf differentiates between the feudal system in Europe and

Iran's landownership institutions. He further argues that since theoretically speaking the Shah owned all arable lands and water resources, his arbitrary power to confiscate and redistribute the land prevented the emergence of a strong landed aristocracy as was the case in feudal Europe. Finally, he realizes the coexistence of "a trichotomous social system of urban, rural and tribal communities" in the Iranian society under a social system that fluctuated between centralization and decentralization of power (Ashraf, 1970: 313).

While Ashraf emphasizes more the "bureaucratic" nature of land tenure in Iran, Abrahamian (1974) focuses on the "fragmented" nature of the social organization in the Asiatic mode of production. Following Marx who sought the foundations for Asiatic despotism in the small "stereotypes" of social organisms such as clans, tribes, and villages (Marx, 1964: 69–71), Abrahamian pictures the 19th century Iran as a collectivity of social units that were economically self-sufficient and yet tied together by blood relations. Although he sees some similarities between feudal Europe and pre-capitalist Iran in terms of the existence of a ruling elite, a hierarchical social strata and ties of personal dependence between the lords and peasants; the political structure of the "Asiatic" societies in the Middle East is nonetheless different from the feudal monarchies of Europe in that the latter were "limited monarchies restricted by a hereditary and independent class of aristocrats" (Abrahamian, 1975: 129–30). Furthermore, Abrahamian argues that the "bureaucratic" theory of Oriental Despotism is useful in analyzing empires such as Egypt, India, China and ancient Iran, where "there were despots, bureaucrats, and irrigation works." But the same theory does not apply to 19th century Iran under the Qajars, where "the ruler was neither involved in irrigation works nor in control of large-scale bureaucracies" (Abrahamian, 1974: 8).

The second approach includes the works of Petrushevsky et al. (1967), the Soviet era Iranologists, who, based on Marx's unilinear theory of historical development divide Iranian history into four stages of primitive commune, slavery, feudalism, and capitalism. Thus Iran from sixteenth to mid-eighteenth century under the Safavids' rule is regarded as a centralized feudal society, while the 19th century Iran under the Qajar Dynasty rule is thought to be a period of the disintegration of feudalism as a result of colonial penetration. In the above context, then, some scholars regard the Iranian society of the 17th and 18th centuries as feudal "tout court" (Critchley, 1978; Jazani, 1978; Keddie, 1960, 1968 & 1972), while others characterize only certain periods as feudal. For example, Nomani (1972) argues that pre-capitalist Iran should be regarded as "feudal" from seventh to fifteenth century. The main characteristic of the Iranian feudal system was a peculiar form of sharecropping called "*Muzara'a.*" Based on this type of contract between the landlord and peasant the latter was obliged to pay rent, usually in kind, such as a share of the crop to the former. Then, during the 10th century, Muzara'a was replaced by a new form of conditional feudal ownership called "*Iqta*." This new form simply was a grant of land or its revenue, or both, which was made by the central government to its regional officers or governors.[4] According to this line of reasoning there are two significant differences between the feudal nature of Medieval Iran and that of Europe, namely, the nonexistence of demesne farming which reduced the landlords' role to an organizer of agricultural production; a combination of large-scale feudal landownership and small-scale peasant production; and 3) nonexistence of labor rent (Nomani, 1978: 119).

Finally, there are those who attempt to analyze Iran's pre-capitalist development within the "modes of production" approach by looking at the dynamics of articulation of different modes of production within the "Iranian social formation" (Lahsaeizadeh, 1984, Mahdi, 1983). Mahdi criticizes those who see pre-capitalist Iran as "feudal" for three reasons. First, while in a feudal economy the landlord is the owner of farmland, the majority of the rural population in Iran lacked any means of production and lived by tenancy and/or as hired laborers on extremely unfavorable terms. Second, based on Lambton's analysis Mahdi argues that the Iranian landlords did not own their land but utilized it under the system of "*iqta*" whereby "the lands were the exclusive property of the state."[5] Thus in many cases the *muqta's* (the holders of iqta) "could transfer their iqta's to their children or even sell them." However, they could do so only with regard to the right of possession and not the property rights, that is, "they could transfer their right of usufruct, but not the ownership rights which they did not have." Third, in contrast to feudal relations in which peasants are dependent on the landlords, in the Iranian situation the state was the sole owner of the land and peasants were being exploited not as an individual but as a member of the village community (Mahdi, 1983: 65–67). Mahdi also questions Marx's concept of the "Asiatic mode of production" which characterizes the Oriental societies as lacking any internal dynamics of their own for change. He utilizes the "Asiatic mode" concept within the "modes of production" approach and refers to the pre-capitalist Iranian society as "Asian." That is, while the Asiatic mode of production was the dominant mode, different modes such as feudalism, pastoral-nomadism and small independent production in both agriculture and handicraft manufacture coexisted with it. To support his claim, he considers the contradictory tendency toward centralization of power through the practice of iqta and decentralization of political authority by means of the development of feudal relations in the provinces as a sign of continued tensions between the ruling classes representing Asiatic and feudal modes of production. Thus in different historical periods, the feudalization of social relations has signaled the structural disintegration of the central state and vice versa (ibid., pp. 112–117).

A careful study of pre-capitalist Iranian history reveals the fact that indeed tribal forces have always been an important element of conflict in the quest for domination and political power. Following Smith (1978) and Lambton (1970), Mahdi (1983: 123–24) points out that many Iranian dynasties have come to power on tribal support. For instance, from the Arab conquest in the seventh century up to the early decades of the sixteenth century the Iranians have been ruled by tribesmen of foreign origin. From then on, they were subjected to the whims and wishes of Iranian tribesmen such as the Safavids (1502-1736 A.D.); the Afsharids (1736-1747 A.D.); the Zands (1751-1795 A.D.) and the Qajars (1796-1925 A.D.). The economic backbone of tribal life in Iran was pastoral-nomadism, a distinct mode of production with its own laws of motion and operating under three conditions: 1) lack of a clear conception of land-ownership; 2) a mode of production based on appropriation and exploitation of animals and pastures through organization of patterns of movement and residence; and 3) lack of market and monetary exchange among nomadic tribes (Mahdi, 1983).

The assumption of political power by the ruling strata representing a pastoral-nomadic socioeconomic system manifests itself in the ideological tenets of a ruling elite of pastoral-nomadic origins. Describing a complicated system of land tenure among an Iranian Kurdish tribe in the first half of the 19th century, Rawlinson (cf. Lambton, 1953: 142-43) provides a vivid example of the nature of land assignments based on pastoral-nomadic social relations:

> The country, acquired in war, was originally held as direct property of the chief. From him it descended to his family, and thus, at the present day, the proprietorship of almost the whole of this extensive country is in the hands of a single family, the Baba Amireh. . . . This small family, which does not number above fifty or sixty people, cannot be supposed capable of cultivating all the lands, and a system has been introduced, by which the chief of the tribe can assign any portion of the country that he pleases to the care of other inferior leaders, called Aghas, with or without the consent of the proprietor.

Related to pre-capitalist Iran, it is my contention that what in fact in the Marxist analysis is recognized as the "Asiatic mode of production," was the historical necessity of the existence of an organizing bureaucracy by a ruling stratum with tribal origins. Continuous conflict between feudal relations of production in terms of land ownership and a decentralized political power in rural Iran on the one hand, and pastoral-nomadic relations represented by the system of iqta and an over-arching centralized state on the other testify to the constant tension both at the infrastructural (economy) and super-structural (polity) levels in pre-capitalist Iran. This required a strong and efficient administrative body capable of maintaining control over fragmented socioeconomic enclaves that were comprised of a complex of villages, towns and tribal communities. Each of these socio-economic entities had their regional networks of interaction that often functioned under various socio-economic and political realities. Thus, as I shall discuss in Chapter 4, the emergence of feudal relations of production based on private ownership of land and political-jurisdictional power of local feudal rulers becomes dialectically related to the weakening of a centralized state in the hands of tribal rulers.

## Pre-capitalist Iran's Initial Contacts with Europe

The Iranian pre-capitalist Society came into contact with the newly emerging world capitalist economy in the 16th and 17th centuries. First, by conquering many coastal cities in the Persian Gulf area, the Portuguese entered Iran in the first decade of the sixteenth century. Then, Britain's considerable industrial growth and nascent capitalist development in the 16th century and her urgent need to find external outlets for her surplus woolen products led to her first expedition to extend foreign trade with Iran in the 1550s. This was followed by the Dutch involvement in the region's trade in the 1580s as well as the French in the 1660s (Savory, 1980; Mahdi, 1983; Glamann, 1958; Peretz, 1963).[6] However, Iran's early involvement in the world capitalist economy was primarily commercial and limited to the coastal regions in the Persian Gulf.

By the end of the 18th century, Iran's economy and politics were increasingly influenced by two major factors: 1) consolidation of British power in India; and 2) emergence of Russia as a competitive economic and political force in international affairs particularly related to Iran, Afghanistan and Central Asia. In regards to Iran, Russia's imminent threat to the interests of the British in the region forced the latter to change her regional policy in the early 19th century from promoting free trade to a more structured political and economic strategy with Iran.

Internally, as a result of an ongoing conflict and rivalry within the Qajar tribe itself, and between the Zand and the Qajar tribes, the latter assumed political power in 1796. In order to control and run the country, a centralized administrative system was established by the Qajars which consisted of two segments: 1) the central government comprising the ministerial offices headed by the office of the "grand vizier" (prime minister); and 2) provincial governments which were run and controlled by the central government's appointed governor-generals. The regional governor-generals were either the local feudal nobles or tribal leaders, signaling the contradictory nature of political control in pre-capitalist Iran (Avery, 1965: 83–87).

That is, while through the practice of iqta and tax collection the central government was controlled by the rulers of pastoral-nomadic origin, feudal landowners in provinces made every effort to establish their own local political and economic power if and when they could resist the central government's authority (Keddie, 1960: 6). Thus the weaker the central government, the stronger the feudal governors became and vice versa.

It was within the above internal and external historical conditions that the Russian and British imperial powers sought to maintain their political and economic influence in Iran's internal affairs. As an outcome of this colonial rivalry Iran never became a formal colony. Rather, as one interpreter of 19th century Iranian politics explains, she "survived as a buffer state between the expanding Russian appetite for the South, and the British policy of the defense of India" (Ashraf, 1971: 30). For example, in 1801 the British sent an urgent mission to Iran pursuing three clear objectives—to obtain Iranian military assistance to suppress the political Afghan threat to her Indian interests; to neutralize the French in their plan to seek Iranian military assistance in a joint-operation with Russia against Indian territories; and to obtain new commercial agreements allowing free operation of British merchants in the Iranian territory (Mahdi, 1983: 462). Eventually, in 1872 Iran granted a mineral exploration concession to the Britisher Baron de Reuter which was the most comprehensive and extraordinary "surrender of the entire industrial resources of a kingdom into foreign hands." The concession gave de Reuter an exclusive right to construct the Iranian railway system and all the needed public land; to exploit all mines except precious metals and stones; and to establish a new privately owned and operated banking system (Corzon, 1966: I, 480).

Related to Russian colonial interests beyond her southern borders, after Iran's defeat in the Russo-Iranian battle of Aslanduz in 1812 a vast part of the Northern Iranian territory was ceded to Russia under the terms of the infamous Golestan Treaty. Russia's violation of this treaty erupted into another conflict that ended with Iran's defeat and culminated in the second Russo-Iranian treaty of "Turkomanchay" in 1828. In addition to lost territories Iran agreed to grant "extra-territorial rights to Russian citizens living in Iran, such as owning homes, shops and warehouses; and granted Russians a low fixed custom duty on goods exchanged between the two nations." (ibid., p. 467).

The above-mentioned political and economic subordination of the Iranian government to the British and Russian interests in the region is what Ashraf (1971), Mahdi (1983), and Mehrain (1979) call the "semi-colonial situation" in Iran.[7] Mehrain (1979: 54) brings four reasons for Iran's semi-colonial situation, namely, presence of a centralized state, a dispersed population residing on a vast territory, lack of desired natural resources (at least until the end of 19th century), and demands of the British/Indian and Russian economies "which were more for markets attainable through trade concessions and less for capital investment outlets which would have required more direct administrative control."

The consequences of this semi-colonial situation were severe and manifested themselves in the peculiar economic and political relations in 19th century Iran. First, while the competition among rival colonial powers helped the central government to maintain its grip over the country, the ruling elite had to adopt a careful foreign policy in order to maintain a delicate balance between the two major powers. This consequently led to their increasing dependence on one or the other colonial power and assumption of a clientele role (Ashraf, 1971: 22). For example, on three occasions of succession during the Qajar dynasty's rule, namely, Mohammad Shah in 1834, Nasser od-Din Shah in 1848, and Muzaffar od-Din Shah in 1896 the "open show of support" by the British or Russian governments was necessary for each of these successions to take place (Avery, 1967: 47). Iran's piecemeal integration into the world capitalist economy also resulted in the gradual disintegration of inflexible local markets and underdevelopment of indigenous local industries, as the fixed custom duties put the Russian and British merchants in an advantageous position in exchange of goods with their Iranian counterparts (Ashraf, 1971: 467; Mahdi, 1983; 467).

## Rural Iran: The Politics of a Rugged Terrain

Physically, a complex of mountain chains makes up much of the scenery of Iran and encloses a series of interior basins. But one can identify four distinct physiographic units in the country. First, the Zagros mountain range that extends from northwest to southeast occupying the entire western part of Iran. Second, the northern highlands of the Alburz range that functions as a continuous wall separating the northern Caspian Sea provinces from the interior desert basins to its south. Third, the eastern and southeastern Iranian region consisting of a number of "upland massifs," and finally the interior desert basins contained within the surrounding mountain ranges of Zagros, Alburz and eastern highlands. This interior basin receives a low rainfall, of about 1-6 inches per annum and covers an area of over 300,000 square miles, or more than one-half of the total land area (Fisher, 1968) (see Figure 3.1).

While Egypt, for example, had the Nile as her prime means of internal communications, in the absence of roads and navigable rivers, the Iranian provinces were separated and isolated from each other by natural barriers. Except for the Alburz region and north-west Zagros area, the aridity of the Iranian climate, the huge size of the territory, and the ruggedness of its terrain made it a difficult task for the central governments to have a firm grip over the Iranian territory. However, up until the sixteenth century Iran's location on the well known overland trade route known as the "Silk Road" that linked the Near East to Central Asia and China to certain extent offset the consequences of geographical isolation. The shift in world

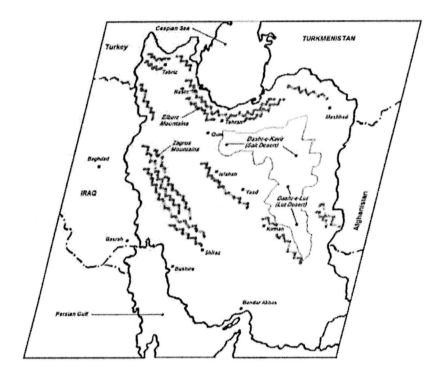

**Figure 3.1. Iran's Physiographic Map**

trade routes from land to the sea during the 16th century negatively affected Iran's
advantageous trade position in the region, which was once bringing prosperity to
several Iranian cities such as Kermanshah, Hamadan, Marv and corresponding
regions, (Issawi, 1971: 3).

The spatial configuration of pre-capitalist Iranian territory is conceived by
many scholars as a "trichotomous" socioeconomic and political system of urban,
rural, and tribal units. Following Marx, some see the units as fragmented social
organizations which in most part were self-sufficient and coexisted under an
over-arching state apparatus or "patrimonial ruler" (Ashraf, 1971; Abrahamian,
1974; Mehrain, 1979; Mahdi, 1983). Others look for the regional integration and
interdependence of the three units in different parts of Iran. In his now classic work
"City and Village in Iran," English (1966) considers the relation between the three
as an "ecological trilogy" which is dominated by urban centers. This dominance
was extended through the concentration of decision-making strata of rulers, land
holders and merchants in urban centers, and their control over agricultural pro-

duction, craft industries, and animal husbandry (ibid., pp. 87–97). The urban-rural-tribal trilogy can be best described as spatial manifestation of the presence of two modes of production, namely, pastoral-nomadic and feudal, as well as Iran's involvement in international trade.

Unlike Egypt, pastoral-nomadic way of life greatly affected political and economic relations in pre-capitalist Iran. Due to the lack of readily available arable lands and constant water supplies on much of the Iranian territory, the sedentary life over greater parts has always been difficult if not impossible. Instead, environmental limitations for a viable sedentary way of life made pastoral-nomadism a feasible alternative. The social organization of pastoral- nomadism has evolved in time and in line with the development of a hierarchical social structure. At the upper level of tribal social hierarchy there existed a "camp" headed by a recognized leader (*Khan*) who was usually the head of the most prominent tribal family (Mehrain, 1979: 59–61). Under this central authority there were various sub-tribes (called "*tayefeh*," "*dasteh*," or "*tireh*") headed by sub-tribal leaders (*Kalantar*). The Kalantars were directly responsible to the Khan who was assisted by a small group of functionaries (Barth, 1961). The kinship ties were the most important regulatory factor in tribal affairs, defining who belonged to what community and mediating between the tribe and external communities.

With regard to the land ownership question, all tribal lands in pre-capitalist Iran were "crown lands" belonging to the central authority, whereby the tribes were assigned rights of usage in return for payment of taxes (Mehrain, 1979: 63). But in some parts of Iran such as the Fars province the tribal pastures legally belonged to tribal leaders in whose names they were registered (Lambton, 1953: 284). In most cases powerful khans also monopolized the control over the organization of production and the extraction of surplus production. This at times was expanded over certain villages in which peasants gave dues, mostly in kind, to the khans in return for an agreement for peaceful coexistence and non-interference. Thus the practice of iqta made the tribal khans hardly distinguishable from feudal landed proprietors (Sunderland, 1968: 638).

The spatial configuration in pre-capitalist Iran was also affected by socioeconomic interaction between people who operated under different social relations pertaining pastoral-nomadic and feudal modes of production. In times of difficulty due to droughts and epidemics, the village life seemed to be more attractive to the pastoral-nomadic population as compared to their own less secure life-style. On the other hand, harsh treatment and exploitation of villagers by the central government and their agents in provinces induced peasants to leave the land and adopt a nomadic way of life. Sometimes this "nomadization" was imposed upon the settled population by force due to the ravages and devastation caused to their settlements by tribal raids. The Mongol invasion is a prime example of a forced nomadization (de Planhol, 1968: 414). However, since it was economically difficult for tribal units to integrate peasants who owned few or no animals to their system of production, the general trend was mostly the movement from nomadic to settled communities (Sunderland, 1968: 641) (see figure 3.2).

Social interaction between nomads and villagers, however, was not always based on amicable terms. In fact, there has always been a conflict of interests between pastoral-nomadic and the settled populations in villages and towns. In many areas, when the tribe's migration route passed through cultivated areas considerable damage was inflicted to the crops. Due to the precarious nature of nomadic life and periodic hardships the Iranian tribes in various occasions have also assaulted the settled population and robbed them off their food supply (Mahdi, 1983: 145). On the other hand, at the economic level the village communities were in need of pastoral produce such as animals and animal byproducts, and the tribes were dependent upon village commodities such as handicrafts and tools. This mutual interdependence in the form of economic exchange kept in check the violent conflicts between the settled and nomadic groups.

## Socioeconomic and Spatial Characteristics of Iranian Villages

Because of the arid climate over much of the Iranian territory, most of the cultivation depended on obtaining water in the highlands either from rivers or through construction of elaborate underground conduits or "*qanat.*" But qanats required a great deal of maintenance and organized collective activity in order to secure an adequate water supply to a village community.[8] Thus in the absence of large rivers and because of a chronic shortage of water, agricultural irrigation networks always played a significant role in the maintenance and survival of rural communities (see figure 3.3). The scarcity of water and its limited availability for agriculture became a significant factor in determining the site of rural settlements. Putting aside the exceptions, the majority of villages in nineteenth century Iran were small, and a large number of them were comprised of fewer than a hundred inhabitants. Most villages were small clusters of dwellings with a few facilities such as a mosque, few shops and a community bathhouse (Behnam and Rasekh, 1969: 193).

In general, the peculiar geographical conditions in Iran were a decisive factor in creation of small, isolated and economically self-contained village communities. Despite the recognition of private landownership by Islamic laws, the agricultural land belonged to the entire Muslim community. But in reality the control and utilization rights belonged to the king and his appointed regional functionaries. Thus the peasants in most cases enjoyed usufruct rights only, but were obliged to pay hefty taxes. During this period the peasants consisted of four distinct groups: 1) rich peasants who employed the landless peasants and peasants had agricultural

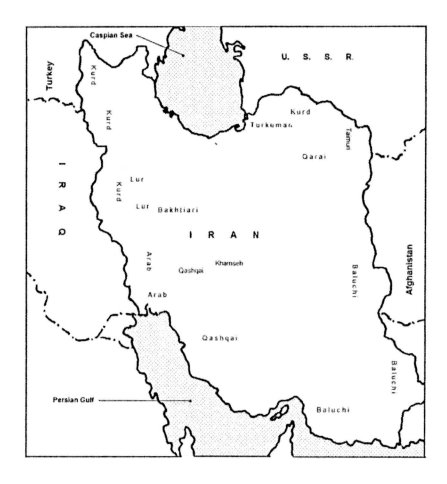

**Figure 3.2. Geographical Location of Various Tribes in Iran (1945)**
Map created based on information from: United States, Office of Strategic Services.
Research and Analysis Branch (1945). Original map courtesy of the Map Collection
Library, University of Iowa.

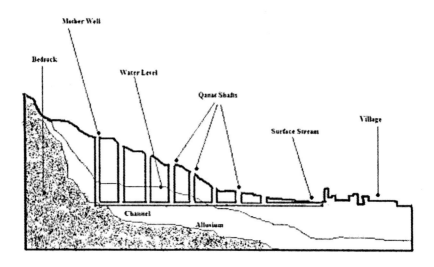

**Figure 3.3. Cross-section of a Typical Iranian Qanat**
(image adopted from a sketch in Corliss, 1999).

cultural surplus; 2) middle peasants who worked on their own land as well as on the landholders'; 3) poor landless peasants who comprised the majority of rural population and enjoyed the right to use the landlord's land; and 4) landless agricultural workers who lived through the sale of their labor power in return for money or contributions in kind (Vali, 1980: 26–29).

The social organization in the villages was similar to that of the tribes, that is, like tribal kalantars one agricultural and judicial headman or "*kadkhoda*" was in charge of the village affairs. In addition, kadkhodas were usually assisted by a "*mirab*" and a "*mullah*," the former in charge of distribution of water supply for irrigation, and the latter serving as a religious, judicial and educational authority in the village. This trilateral local power structure facilitated tax collection and helped the peasants to build and maintain rural infrastructures such as irrigation canals and community buildings (Mehrain, 1979: 67). While the trilateral alliance mainly functioned to organize economic production process at the village level, the real economic power and political authority remained in the hands of official represent-tatives of the provincial or central governments.

## Urban Iran and the Question of the Unity of Town and Country

One of the major differences between spatial organization in pre-capitalist Iran and that of feudal Europe was the relation between town and country. Many Medieval cities in Europe were autonomous and independent units functioning as centers for craftsmen and traders, while the real political power resided in the villages where the feudal lords built their fortified castles. Thus town and country were separated and this enabled the townspeople to challenge the feudal lords and develop autonomous cities. This observation of the historical development in the West has led many to the conclusion that the contradiction between town and country is a universal phenomenon since they are two different and independent entities. In his early writings, Marx (1980: 27–29) also considered the separation of town and country as the "most important division of material and mental labor" and as a clear outcome of the separation of capital and landed property. But the absence of private landownership in most Asian societies led Marx to clarify them by some specifications other than those of the European communities:

> Ancient classical history is the history of cities, but cities based on land-ownership and agriculture; Asian history is a kind of undifferentiated unity of town and country (the large city, properly speaking, must be regarded merely as a princely camp, superimposed on the real economic structure); the Middle Ages (Germanic period) starts with the countryside as the locus of history, whose

further development then proceeds through the opposition of town and country; modern (history) is the urbanization of the countryside, not, as among the ancients, the ruralization of the city (ibid., pp.77–78).

Many observers and travelers have considered the walled cities and villages in the "Islamic Orient" as independent socioeconomic units, each with its own independent and self-contained structure. But similar to Marx's argument, some scholars of the nineteenth century Iran have viewed this rural-urban reality differently. For instance, in his analysis of the spatial characteristics of pre-capitalist Iran, Ashraf (1974: 42) asserts that: 1) the town-country relation was one of contradiction and mutual interdependence; 2) town and country shared similar cultural traits despite their alleged cultural diversities; and 3) there was no distinct spatial separation or concentration of agricultural activities in the country-side, and those of industries and trade in the cities. This also indicates the lack of a distinct division of labor between town and country in pre-capitalist Iran.

There exist numerous historical evidence to support the fact that many cities had rural functions, and that many villages served as centers for local industry and regional trade. In some cases cities emerged out of the spatial junction of several villages. Provincial cities of Qazvin and Kazerun are prime examples in which one could not distinguish the separation between town and countryside, since each village unit was transformed into a neighborhood in the newly formed "urban" conglomerate. In addition, the walled city suburbs were utilized for gardening and other forms of agriculture, and in some cases agricultural production took place within the city boundaries (Lapidus, 1969: 64; Ashraf, 1974: 42). In fact, many Iranian cities have been surrounded by crop fields and fruit gardens. Mosto'fi (1957: 53, 65) describes 19th century Isfahan as "comprised of four villages with plenty of vegetable and fruit produce," or Qazvin as "the city of fruit gardens and vegetable plots."

Economic trade and commodity production was not the only prevalent activity among the city dwellers either. Many artisans and traders were part-time peasants who produced agricultural products for each city's market or "bazaar." For example, in the early 19th century the majority of the 50,000 inhabitants of Tabriz, Iran's largest and most important commercial center in the northwest were involved in agricultural and not industrial production (Ashraf, 1974: 44). Conversely, many settlements considered as villages, presumably because of their relatively small size, were centers of industrial activities, periodic markets, and external trade (Lapidus, 1969: 65–66). In studying Ferdaus, an "urban region" in northeastern Iran, Ashraf (1974: 46–47) also finds the existence of this unified rural-urban entity with regard to agricultural, industrial, and trade activities. English (1966) in his study of the Kerman Basin and Lapidus (1969) in his analysis of Muslim Cities have come to similar conclusions, that is, the existence of composite "urban regions" comprised of several villages and towns; and the lack of a clear distinction between town and countryside.

In spite of the distinct spatial and functional similarities between town and countryside in Iran, certain urban localities served as centers of economic and political control. Cities like Tehran, the seat of the central government and the Court, and major urban provincial centers like Tabriz, Mashhad, Isfahan and Kerman also developed rather complex social systems comprised of various social classes and sub-strata (see Figure 3.4). Three distinct classes can be identified in major urban centers. First, the collectivity of feudal landowners and tuyulholders including the king, the princes and influential courtiers of the Qajar Dynasty, political governors, tribal chiefs (khans), state-appointed religious officials (imam jum'es), and top-ranking administrators who comprised the ruling classes and particularly resided in Tehran (Abrahamian, 1980: 33). This concentration of landowning and landholding class in urban centers puts Iranian cities in sharp contrast with European feudal cities (Lambton, 1963: 113), and also confirms Marx's definition of Asian cities as being "princely camps" (Marx, 1980). Next were the propertied urban merchants (*"tujjar"*), shopkeepers, small workshop owners and craftsmen who belonged to the bazaar community (ibid.). The urban merchants were involved in trade of commodities both with internal and European and Asian markets, and carried out banking and brokerage activities without paying any taxes to the state, almost functioning as independent capitalists of the 19th century Iran (de Gobineau, 1971: 36). Finally, there were the urban wage-earners such as hired artisans, apprentices, construction workers, journeymen and low-ranking clerics as the subordinate urban class.

## Population Distribution and Urban Hierarchy

It is difficult to study demographic changes and spatial distribution of population in different localities in 19th century Iran. This is due to the fact that no general census has been taken in the 19th century. Initially, the central government's interest in having an accurate number of inhabitants for taxation led to an attempt for a general census in 1860. However, it ended in complete failure because male heads of families for various religious, economic and cultural reasons were reluctant to reveal the number of family members, particularly women in their households (Issawi, 1971: 33). Thus all population figures and estimates for the past century remain sketchy and highly unreliable. Most available figures are merely "guess estimates" of travelers, foreign advisors, and army officers of foreign missionaries who lived in Iran in different time periods, often providing contradictory estimates of urban population. However, based on the estimates given by Schindler, Zolotoliv, Curzon, and Medvedev in Sobotsinskii (cf. Issawi, 1971: 33–35) and

Shiel (op. cit., p. 28), it is possible to sketch Iran's population distribution and demographic changes in the second half of the 19th and early 20th centuries (see table 3.1).

**Table 3.1: Spatial Distribution and Estimation of Population in Pre-capitalist Iran, 1867–1913 (in thousands)**

| Year | Estimated By: | Tribes | | Villages | | Towns | | Total Population |
|------|---------------|--------|-----|----------|-----|-------|-----|------------------|
|      |               | Pop.   | %   | Pop.     | %   | Pop.  | %   |                  |
| 1867 | Shiel[1]      | 1,700  | 39  | 1,700    | 39  | 1,000 | 22  | 4,400            |
| 1884 | Houtum-Schindler[2] | 1,910 | 25 | 3,780 | 49 | 1,964 | 26 | 7,654        |
| 1888 | Zolotoliv[3]  | 1,500  | 25  | 3,000    | 50  | 1,500 | 25  | 6,000            |
| 1891 | Curzon[4]     | 2,250  | 25  | 4,500    | 50  | 2,250 | 25  | 9,000            |
| 1913 | Medvedev[5]   | 2,500  | 25  | 5,000    | 50  | 2,500 | 25  | 10,000           |

Sources:
(1) From J. Shiel's, "Notes on Persian Eelyats" (cf. Issawi, 1971: 28).
(2–5) From A. Sobotsinskii (cf. Issawi, 1971: 33).

Related to the changes in tribal, rural and rural populations no firm conclusion can be drawn in light of the unreliability of all estimates. However, based on the figures presented in table 3.1, we can speculate that no spatial displacement and redistribution of population among tribal, rural and urban units seems to have happened during the 1884–1913 period. There are also indications that population movement took place within each spatial unit, particularly among urban areas. For instance, there seems to be a slight rise in the population of major Iranian cities in the second half of the 19th century (see table 3.2).

A closer look at table 3.2 indicates that while the total population had a growth rate of 118 percent from 4,400,000 in 1867 to 9,600,000 in 1900, several cities such as Tehran, Shiraz, Barfroosh, Rasht, Kashan and Khoi exceeded this mark. Various economic and political factors contributed to this lopsided urban growth. As the nation's capital, the seat of the Qajar Court, and an important center of regional trade Tehran had a considerable population increase during the 1867–1900 period. On the other hand, the main reason for the growth of Rasht and Barfroosh in northern Iran was the increasing volume of trade with Russia via the Caspian Sea. Likewise, Shiraz and Kashan owed their importance to a prosperous regional trade via the Persian Gulf. In brief, urbanization in 19th century Iran was directly related to the growth of cities located on regional and international trade routes (See figure 3.4).

In contrast to the urban centers of regional and international trade, most cities which served as the centers of "urban regions" in the provinces such as Tabriz, Mashhad, Isfahan, Yazd, Kerman, Kermanshah, and Hamadan experienced a lower growth rate as compared to that of general population. Among the cities of the latter category, Tabriz, however, remained as one of the most important urban centers in Iran. The importance of Tabriz and its growth during the same period was exacerbated by its being the capital city of various pastoral-nomadic rulers such as the Mongols, the Qara Qoyunlu, the Aq Qoyunlu, and finally the Safavids. Anxious both to be near their tribes and to escape the excessive heat of the southern regions, the princes of these nomadic tribes settled in Tabriz. Until the beginning of the 20th century Tabriz was also a major center of foreign trade with Europe and Russia (de Planhol, 1968: 432–440). However, designating Tehran as the capital city by the Qajars and diversion of trade from the Tabriz-Trebizond route to the Persian Gulf route in the aftermath of the opening of the Suez Canal reduced the prosperity and economic importance of Tabriz and caused its stagnation and relative decline (Issawi, 1971: 26–27).

During the same period many other principal centers of urban regions either declined or stagnated. For example, while Isfahan's population doubled from 100,000 to 200,000 between 1800-1815, its population dropped to 60,000 in 1867 and rose only to 100,000 by 1900, with almost no change within a century (Issawi, 1971: 26). Similarly, Yazd's population which may have reached as high as 100,000 in 1800 declined to a low 40,000 and recovered somewhat by 1900. Anoher city with considerable population decline was Astarabad (present-time Gorgan), a major residence for the Qajar tribe and a key provincial center that facilitated trade between Russia and provinces of Mazandaran and Khurasan. The city's drastic rate of decline may be attributed to the completion of the Trans-Caspian railway by Russia in 1888, terminating at Uzunada on the eastern coast of the Caspian Sea. The Uzunada connection furnished Russian merchants with direct communication and contact with the Khurasan province and effectively diverted considerable volume of trade from Port of Gaz (Bandar Gaz) on the Caspian Sea, the port of entry for Astarabad's trade (Kazembeyki, 2003: 106). The other principal cities of Mashhad, Kerman, Kermanshah, and Hamadan also seem to have stagnated with an average growth rate similar to that of the total population.

**Figure 3.4. Major Urban Centers in 19th Century Iran**

**Table 3.2: Population of Principal Iranian Cities of 10,000+ Inhabitants in the 19th Century**

| City | 1867[1] (in thousands) | 1900[2] (in thousands) | % Change (1867–1900) |
|---|---|---|---|
| Barfroosh | 10 | 40 | 300 |
| Kashan | 10 | 30 | 200 |
| Shiraz | 25 | 60 | 140 |
| Khoi | 25 | 60 | 140 |
| Tehran | 85 | 200 | 135 |
| Rasht | 18 | 40 | 122 |
| Kermanshah | 30 | 60 | 100 |
| Kerman | 30 | 60 | 100 |
| Yazd | 40 | 75 | 87.5 |
| Tabriz | 110 | 200 | 82 |
| Boroojerd | 10 | 17 | 70 |
| Isfahan | 60 | 100 | 67 |
| Hamadan | 30 | 50 | 67 |
| Qom | 12 | 20 | 67 |
| Qazvin | 25 | 40 | 60 |
| Rezaieh | 30 | 35 | 17 |
| Sabzevar | 12 | 15 | 25 |
| Mashhad | 70 | 75 | 7 |
| Dezful | 15 | 16 | 6 |
| Maragheh | 15 | 15 | 0 |
| Qoochan | 10 | 10 | 0 |
| Ardebil | 10 | 10 | 0 |
| Bushehr | 18 | 15 | -17 |
| Zanjan | 25 | 20 | -20 |
| Shooshtar | 25 | 20 | -20 |
| Saree | 15 | 8 | -47 |
| Torsheez | 10 | 6 | -60 |
| Astarabad | 18 | 6 | -67 |
| Total | 4,400 | 9,000 | 118 |

Sources:
1) Based on Thompson's estimate, cf. Issawi (1971: 28).
2) Based on Bharier (1977: 333–34).

The most remarkable growth was that of Tehran, beginning with the Qajar Dynasty's founder Aqa Mohammad Khan's decision to make it the capital city in 1786. Having about 50,000 inhabitants in the early 19th century, Tehran's population reached 90,000 in the 1850s and 156,000 in 1884 (Amani, 1970: 89). throughout the 19th century Tehran lagged behind Tabriz in both population and commercial importance but gained momentum from the early 1900s onward.

A striking feature of Iran's urban history in the 19th century is the under-development and stagnation of port cities. This is attributable to the nonexistence of an export-oriented economy in Iran, resulting in the stagnation of port cities along the coasts of the Persian Gulf in the south and the Caspian Sea in the north. For instance, Bushehr, the main port city on the Persian Gulf did not pass the 20,000 mark by 1900, and It was only with the oil discovery and development of the oil industry in southern Iran that the southern port city of Abadan on the Persian Gulf was established and experienced a considerable growth later in the twentieth century.

## The Effects of Foreign Trade on Urbanization

The growth, development and/or decline of the 19th century Iranian cities was to a great extent related to trade routes that connected Iran to regional and international markets. Marx was among the first European thinkers who perceived of the relationship between the formation of Asiatic cities and external trade in general and long-distance trade in particular. According to his analysis, the economic-strategic locations and a favorable geographic landscape such as access to water supplies were the main factors for the survival of Asiatic cities:

> Cities in the proper sense arise by the side of villages only where the location is particularly favorable to external trade, or where the head of the state and his satraps exchange their revenue (the surplus product) against labor, where they expend it as labor-funds (Marx, 1980: 71).

In general, Iran's foreign trade was carried on through four major trade routes during the 19th century. The first was the Constantinopole-Trebizond-Erzerum-Khoi-Tabriz-Tehran route. This was the most important land route for the European markets, particularly the British, in the 1800-1860 period. It also explains the enormous growth of Khoi, Tabriz, and Tehran during the 19th century. Second, Iran's urban trade centers were connected to Russian markets via the Caspian Sea through two routes: the Nizhni Novgorod-Anzali-Rasht-Tehran route on the on hand, and the Mashhadsar (Babolsar)-Barfroosh (Babol)-Asterabad-Mashhad connection on the other. The first route connected Russian markets to Central Iran via Tehran; and the second linked Russia to Iran's northeastern provinces. Third, the

Baghdad-Kermanshah-Isfahan route which brought British goods into Iran via the Persian Gulf. Finally, the Bombay- Bushehr-Shiraz-Yazd route which connected the British markets in India to that of Iran via the Persian Gulf (Polak, 1971: 278). Although of lesser importance, there were two other routes that connected the British-controlled Indian markets to Iran: the Herat-Mashhad route in the North and the Bombay-Bandar Abbas-Yazd- Kerman route in the south (see figure 3.5).

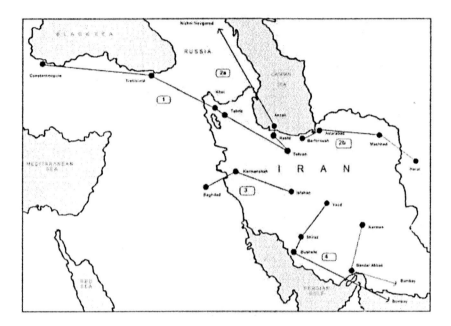

**Figure 3.5. Major Inland and Sea Trade Routes in 19th Century Iran**

Among Iranian cities, Tabriz was the leading trading center and the "depot" of the European trade with Northern Iran mainly because of its geographical location situated at the junction of the routes from Tiflis in Russia on the north and Trebizond in Turkey on the West, both leading to the capital city of Tehran. The increased importance of Tabriz during the first half of the 19th century was also due to an increase in the output and export of silk, and the channeling of European trade through Trebizond in Turkey. As a result, Tabriz handled between a quarter and a third of Iran's total trade in the late 1830s and early 1840s (Issawi, 1971: 108). Most European merchants also resided in Tabriz, with few others in Rasht and Tehran.

The importance and growth of Tabriz was later undermined due to three factors: 1) the failure of the silk crops in 1867 and hence a sharp decline in its trade; 2) the Russian conquests in Turkestan (Northern Iranian territories) which closed that market to foreign commodities and reduced Tabriz's share of that trade; and 3) the opening of the Suez Canal in 1869 that provided a new sea route through which European commodities and Iranian Products were transported more securely and cheaper than the overland Trebizond-Tabriz route. This in turn increased the importance of the Baghdad-Kermanshah and Bushehr-Shiraz routes. Hence, Shiraz in central Iran gained the status of the main "entrepot" of trade in the second half of the 19th century (op. cit., p. 110).

The volume of Iran's foreign trade during the 19th century grew steadily as a result of the increasing interest and influence of colonial powers in the Iranian economy. Issawi (1971: 70) puts this increase during the 1800–1914 period as twelve-fold. Notwithstanding this growth, there were periodic crises and setbacks as well. For example, the failure of the silk crops in Gilan Province along Caspian Sea in 1865, reduction in imports due to overstocking of local markets in 1852 and the American Civil War which resulted in a drastic drop in the export of cotton for European textile industry all negatively affected the Iranian economy (ibid.).

The fiscal consequences of trade with the world capitalist economy were significant for Iran. On the one hand, there was a sharp rise in cash crops such as opium for consumption in the Chinese and European markets. On the other hand, Iran increasingly became a net importer of commodities from capitalist markets. For instance, once an important export item to Russia and Central Asia, Iran's domestic textile industry was gradually destroyed by the import of European and Russian textiles that dominated Iranian markets. Imported processed food items such as cereals and other colonial commodities such as sugar and tea from India also saturated Iranian markets. In the absence of any viable industrial capitalist enterprises in nineteenth century Iran the imports of machinery for both capital- and producer-goods industries remained negligible (ibid., pp. 71–72).

The terms of conducting foreign trade, such as removal of prohibitions, provision of five percent ad valorem duty on both exports and imports for foreign capitalist firms; and freedom of action and movement for foreign merchants were set by Russia through the provisions in the Treaties of Gulestan (1813) and Turkomanchay (1828). This put the Iranian merchants in a disadvantageous position compared to that of their foreign counterparts since they had to pay various road taxes and imposts. Interestingly, most of the trade with foreign countries remained in Iranian hands. This indicates the importance of Iranian merchants as an influential economic and political group on the rise. The head-quarters for handling Iran's foreign trade were mainly in Tabriz and Tehran, where foreign firms were also located. According to Issawi (1971: 101) in the 1840s there were three Greek firms, one Austrian firm, and four Russian firms with headquarters in Tabriz. In addition, at least three Armenian and four Iranian firms were operating in that city.

Tehran was less significant, where only one Austrian and three Russian-Armenian firms had their headquarters in the capital city. This clearly corresponds with a striking feature of 19th century Iran (as compared with that of Egypt, for example) which is the lack of presence of foreign residents and merchants in major urban centers. Isaawi (1971: 230) puts the number of foreigners in the 1860s as twenty five British, fifty French (mostly missionaries), and eighty-six Indians. Even the establishment of telegraph and Anglo-Persian Oil Companies, foreign consulates, hospitals and more trading firms in the early 20th century did not bring the number of foreign residents to more than a few hundreds.

## Early Industrialization Efforts and Their Effects on Urban Development in Pre-capitalist Iran

Historically, Iranian crafts and small-scale manufacturing during the Safavid era (1502–1736) reached a technological level comparable to that of the most advanced capitalist countries of the time. But a period of civil wars and devastating tribal invasions virtually crippled the handicrafts industries in many cities such as Shiraz, Isfahan, and Kerman. The relative strengthening of the central government under the Qajars, coupled with a reduction in European exports due to the Napoleonic wars created a peaceful environment in which most crafts and domestic industries in Iran recovered and flourished. However, this period of rehabilitation was brief and the Western penetration which was achieved through colonial concessions and superior Western technology gradually destroyed the Iranian manufactures and their capability to compete with machine-made goods. In addition, local tax immunities and low custom duties enabled foreign capitalists to practice dumping and hence to force the Iranian products out of market. For example, Kashan's large local factories were systematically destroyed in the 1890s because of this practice (Flandin, 1957: 107). Once the leading city in local industries in central Iran, Isfahan also became a "consumer of manufactured goods, almost wholly from Manchester and Glasgow" (Curzon, 1966, II: 41). In Yazd, another major urban center, local industries were replaced by cultivation of poppies and production of opium in response to an increasing demand in the world market (ibid., pp. 211–212).

While efforts to introduce modern industries in the 19th century Iran were not successful, pre-capitalist local industries such as carpet weaving managed to survive and at times flourish in some areas. In general, the centers of manufacture and commodity production in pre-capitalist Iran during the first decades of the 19th century were chiefly the cities of Isfahan, Yazd, Kashan, Shiraz, Hamadan, and Rasht. Although of trade importance, the cities of Tehran, Qazvin and Kermanshah did not have any significant industries. Various types of pre-capitalist commodities in different cities are identified in table 3.3.

**Table 3.3: Centers of Manufacture and Commodity Production in Pre-capitalist Iran (Circa 1800)**

| City | Type of Manufacture | Remarks |
|------|--------------------|---------|
| Isfahan | gold brocades, lambskin, cotton, clothes, saddles, swords and utensils | the most important city in Iran |
| Yazd | silks, carpets, namads (rugs), woollen shawls, cotton cloth | |
| Shiraz | guns, pistols, swords and other military arms, glass-ware, sheep- and lambskin, enamelled work, coarse cloths | trade of Shiraz has decreased since it ceased to be the seat of government |
| Kashan | silk and carpet | |
| Hamadan | leather, namads, saddles and coarse cloths | |
| Rasht | silks, saddle cloths | |
| Kerman | shawl manufacture | |

Source: Malcolm (1971: 262–63)

One point has to be made in this juncture: the increasing demand for some Iranian products in the world capitalist markets to certain degrees transformed the pre-capitalist organization of commodity production and introduced new provisions for a more rational division of labor. For example, at the end of the 19th century Persian carpets were in high demand in the world markets due to their superior quality. This necessitated the transformation of small-scale, domestic carpet weaving workshops into large-scale carpet factories employing up to one hundred workers. Abdulayev (1971: 297–98) clearly describes the extent of division of labor in the reorganized carpet industry:

(I)n some large carpet workshops there were specialists who dyed the yarn, which apprentices gathered in skins. Often large merchants who owned carpet manufactories bought up raw wool and put it out for spinning into yarn at home; the merchant owning a large carpet workshop also put out raw wool to carpet weavers who worked at home.

Aside from pre-capitalist commodity production, few efforts were made in the early 19th century to introduce industrial production based on modern capitalist technology. For example, in the 1830s a factory in Tabriz produced cannon and ammunition. Later, in 1849, textile, paper, and glass works were established under Amir-i Kabir's efforts, who was the prime minister in the Nasser od-Din shah's Court, but most of his projects ended in failure. Attempts by foreign capitalist enterprises were also made in the 1880s but with little or no success (Issawi, 1971: 260–61).

The reasons for the failure of modern industries may be attributed to several factors: 1) the persistence of subsistence economy at the village unit and small town levels and underdevelopment of a national, market-based economy; 2) lack of a skilled industrial labor force; and 3) non-existence of banking and credit institutions to support capital investments. In addition, the difficulties involved with the importation of machinery and spare parts such as lack of adequate and safe inland roads made any industrial operation expensive and unprofitable for foreign capitalists (Polak, 1971: 268).

## Notes

1. See for example Razi (1968) and Afzal al-Mulk et al. (1982).

2. For this part, I am indebted to the works of Ashraf (1970) and particularly Mahdi (1983) for his historical review of the literature. Vali (1993) also provides an excellent review of literature pertaining to pre-capitalist Iranian history and political economy.

3. Marx argued that "climate and territorial conditions, especially the vast traces of desert" necessitated "artificial irrigation by canals and water works." He also contended that vastness of the territories and the need for artificial irrigation due to water shortage manifested in the "interference of the centralizing power of the government" and absence of private ownership of land, hence necessitating communal property in the "Orient" (Marx & Engels, 1972: 37, 315). Furthermore, the shortage of water resources and the need for organization of agricultural production resulted in the absence of private ownership of land in the "East," and the importance of communal property. By giving the Indian example, Marx & Engels assert that the stagnant character of pre-capitalist Indian society was due to the self-sufficient nature of villages and towns which formed separate units of production but at the same time were dependent on the central government for

public works.

4. According to Lambton (1953) the term "iqta" or land assignment was gradually replaced during the Ilkhan period (1256-1336 A.D.) by "tuyul" and was carried on to the Qajar period. For a detailed explanation of various types of tuyul during the Qajar period see Ibid. (139-140).

5. For a detailed analysis of iqta see Lambton (1953: 53–77).

6. For a detailed analysis of Iran's early involvements in the world capitalist trade see Mahdi (1983: Chapter 4).

7. Originally, the concept of "semi-colonialism" was used by Lenin (1964:151) and Mao-tse Tung (1965: 196–99) to distinguish societies which maintained their formal political independence under colonialism, from those which were completely colonized (e.g., Egypt during the 1882–1922 period) and lost their independence.

8. For a detailed explanation of qanats and their importance for agricultural production in Iran see the works of English (1966: 30–38) and Mahdi (1983: 212–220).

## Chapter Four

# Development of Commercial Capitalism and Dependent Urbanization in Iran (1880–1953)

By the mid-19th century the Iranian pre-capitalist economy was in shambles. The fiscal crisis of the central government and its need for extra income in the second half of the 19th century led to the sale of local governorships to the highest bidder. Since the governors were most concerned with increasing their income in order to keep up their bids, they recruited village officers on the basis of their promised monetary return. Officials at each level retained profit from collected taxes and the peasants had to support a hierarchy of government officials (Keddie, 1960: 4-5). The foreign powers' involvement with the Qajar kings and government administrators in proposing and concluding treaties and obtaining concessions effectively weakened the relative autonomy of the Iranian state apparatus and created discontent among merchants in "*bazaar*" which initially burst into the open by Naser od-Din Shah's sale of a major concession to the Britisher Major Talbot in 1891. The concession granted a fifty-year monopoly over the production, distribution, and exportation of tobacco. In return the Shah was to receive a 25,000 Pounds personal gift, and the government was set to get an annual rent of 15,000 Pounds plus 25 percent of the yearly profit earned from tobacco trade (Katouzian, 1981: 55; Abrahamian, 1979: 399). The British monopoly over this cash crop effectively deprived Iranian merchants of a lucrative market, provoked a mass protest movement in 1891-92 and led the Grand Ayatollah (Mirza Shirazi) to issue a religious decree (*Fatwa*) against using tobacco. The crisis was ignited with the arrival of the British company agents in Shiraz, the urban center of a major tobacco region, and subsequent local strike waged by merchants and craftsmen in the city's bazaar community. The strike was soon spread through all bazaars in major cities such as Tehran, Tabriz, Isfahan, Mashhad, Yazd, Kermanshah and Qazvin. Eventually, by having the support of the leading clergy the strike turned into a nation-wide consumer boycott and mass demonstration, forcing the Shah to annul the concession.

The outcome of the tobacco crisis was in fact an early sign of disintegration of Iran's pre-capitalist state and its vulnerable position within the world capitalist economy in light of a mounting internal pressure. Because of the role of Russia and Britain in handling Iran's foreign trade activities, the last two decades of the 19th century also witnessed the increasing discontent of the propertied class of merchants, craftsmen and guild members. In particular, the active role played by the Russian government in promoting the commercial activities of its subjects in Iran was alarming. Beginning in the 1880s the Russian government introduced easy loans and provided bonuses for Russian merchants trading with Iran, enabling the latter to sell their products in Iran well below the market prices. As a consequence, not only were the Iranian commodities unable to compete with the Russian goods, Russia's dominance and control over Iran's foreign trade also drove the other rival power Britain out of the Iranian market (Nashat, 1981: 76-7).

The growth of foreign trade toward the end of the 19th century contributed to the emergence of a sizable new Iranian merchant class who began to control both internal and external markets while at the same time increasing their political power. With the public discontent on the rise, the final blow to Iran's economy came from a chain of events in the first decade of the 20th century, including "a bad harvest and a sudden disruption in the northern trade caused by a cholera epidemic, by heavy snows, by the Russo-Japanese wars, and by the subsequent revolution in Russia" that led to a runaway inflation particularly in major urban centers such as Tehran, Tabriz, Rasht and Mashhad (Abrahamian, 1979: 404). Unable to cope with increasing influence of colonial powers the government held Iranian merchants responsible for price inflation while raising tariffs on imported goods. The increasing discontent among the bazaaris who were supported by both intellectuals and the clergy triggered three public protests which culminated in the Constitutional Revolution of August 1906.[1] The foreign powers' reaction to these events reflected their colonial interests in Iran: while the Russians stood behind the Shah and the Court by opposing the demands of the Constitutionalists; the British tried to maintain their alleged neutrality by giving a subtle but very effective support to the merchants (bazaaris) on the one hand and also providing sanctuary for the defiant merchants and craftsmen on the other. The subsequent British support ended in the sanctuary of 14,000 people, mostly from the bazaar community, in the summer residence of the British Legation near Tehran. The sanctuary forced the reigning King, Muzaffar od-Din Shah, to sign a proclamation for the convening of a Constituent National Assembly.

The Constitutional Revolution caused an immediate shift in control over state power from the Qajar Shah and his Court to the new National Parliament that was initially dominated by urban merchants and guild members. This was reflected in the social composition of the First National Assembly's deputies. Based on one estimate, guild members comprised 26 percent of the deputies while merchants and clergymen associated with the bazaar community comprised 15 and 20 percent, respectively (Shaji'i, 1965: 176). Despite this shift of power and empowerment of the National Assembly or *"Majlis"* by the newly enforced Constitution to control over financial legislation, the Majlis never directly attacked the foreign powers' colonial interests. In fact, the colonial powers and the court remained in control of financial institutions, trade regulations, and above all the military and coercive apparatus (Mehrain, 1979: 185). As a consequence, although urban petty commodity producers and bazaar merchants gained a limited but yet significant political power, they nonetheless remained on the margins of political power struggle in pre-capitalist Iran.

Deprived of its control over the legislative process, the *"Asiatic"* faction led by the Shah and supported by the Russian Government waged a coup d'état in 1908. Aimed at eliminating the Parliament in order to gain total control over the judicial, executive, and military power, the Shah's coup d'état mobilized the entire society along clear factional and class interests. It was at this historical junction that the feudal and rival tribal factions opposing the Qajar rule directly entered the scene to support the newly established parliament and the bazaar community. The political and military intervention by feudal leaders led to final defeat of the Russian-trained Cossack Brigade (the Imperial Guards) and consequent expulsion of Mohammad Ali Shah to Russia in 1909. This victory was gained through military intervention of three provincial armies: 1) the Tabriz Revolu-tionary Army led and supported by petty commodity producers and the bazaar community; 2) the Gilan army led by Sepahdar-i A'zam, a landed elite; and 3) the military forces of the Bakhtiari tribe mobilized by Sardar As'ad, a defiant tribal leader.

The provisions of the Constitutional Revolution for the creation of a National Assembly was an ideal opportunity for provincial feudal landlords to share state power and strengthen their position within their own immediate rural regions of influence. A closer look at the social composition of the Revolutionary Committee which ousted the Shah and appointed the members of the first cabinet indicates the increasing influence and political power gained by the landed aristocracy and provincial khans.[2] Based on one account, the rival feudal landlords and tribal khans dominated the Revolutionary Committee (87 percent), while prominent merchants, affiliated clergy and intellectuals only comprised about 12 percent of the membership (Mehrain, 1979: 191–192). Furthermore, three of the six-member cabinet appointments went to the top landed bureaucrats of the Qajar Court; two feudal landlords from the Gilan province and one Bakhtiari tribal khan (Shamim, 1963: 321–24). The failure of the Constitutional Revolution in fulfilling the demands and interests of the bazaar community and the consequent state takeover by the feudal faction was clearly reflected in the composition of the second Parliament when the merchants and guild members' representation dropped to only 7 percent as compared to 37 percent in the first Parliament (Shaji'i, 1965: 176).

### Disintegration of the Iranian Pre-capitalist Society and its Effects on Urban Development

In the aftermath of the Constitutional Revolution the Iranian territory was parceled out by various tribal factions and feudal lords in the provinces, who, caught up between the Russo-British rivalry in the region were forced to affiliate themselves to one or the other colonial power in order to secure their fragile status. The British colonial interests and policies in Iran took a divergent path when vast reserves of crude oil were discovered in southern Iran. The oil discovery in Iran dates back to the late 19th century and the investigations of a French government scientific mission in 1892. But it was not until 1908 that the extraordinary amount of Iranian oil was discovered in Masjed-i Soleiman in southwestern Iran by the Britisher William Knox D'arcy. The concession clearly specified that Iran was to obtain 16 percent of the profits out of the sale of crude oil, but in reality this was never fulfilled. In order to preserve their vital interests in Iranian oil, the British were determined to utilize any possible means to fulfill their colonial objectives. In 1909 the Anglo-Persian Oil Company (APOC) was established in order to take over the Iranian oil operations, and it was at this time that the British government took a keen interest in the management and financial control of Iran's oil revenues, and consequently financed APOC and virtually controlled its operation based on D'arcy's original concession.[3]

The October Revolution of 1917 in Russia eliminated the Czarist imperial interests in Iran and created a power vacuum in the region, enabling the British to coerce Iran into accepting a protectorate status in 1919 in the guise of a bilateral treaty of technical assistance and economic cooperation. Provision of a loan by Britain to Iran and employment of British military and civil advisors by the Qajar Court were the main points of this agreement. This caused both internal opposition by nationalist and anti-imperialist sentiments and external reaction resulting in the Soviet Union's invasion of northern Iran and her threat to establish a Soviet republic in the northern province of Gilan. Faced with the imminent Soviet presence and anxious to safeguard their interests in the Iranian economy the British responded through their subtle but active support of a military coup d'état. The military coup ended the reign of the Qajar Dynasty and brought Reza Khan to power who later founded the Pahlavi Dynasty.[4]

By the 1920s the British colonial policy in Iran was focused on achieving two main objectives: 1) to control the extraction and export of crude oil; and 2) to facilitate Iran's gradual integration into the world capitalist system as a potential market for colonial goods and commodities. These objectives necessitated the introduction of capitalist relations of production to prepare the Iranian economy for its entry into the world market. To achieve these objectives two preconditions had to be met: 1) accumulation of money capital in the hands of non-productive labor which has also control over the means of production; and 2) separation of direct producers from their means of production in order to create wage-laborers for capitalist production and consumption. The former prerequisite was met by the increasing oil revenues in the hands of the state and the ruling elite, as well as an inflow of foreign-controlled money-capital in the forms of foreign aid, foreign bank loans and foreign direct investments. The latter had to be met through state intervention and a variety of strategies such as taxation, land redistribution, infrastructural projects (roads, railways, health care, etc.) and gradual elimination of certain relations of production which were not conducive to capitalist development. In general, six major social processes and policies led to Iran's transition from a pre-capitalist economy to one that accommodated European colonial interests and also contributed to urbanization in Iran, which I will discuss them in the following section.

**Legal Recognition of Land Ownership and Property Rights**

Historically speaking, since the Arab conquest of Iran in the 7th century the right to private property was both recognized and approved according to Islamic laws (*Shari'a*). Private property rights were held to be inviolable except "when it was necessary to resort to expropriation" either legally or illegally (Lambton, 1953: 16-17). The institution of private landownership thus had existed hand in hand with other forms of landholding such as crown lands, state lands, communal lands administered by the "*imam*" or spiritual leader, and land assignments or "*toyul*" as rewards to individuals in return for their military, administrative and financial services (Lambton, 1953: 20; Ashraf, 1971: 151; Mehrain, 1979: 78–80). The legal recognition of private ownership of land in the form of land registration is documented since the Mongol's period in the 13th century. Prior to that, the landholders had some sort of title-deed in their possession, but this did not prevent the transfer and/or cancellation of titles "when the property was transmitted from one holder to another" (Lambton, 1953: 69). Recognition of private property in general and legalization of land ownership and registration in particular entered into a new stage of development during the 19th century. The increasing political and economic pressures by colonial powers and the weakening of the central government during this period paved the way for the growth and reinforcement of landownership in Iran. On the one hand, the tribal system of land assignment (toyul) inherently had a tendency to alienate large areas of the country from direct administration by the central government. This resulted in usurpation of large portions of arable lands and their conversion into de facto private property by toyul holders, whenever the central government was unable to maintain its control and power in the provinces (Lambton, 1953: 139). The interests of foreign powers in commercial activities and trade with Iran also necessitated the establishment of monetary relations and recognition of private ownership rights in the second half of the 19th century. In one occasion, the British put pressure on Nasser od-Din Shah, the Qajar King who ruled from 1848 to 1896, "to issue the decree on the security of life and property" of all subjects (Ashraf, 1971: 1522–53). Foreign pressure, coupled with the fiscal crisis of the state and the challenging of the Shah's authority by regional rulers gradually weakened the central government and eroded its political power. Deprived of a previously secured source of income and apprehended by an unknown political future, the Qajar kings were compelled to "sell a portion of the available crown and public domains," and then "to confiscate and incorporate a portion of toyuls and private lands into state lands for further sale" (ibid.). Related to the land question, the 19th century Iran has to be regarded as a transitional period during which the feudal principles of landholding gained momentum while the pastoral-nomadic institution of toyul was increasingly undermined. The institutionalization of private landownership reached its peak in 1907, when the first Iranian Parliament abolished toyul, the nomadic tradition of landholding, and recognized all toyul holders as private landowners (Lambton, 1953: 178–179).

**Modern Banking**

The recognition of private property rights, Iran's involvement in foreign trade and consequent penetration of Iranian economy by foreign capital necessitated the introduction and institutionalization of modern banking. The first bank in Iran was a branch of the British-based New Oriental Corporation which opened in 1888 with offices in Tehran and other major cities. This was followed by the establishment of another British-owned financial institution, the Imperial Bank of Persia in 1889, and the Banque d'Escopmte de Perse in 1899, a branch of the Russian State Bank (Issawi, 1971: 346–47). However, it was not until 1927 when banking came under national control with the provision for a National Bank (Bank Melli). As a process of indigenization of capitalist development, in 1930 the right to issue bank notes was also transferred from the British Imperial Bank to the National Bank of Iran (Bank Melli). The government gradually expanded its control over financial matters by forming the Agricultural and Industrial Bank in 1933 and the Loan Bank in 1939. The initial capital was provided through taxing the population and specifically the poverty stricken peasants, urban petty commodity producers and workers (Keddie, 1981: 102). However, despite Reza Shah's attempts for con-centration of money capital in the state-controlled banks, Iranian merchants for a long time afterwards remained dependent on financial services provided by pre-capitalist money lenders or "*sarrafan*," Iranian counterparts to the European goldsmiths (Katouzian, 1981: 112).

**The Sedantarization Process**

As I discussed earlier, the Constitutional Revolution of 1906 undermined the economic and political foundations of the pastoral-nomadic economic relations through the abolition of tribal landholding tradition of "tuyul" and gradual exclusion of tribal leaders from political power. However, the final blow came with Reza Shah's policy of forced sedentarization of tribes with the objective of establishing a strong centralized state free from tribal and regional threats. Communal land ownership, a distinct characteristic of the tribal culture and economic survival was viewed by the new government as a major obstacle to the expansion of capitalist relations and private landownership in Iran. To this end, many tribal leaders were executed, imprisoned, tortured, or were brought to the capital city of Tehran and kept as hostages in order to force the tribes to cooperate with the central state (Mahdi, 1983: 127). The pastoral-nomadic lifestyle which was based on an orderly seasonal migration throughout the year was deliberately disrupted by the agents of central government through the use of force. In many occasions the central government attempted to settle nomads in newly established villages which were built mostly on unsuitable lands (Sunderland, 1968: 641–42). As a consequence, Reza Shah's conscious policy of sedentarization led to a considerable loss of livestock and undermined pastoral- nomadic relations of production. Separated from their means of production such as the livestock and communal grazing lands, the tribal populations were gradually and forcibly converted into seasonal wage-laborers who had to seek employment within a stagnating rural economy, the petty commodity production sector, and in construction activities in major cities and urban centers (Smith, 1978: 80; Mahdi, 1983: 127). Information about changes in the nomadic population is sketchy, but available data indicate a sharp decrease in the nomadic population during the 1910–1956 period. As is shown in table 4.1, destruction of pastoral-nomadic lifestyle and economy and decline in Iran's nomadic population is demonstrated in the changing ratio of nomadic population to total rural population. The only exception is the 1940s period during which the abdication of Reza Shah in 1941 and weakening of the central state enabled many settled nomads to take advantage of a chaotic social situation and return to pastoralism.

Furthermore, during the 1900–1952 period there was considerable increase in the number of small villages having 50–1,000 inhabitants throughout Iran, as compared to the larger villages and regional centers. Based on Bharier's estimation (1977) there were about 15,000 villages in 1900 as compared to 39,099 in 1956. Within this context, small-size villages with 50–1,000 inhabitants had an 8 percent proportional increase in their numbers as compared to 8 percent decline for larger villages having 1,000–5,000 inhabitants. Although it is hard to come by reliable data and information about the spatial movement of tribal population, it appears that destruction of pastoral-nomadic life style forced the nomadic people to settle in small villages in the first place, as is supported by figures in table 4.2. Thus it is reasonable to contend that particularly during the 1930s the sedantarization process was not a decisive factor in an increase in urban population, and that population movements took place mainly in rural areas.

**Table 4.1: Pastoral-Nomadic and Rural Population in Iran: 1910-1956**

|                                | (in millions) | | | |
| Year                           | 1910 | 1932 | 1945 | 1956 |
| --- | --- | --- | --- | --- |
| Total Rural                    | 8.36 | 10.24 | 11.7 | 14.6 |
| Pastoral-Nomadic               | 2.65 | 1.0 | 2.0 | 0.24 |
| Settled Rural                  | 5.71 | 9.24 | 9.7 | 14.36 |
| % Pastoral-Nomadic to Total Rural: | 31.6 | 9.8 | 17.0 | 1.6 |

Source: Table based on information in Bharier (1977: Table 3, p. 335; and p. 338).

**Table 4.2: Size Distribution of Villages in Iran, 1900 and 1956**

| Village Population Size | 1900 % | 1956 % |
| --- | --- | --- |
| 50–999 | 87 | 95 |
| 1,000–4,999 | 13 | 5 |

Source: Table constructed based on information given in Bharier (1977: 339).

**Taxing the Peasants: A Prelude to Rural-Urban Migration**

Another strategy for paving the way for a nascent, state-controlled capitalist development in Iran was imposition of a wide variety of taxes on peasants, their lands and agricultural produce. This undermined peasants-producers' ability to exchange their products in the market for an adequate return, and hence forced them to sell their labor power in order to survive (Taylor, 1979: 209-10). In addition, tax revenues provided the much needed capital for the state-sponsored economic development and infrastructural projects. To this end, financial planning in the 1920s was aimed at devising a more efficient method of collecting taxes on land, animals and agricultural products. Based on the land tax law of 1926 those peasants working on both the irrigated and unirrigated lands were to pay a fixed 3 percent tax on the gross produce before the crop was divided between the landlord and the farmer (Lambton, 1953: 184). Later on, this law was replaced by a new provision in

1934 which increased the burden of taxation on peasants. That is, rural producers were to pay a 3 percent tax in kind on all agricultural and animal products upon entry to a town or a market place (ibid.). The widespread practice of agricultural production in Iran was sharecropping, which was sharing the crop yield according to the extent of landlord's or peasant's control over land, seed, oxen, water, and labor. This perpetuated the poverty of the majority of rural population who only had control over their labor power, while about 75 percent of all lands were owned by large land owners, the state, the Shah, and religious institutions (Sunderland, 1968: 624). The destructive effects of taxation have to be examined within above-mentioned system of agricultural production during this period (see table 4.3). Taxation along capitalist lines was further reinforced with the abolition of payments in kind in the late 1930s and the introduction of income tax in 1942. Shopkeepers and craftsmen were also subjected to taxation with taxes being collected through their guild organizations, and indirect taxes on items of public consumption such as tobacco, opium, sugar and tea were being derived more efficiently (Avery, 1961: 262–63).

**Table 4.3: Estimates of the Distribution of Landownership in the Period Prior to the 1961 Land Reform in Iran**

| Type of Ownership | All Land Owned (%) | All Villages (%) |
|---|---|---|
| Large Landowners | 56 | 34.43 |
| Small Landowners | 10–12 | 41.93 |
| Royal Holdings | 10–13 | 2.06 |
| Religious Endowment | 1–2 | 1.81 |
| Tribal Holdings | 13.0 | — |
| State-owned Lands | 3–4 | 3.67 |
| Other (mixed and unknown ownership) | — | 16.10 |

Source: McLachlan (1968: 686).

What made the situation even worse, was that large land owners who owned 56 percent of cultivated land comprised only 1 percent of the population, at a time when 95 to 98 percent of rural population was reportedly landless (McLachlan, 1968; Lambton, 1953: 262–63). In many rural areas, the poor peasants were perpetually indebted to the landlords by receiving an allocation of grain in advance (Sunderland, 1968: 624). Thus, in a situation where the majority of the rural population was tied to the land through their indebtedness to landlords the effect of state-imposed taxation on peasants should have been devastating. As I will discuss in chapter 5, excessive taxation and impoverishment of Iranian peasantry eventually led to massive rural to urban migration which continued to be the case up until the 1979 Revolution, and even to the present time.

## The Emergence of an Urban Industrial Working Class

Despite several attempts to promote industrialization in Iran during the early decades of the twentieth century, the extent of industrial production and Iran's involvement in the world capitalist economy was fairly limited. Estimates for the pre-World War I period indicate that only 1,700 workers were employed in "modern" factories, of whom 400 worked in cotton gin workshops and 300 in sugar products. In the absence of an indigenous industrialization process, foreign-owned and operated commercial and industrial activities were the principal employers of a nascent class of industrial workers. For example, Some 7,000 to 8,000 workers were employed by the Anglo-Iranian Oil Company, and 5,000 Russian subjects worked in Russian-owned enterprises involved in fishery and road construction activities. However, during the same period small-scale local industries and petty commodity production sector employed about 100,000 workers, of whom 65,000 were engaged in carpet making and another 20,000 in weaving industries (Abdullayev, cf. Issawi, 1971: 261).

Like many other countries in the periphery with dependent economies, Industrial development in Iran began during the 1930s when a state-initiated program of import-substitution industrialization produced goods mostly for internal markets. By 1941, the large modern factories employing fifty or more workers provided jobs for about 50,000 workers. Industrial activities included light consumer goods industries such as soap, glass, paper, etc., and processing industries for various agricultural products. Abrahamian (1980: 147–148) estimates that in 1941 a total of 170,000 wage-earners were employed by modern factories. But this new working class comprised only less than 4 percent of the total labor force. Furthermore, the dependent and uneven nature of Iran's capitalist development resulted in concentration of over 75 percent of industrial activities in a few major cities such as Tehran, Tabriz and Isfahan. Tehran alone employed 64,000 wage-laborers in its 62 large-scale plants and numerous small- scale industries (ibid.).

The state-initiated industrialization should be considered as the first step for Iran's dependence on Western capitalist economies for technological know how, parts and capital goods producing machines (machines that produce machines); while the state controlled industrial-commercial activities, foreign trade and agricultural production almost completely remained in private hands. But import-substitution industrialization did not transform the Iranian pre-capitalist economy, and its effects on the overall process of capital accumulation and capitalist development remained minimal. The sale of state lands, institutiona-lization of private landownership and the state's monopoly over trade forced the owners of capital (landowners and merchants) to look for profit in land speculation and investment in real estate activities, instead of investing in the new but fragile modern industrial sector.

## Railroad Networks and Urban Growth

Construction of railways in many colonies started in the 1890s and even earlier in order to facilitate export of raw materials and colonial products to the European colonial centers. But because of Iran's semi-colonial status and out of colonialists' fear of its becoming a tool for the rival power's expansion in the region, construction of the railway system became the object of colonial rivalry. This also prevented foreign capital investment in the Trans-Iranian Railway network later in the 1920s. Reza Shah's policies of state-capitalist development included an ambitious scheme for connecting the north and the south by rail. But in the absence of available foreign capital, Reza Shah had to finance the project through monopolization of imports of tea and sugar and revenue generation through their taxation (Banani, 1961: 132–34).

In order to thwart any advantages imperial powers might have expected to get from it, Reza Shah constructed the Trans-Iranian Railway (1927–1938) based on a quite irrational scheme which served neither domestic need nor helped the development of external trade. First, it was standard gauge as opposed to the Soviet's broad gauge system and Iraq's British-built narrow gauge system. Second, eight of the fifteen principal cities (Isfahan, Yazd, Kerman, Shiraz, Mashhad, Tabriz, Hamadan, and Kermanshah) were not served by the initial network (Avery, 1968: 301–304).[5] But apart from Reza Shah's relatively independent political stand in regard to the railway project, the irrationality of this project has to be understood in the light of its importance for the creation and training of wage-laborers in a predominantly pre-capitalist economy. As Taylor (1979: 212) puts it,

> construction of railways, apart from providing a secure productive investment for finance capital-- since the state generally had ultimate control over the project and opening up of markets and new sources of raw materials, provided the basis for a general system of recruitment, in which the state supervised a forced migration of labor into isolated pockets of infrastructural development which depended on the very form of wage-labor that imperialist penetration had to create.

Thus in a situation where there was neither a capitalist economic infrastructure nor a plausible justification for such a large scheme in terms of transporting, exporting and importing of goods, railway construction along with other infrastructural project such as ports and roads served as a "bridgehead" to create a new breed of wage-earning workers. While the new railway network bypassed many provincial centers, it contributed to the growth and development of several others. For example, on its way to Tehran from Bandar Shahpur, an inlet of the Persian Gulf in the Khuzestan Province, the railroad by-passed Hamadan and Isfahan but connected the oil city of Ahvaz to the network and contributed to its considerable growth. The major beneficiary of the railway system was Tehran, which became the center of concentration for trading, manufacturing and service-related activities. Almost all imports were transported from southern ports to Tehran to be dispatched to provinces for final redistribution. As a result, Tehran in the 1940s handled nearly half the retail trade turnover of imported merchandise (Melamid, 1968: 558–59).

## Uneven Nature of Urban Development in Iran

As was the case for the 19th century Iran, there is no systematic and comprehensive information about population changes, movements and socioeconomic conditions in towns and villages for the first half of the 20th century. The first national census was not conducted until 1956, and therefore most of the available data should be considered as "guess-estimates" and dealt with caution. The only viable study of the population changes and growth of towns and villages for this period is a quantitative analysis by Bharier (1977), who, based on independent estimates of urban and rural population for the years 1900, 1934, 1940, 1956 and 1966 examines patterns of inter-urban and rural-urban migration. His definition of an urban place is based on the Iranian government's official categorization which considers all places of 5,000 or more inhabitants as "urban." This by all means is a vague definition, as in the absence of a clear distinction between town and countryside in Iran up until the 1930s many large rural settlements could have easily passed as "urban" centers (see table 4.4). In fact, between 1900 and 1950 a total of 85 villages with 2500-5000 inhabitants gained the status of an "urban place" by official definition (ibid.). Despite apparent shortcomings of Bharier's analysis I can safely make two conclusions. First, as is illustrated in table 4.4, population movements up until the mid-1930s were mostly of inter-urban and inter-rural nature. Second, urban growth and rural-urban migration in Iran started to take place in the late 1930s and certainly throughout the 1940s.

Reza Shah's ascendance to power and his state-supported and initiated strategies to introduce capitalist relations of production from early 1930s onward affected the nature and direction of growth for many Iranian cities. As I argued earlier, besides concentration of money capital in the hands of the state, in the absence of a viable capitalist class (*bourgeoisie*) in Iran the imposition of capitalist relations became the state's prime objective with the oil income at its disposal. To this end, the state bureaucracy, foreign consulates, the army, industrial activities and most of the trade were concentrated in the capital city of Tehran for the apparent reason of efficiency and practicality. Yet despite import-substitution industrialization schemes Iranian merchants favored investment in commercial activities, and were both reluctant and skeptical to invest in the newly created industrial sector. For instance, in 1940 for each industrial enterprise there were two corporations involved in commerce, almost all of them concentrated in Tehran. In the same year 58.5 percent of all domestic capital was also invested in the capital city (Bank Melli Iran, 1941-42: 312).

**Table 4.4:  Annual (Compound) Rates of Population Growth for Iran**
**For Selected Periods**

| Period | Urban | Rural | Total Population |
|---|---|---|---|
| 1900–1926 | 0.08 | 0.08 | 0.08 |
| 1927–1934 | 1.50 | 1.50 | 1.50 |
| 1935–1940 | 2.30 | 1.30 | 1.50 |
| 1941–1956 | 4.40 | 1.40 | 2.20 |

Source:  Bharier (1977: 335).

The outbreak of the Second World War and Iran's occupation by the Allied forces provided new opportunities for urban merchants and the bazaar communities to profit from the war economy. The demands of the Allied troops for consumer goods contributed to an increase in urban economic activities. Specifically, those cities which were located along the Trans-Iranian Railway and major roads benefited from the war traffic between the Persian Gulf and the Soviet borders (Keddie, 1981:   113–116). In addition to Tehran, the growth of Arak, Khorramshahr, Ghom, Dezful, Khorramabad and Mianeh was to a great deal related to the war economy. As I argued earlier, the town and country during this period remained mostly undifferentiated due to the dominance of feudal relations of production in Iran. Except Tehran that experienced a limited degree of urban transformation and modernization, many provincial cities maintained their rural character for the most part of this period. Apart from the rapid growth of towns which served as railway stations and marketplaces for the occupying army, the only change in Iranian cities during the 1921–1941 period was state-sponsored plans for urban beautification and modernization of their appearance. Plans for urban beautification were mostly concentrated in Tehran, where "spacious circles and squares with fountains, landscaping and statues of Reza Shah in every conceivable pose, added to the European aspect of the Capital" (Banani, 1961: 143).[6] While the majority of Iranian cities remained undifferentiated from rural settlements as "cities of peasants," to use Bryan Roberts' phrase (1978), Reza Shah's attempts for urbanization and physical transformation proved futile and served only as "window dressing" to impress foreign visitors and colonial functionaries who mostly stayed in Tehran. Banani (1961: 145) gives a clear picture of Reza Shah's urbanization:

> To the Westerner who visited Iran for the first time in 1941, it was a land
> somewhere between the East and a shabby West. To many Iranians who had
> studied or traveled in the West, the chasm between the national progress of the
> West and their own country was a source of frustration and defeatism.

Although in its embryonic form, by the early 1940s one could detect the spatial
manifestation of a new capitalist economy in the way the government perceived
urban development in Iran: while Tehran's modernization took the form of a rapid
northward growth outside the gates of the old pre-capitalist city quarters,
"modernization" in provincial cities was limited to the superimposition of two wide
main streets intersecting at right angles over the old, pre-capitalist urban fabric. The
latter was an apparent response to the presence of automobiles; especially trucks
and buses which could not pass through narrow and zigzagged alleys of pre-
capitalist urban fabric.[7]

Finally, compared to the first period (1800–1880s), there was a clear shift
toward an increase in urban population during the 1900–1952 period particularly in
the capital city of Tehran. However, by 1956 of the total of 100 places defined as
urban in 1900 (having 5,000 or more inhabitants) only 25 cities had a growth rate
higher than that of total population. This means that only 25 towns had immigrants
from other places, and the rest had lower growth rates compared to that of the total
population. That is, either they stagnated or lost their population, all of which
indicating a process of urban out-migration and de-urbanization (see Bharier, 1977:
333–34). For instance, while the declining cities had a total population loss of
1,074,000, the growing cities gained by 1,759,000 population during the 1900–
1956 period. Thus the net rural-urban migration can be estimated at about 685,000
people. This indicates that 61 percent of population movement was inter-urban
while 39 percent was the result of rural-urban migration (ibid.: 339). Related to
urban out-migration, according to Bharier four urban centers accounted for 31
percent of net loss, namely, cities of Tabriz (10 percent), Khoi (8 percent), Yazd (8
percent), and Kerman (5 percent). The first two cities lost population because of a
decline in trade on the Tabriz-Trebizond route, and the latter two lost their
prominence related to the decreasing importance of the Basra-Kermanshah-
Isfahan-Yazd trade route. On the other hand, 60 percent of migration was targeted
at the Capital, while the oil towns of Abadan and Ahwaz accounted for another 22
percent of in-migration. Not surprisingly, according to the 1956 Census the main
centers of attraction for life-time migration were also the cities of Tehran, Abadan,
and Ahwaz. This clearly reflects the nature of an economy being dependent on oil
export and a foreign trade controlled by colonial interests, since Tehran functioned
as the center of industrial, commercial, bureaucratic and service activities and
Abadan and Ahwaz served as centers for the extraction, production and exportation

of oil-related products. Related to other urban centers, the main impetus for urban growth appeared to be the Trans-Iranian railway, since twelve out of 27 cities experiencing urban growth during this period were along the new railroad network. This effectively contributed to the decline of urban centers such as Hamadan, Isfahan, and Kermanshah which did not benefit from the Trans-Iranian railroad network.

## Notes

1. For a detailed account of the events leading to the Constitutional Revolution see Abrahamian (1979) and Kasravi (1961).

2. After Mohammad Ali Shah's escape to Russia (1909) the Revolutionary Committee was created to function as a regent since the heir to the Shah was a minor. The RC was also responsible for selection of the new cabinet.

3. For a historical account of the events leading to the 1921 coup see among others, Makki (1945, Vol. 1), Katouzian (1980; 75–100), and Abrahamian (1980: 102–118).

4. It has to be noted that D'arcy's quest to obtain concessions from the Iranian government at the time was fulfilled in 1901 for a 60-year period of exclusive privilege to search for, obtain, exploit, develop, render suitable for trade, carry away and sell natural gas and petroleum throughout the Iranian territory with the exception of five northern provinces (Azerbayjan, Gilan, Mazandaran, Khorasan, and Astarabad) under the Russian influence. Later on, APOC changed its name to the Anglo-Iranian Oil Company (AIOC). See F. Fesharaki (1976: 5–9) for further details.

5. By 1941, however, lines had reached as far as Zanjan on the way to Tabriz, as far as Kashan on the way to Yazd, and as far as Semnan on the way to Mashhad (ibid., p. 304).

6. Two classic examples of Reza Shah's modernization and beautification plans during the 1921–1941 period are Mokhber-al-Dowleh and Hassan Abad squares, both in central Tehran. Visit the following pages for photos taken of each square in 1953 and 1957, respectively:
   http://ivizlab.sfu.ca/arya/Gallery/Tehran/22.jpg, accessed 10-24-2007
   http://ivizlab.sfu.ca/arya/Gallery/Tehran/21.jpg, accessed 10-24-2007

7. An early example is the layout of Zand Street in old Shiraz. Visit the following web page for a 1931 photograph: http://www.iranian.com/Books/2002/September/Shiraz/index.html, accessed 10-12-2007.

Chapter Five

# Dependent Urbanization in Iran: From the Mosaddeq Era to the 1979 Revolution

The Allied invasion of Iran in 1941 was a prologue to a new era in Iran with regard to its position within the world capitalist economy. Iran's occupation by British and American forces from the south and the Soviets from the north was justified as being essential for securing a supply line for the Allied forces. The war economy and invasion, a humiliating and embarrassing episode in Iran's modern history nonetheless proved to be beneficial for some Iranians, as it brought prosperity for some merchants and members of the petty-bourgeoisie who profited from hoarding foodstuffs, black market dealings in industrial goods and accommodating the needs of the occupying armies. Due to the reduction in production of consumer goods in Europe and the United States, Iran's internal markets also remained free of foreign competition and in relative terms domestic industries flourished. But the post-War revival of industrial production in the core (European) countries reversed the trend and a consequent flood of foreign commodities posed a serious threat to domestic industries in the peripheries including Iran (Jazani, 1980: 19, 25).

With Iran's oil being the main item of colonial interest, the British continued to control the oil industry. Although Iran's share of income from oil export was meager due to unfair colonial practices by the British, it nonetheless became the chief source of revenue for the Iranian government. In response to this colonial situation a growing nationalist movement led by Dr. Mosaddeq called for the nationalization of oil industry. In 1951 oil was nationalized but the British Petroleum Company (former AIOC) and the Iranian government failed to agree on the terms of the settlement. Subsequently the BP imposed a world-wide boycott of Iranian oil, and the events to be outlined later in this chapter led to the overthrow of Premier Mosaddeq by a well-known and well-documented CIA-backed coup d'état which consequently reinstated the deposed Mohammad Reza Shah. Later on in 1954 an agreement was signed by the new government under which the oil industry was nationalized on paper, while in practice the effective control over price and output remained in the hands of the new international consortium that replaced AIOC.[1] The replacement of a single company by an international consortium in 1954 was a major turning point that distinguished the post-1954 era from the 1880-1950s period. While in the past Iran's oil resources were being exploited and revenues expropriated solely by a single British-owned company, the post-1953 era witnessed a crucial shift in colonial domination. That is, a weakened British colonial power was forced to share its assets with the United States as the new emerging world power. This also signaled the increasing power and influence of multinational corporations in the control of natural resources and political institutions in Iran (see table 5.1). As is illustrated in table 5.1, Britain's share of Iranian oil was reduced from total control to only 40 percent while American companies picked up a hefty 40 percent, and the rest was divided among the French and Dutch corporations.

**Table 5.1:  Percentage Share and the Nationality of the Consortium Participants in 1954**

| Company | % Share | Nationality |
|---|---|---|
| British Petroleum | 40 | British |
| Royal Dutch/Shell | 14 | Anglo-Dutch |
| CFP | 6 | French |
| Standard Oil of New Jersey | 7 | American |
| Standard Oil of California | 7 | American |
| Texaco | 7 | American |
| Mobil | 7 | American |
| Gulf | 7 | American |
| Iricon Group | 5 | American |

Source:  Fesharaki (1976: 48)

## Introduction of Capitalist Relations of Production in Iran

The nationalist and anti-colonial aspirations of Dr. Mosaddeq and his govern-ment were promptly defeated and popular support for his programs was suppressed, mainly because he favored the development of an independent path of capitalist development in Iran. Popular support for Mosaddeq and his nationalist platform mostly came from guild leaders in Tehran as well as from professional associations of lawyers, doctors and university professors. As a populist, Mosaddeq insisted on taking action on behalf of the nation and not any particular class. His political views were particularly in line with those of the main secular nationalist organization, the Iran Party. Established in 1941, the Iran Party advocated state capitalism based on three clear objectives: 1) a national revolution to undermine the feudal landlords; 2) a state-initiated program for rapid industrialization; and 3) nationalization of major industries in Iran. A closer look at the composition of the early leadership of the Iran Party and also Mosaddeq's own organization, the National Front indicates the predominantly urban middle class base of the movement (see table 5.2).

**Table 5.2: Social Class Origins of the Founders of the Iran Party and the National Front**

| Organization | Urban Middle Class # | Urban Middle Class % | Comprador Class & Aristocracy # | Comprador Class & Aristocracy % | Tribal Nobility # | Tribal Nobility % | Total # |
|---|---|---|---|---|---|---|---|
| Iran Party | 10 | 66 | 2 | 14 | 3 | 20 | 15 |
| National Front | 14 | 70 | 4 | 20 | 2 | 10 | 20 |

Source: Table constructed based on information in Abrahamian (1982: 190–91, 254–55; Tables 4 and 6).

Under Mosaddeq's premiership the structure of the Iranian economy drastically changed, mainly due to a sharp decline in state's revenues from the sale of crude oil. A conscious governmental step was consequently taken in order to stop the import of luxury goods. Also, in order to produce the vital commodities such as sugar and textiles which used to be imported from the West, the Mosaddeq government had to increase the output of exports in order to accumulate foreign currency to purchase the needed machinery and equipment. This led to a positive balance of trade during Mosaddeq's short-lived tenure as Iran's Prime Minister (see table 5.3).

Mosaddeq's personal stance on social issues, the Iran Party's programs for social change and the class composition of the Iran Party and the National Front all represent aspirations of a disenchanted middle class which was caught in the midst of a conflict between the landed aristocracy represented by the Parliament and the ministers and British imperialist interests represented by the monarch, Mohammad Reza Shah. The failure of Mosaddeq's nationalist movement is a classic example of the historical incompetence of the middle class in successfully leading a popular anti-colonial movement without the active presence and participation of industrial working class and peasants.

## Table 5.3: Balance of Trade under Mosaddeq's Leadership in Iran

| Year | Imports (millions of Rials) | Exports (millions of Rials) | Balance of Trade |
|---|---|---|---|
| 1. Pre-Mosaddeq years: | | | |
| 1949–1950 | 6,243 | 3,494 | Negative |
| 1950–1951 | 7,011 | 4,319 | Negative |
| 2. Mosaddeq era: | | | |
| 1952–1953 | 5,031 | 5,721 | Positive |
| 1953–1954 | 5,324 | 8,318 | Positive |
| 3. Post-Mosaddeq years: | | | |
| 1954–1955 | 7,425 | 10,288 | Positive |
| 1955–1956 | 9,125 | 8,033 | Positive |
| 1956–1957 | 20,081 | 7,930 | Negative |
| 1958–1959 | 33,578 | 7,941 | Negative |
| 1960–1961 | 52,657 | 8,360 | Negative |

Source: Table constructed based on Nirumand (1969: 109–111)

In light of historical shift in leadership within the world capitalist system, Iran's post-War economy increasingly became subjected to political decisions made in Washington. Economic planning in Iran after the Second World War also followed the United Nations' Economic and Social Council Resolution 1494, which vowed a unified effort for an all-encompassing national development strategy aimed at bringing about "equality of opportunity and income to the Third World."[2] In Iran's case, the then new World Bank and the American Embassy in Tehran played crucial roles in shaping the planning efforts. However, the new U.S. policy in Iran was opposed and criticized by the British who saw any change in Iran's economic structure as a threat to their vested interests in oil industry and commercial activities (Baldwin, 1966: 24). With the help of the U.S. State Department and the International Bank for Reconstruction and Development (IBRD), the newly formed Plan and Budget Organization laid out strategies for Iran's long-term economic development. The First Development Plan (1949–1955) was expected to be financed largely from oil revenues. But Mosaddeq's attempts for nationalization of the oil industry dried up this source of incomee through the reaction of multinational oil companies (Razavi and Vakil, 1984: 20–22).

The second Development Plan (1956–1962) was drafted in 1954 after Mosaddeq's overthrow and the return of Mohammad Reza Shah through direct assistance of the United States and British governments. A new agreement between the Iranian government and multinational oil companies guaranteed the oil revenues, while the U.S. and IBRD also promised additional loans to fuel the economic development plans. The main emphasis was put on transport, communications and agriculture, and unlike the First Plan industrial development had the lowest priority. For example, construction of large dams absorbed most of the funds allocated to the agricultural sector, obviously preparing a pre-capitalist agricultural sector for future capitalist agri-business operations (see Table 5.4). Emphasis on expanding the transportation networks was also an indication of state planners' awareness of the role of an efficient network of roads in penetrating the country and opening up new markets for consumer goods (Razavi and Vakil, 1984: 22–25).

The Third Development Plan (1963–1967) was born out of the need for comprehensive planning. An overexpansion of credits to the private sector and a severe balance-of-payments crisis forced the government to accept austerity measures imposed by the International Monetary Fund (IMF) in 1959. Like the Second Development Plan, the Third plan's emphasis was also on infrastructure and agriculture with a slight increase in expenditures for industrial development. While the state undertook the task of improving the infrastructure, provisions made in the Third Development Plan called for encouraging private capitalist investments particularly in light industries. The timing of the Third Plan and its emphasis on industrial development coincides with the implementation of land reform laws. Aimed at disintegration of pre-capitalist relations of production in rural areas, the implementation of Land Reform policies gradually detached peasants from the land and created a new pool of rural laborers for urban employment in industrial, construction and service-related activities.

The Fourth Development Plan (1968–1972) has to be considered as a turning point in planning strategies. While previous plans focused on rural economy and aimed at transforming it into a capitalist-based agricultural sector, the Fourth Development Plan's overall objective was to push for rapid industrialization by raising the productivity of labor employed in capital-intensive industries. Compared to previous development plans the "industry and mines" sector received the highest priority (20.8 percent) while the "agriculture" sector's share dropped from 21.3 percent in the Third Plan to a low 8.4 percent (see table 5.4). At the same time, infrastructural development in the areas of transportation, communications and energy retained its high share of expenditures (42.3 percent) (Razavi and Vakil,

1984: 31–35).

**Table 5.4: Allocation of Public Funds for Development Plan in Iran, 1949-1972**

| Sector | % of Total Estimated Expenditures | | | |
|---|---|---|---|---|
| | 1st Plan 1949-1955[1] | 2nd Plan 1956-1962 | 3rd Plan 1963-1967 | 4th Plan 1968-1972 |
| Agriculture and Irrigation | 27.8 | 23.3 | 21.3 | 8.4 |
| Industries and Mines | 20.1 | 8.3 | 11.7 | 20.8 |
| Electricity and Fuel | — | — | 18.0 | 18.7 |
| Transport and communication | 29.3 | 37.5 | 24.3 | 23.6 |
| Social Services | 22.8 | 14.4 | 15.1 | 24.6 |
| Regional Development | — | 15.0 | — | 0.5 |
| Urban Development | — | — | 3.1 | 1.6 |

(1) Revised estimates in 1965

Source: Table constructed based on Razavi and Vakil (1984: 21–33, Tables 2.1–2.4)

The Iranian economic crisis was endemic since 1954 when the government was no longer able to pay for the seven year plan's expenditures out of revenues earned from the sale of crude oil. In the mean time, a bad harvest in 1959-1960 worsened the situation and forced the cost-of-living index to rise by 35 percent (Central Bank of Iran, 1970: 673–93). Foreign reserves were also depleted through heavy borrowing which forced Iran to ask for emergency aid from the IMF and the American Government. In response, the IMF promised $35 million in loans if Iran trimmed its budget and shelved some development projects. In the United States, the Kennedy Administration offered an $85 million aid package on the condition that the Shah brings liberals into the cabinet and imposes land reform to curb any attempts to ignite a social revolution (Abrahamian: 1982: 422). Forced by internal concerns for rural reforms and outside political pressure for hastening the land reform, in 1963 the Shah launched his "White Revolution" as a six-point program of socioeconomic and political reform. The plan's most important measure was the land reform which drastically altered pre-capitalist relations of production in rural Iran. The fact that the land reform was not even conceived by planners of the Third Plan is indicative of its urgency for Iranian policy makers and their foreign advisors to pave the way for foreign capitalist investment and prevent any radical changes in Iran.

## Paving the Road to Dependent Urbanization: Land Reform's Effects on Rural and Urban Social Classes

I consider "dependent urbanization" as an induced process that is the spatial manifestation of implementation of the above-mentioned socioeconomic "blueprints" that aim at establishing a dependent capitalist economy. This process results in transformation of social class structures both in rural and urban areas and in turn leads to the spatial transformation of rural and urban structures. I will argue that land reform policies in the 1960s played a crucial role in Iran's rural and urban spatial transformation, and immensely contributed to the process of dependent urbanization. My concern here with economic development plans and land reform policies is more with the way their implementation affected the class structure of rural Iran and in turn resulted in spatial dislocation of certain segments of the rural population. In this section I will sketch social classes in rural and urban areas and the ways in which they have been affected by land reform policies.

### Social Classes in Pre-Land Reform Rural Iran

There were four distinct classes in rural Iran prior to the implementation of the Land Reform.[3] First, the *landlords* who, ironically in most cases resided in urban areas. Before the reform, the most powerful landlords consisted of 400- to 500 families. The big landowners owned an estimated 80-85 percent of the cultivated land in Iran (Halliday, 1979: 106–7; Bill, 1963: 401). The landowning class had also an effective representation in the government. During the 1941–1961 period 57 percent of the Parliament (*Majlis*) deputies were landowners. At the same time, almost 80 percent of the Senate members during the 1950–1960 period were either large landowners or came from landholding families (Zonis, 1968: 265–67). *Peasants* were the second rural class who comprised 60 percent of rural households. This refers to those who possessed cultivation rights or "*nasaq*," owned some means of production such as seeds and plough animals, and were engaged in either sharecropping or tenancy agriculture. *Independent peasants and petty producers* formed the third class. Comprising only about 5 percent of rural households, independent peasants owned a small plot of land by maintaining their productivity at subsistence level, and independent craftsmen/petty producers manufactured almost all non-food products in the countryside (GOPF, 1976: 22). Finally, there were the *landless rural laborers* who neither owned any means of production such as land, seed and tools, nor did they enjoy the right to cultivate the land. As wage laborers they survived by working for rich peasants or landlords and being compensated in kind or cash, or as seasonal agricultural laborers performing a variety of petty jobs in the countryside. Governmental data indicate that prior to the land reform landless peasants comprised about 2,000,000 households (Ministry of Interior, 1962: 269).

Initiated from above, the Land Reform was carried out in Iran by pursuing four major objectives: 1) limiting the size of individual holdings to only one village, where landlords were required to sell their excess village holdings and land to the government; 2) allocating land holdings among peasants without any changes in the field layout; 3) making membership of peasants in rural cooperatives as a necessary means for their eligibility to receive land; and 4) redistributing land among those peasants who had cultivation rights on feudal lands ("nasaq" holders) (Research Group, 1970; Hooglund, 1982). The Land Reform was planned to be implemented in three distinct phases. The first phase (1963-1967) was naturally the most critical stage of social transformation and introduction of new relations of production in rural Iran. The most important aspect of this phase was the development of rural cooperatives. It was assumed that the cooperatives would provide credit and also general supervision for peasants to obtain seeds, fertilizers, tools and other needed items. The objective was to promote modernized farming and facilitate market relations in rural Iran.

The overall impact of this phase in liquidating the large land holdings was substantial. However, it only affected about 20 percent of villages in Iran. The second phase (1965–1968) aimed to eliminate sharecropping practices, and thus eliminate the pre-capitalist form of rent and pave the way for a large landholding system. All owners whose lands were exempted in the first phase had three major options in the second phase: 1) to lease their lands to the peasants who had worked on them for up to 30 years; 2) to sell their lands to peasants altogether; or 3) to form joint-stock agricultural units with peasants and having shares proportionate to each party's assets of land, livestock and tools (Lambton, 1969: 194-206). Soon it became obvious that the first option was the landowners' favorite. As a result, about 80 percent of the transactions made during this period created tenancies, which in turn denied peasants the ownership rights.

Once the new relations of production and land ownership patterns were introduced, the planners began promoting the creation of farm corporations and agri-businesses in the third phase of Land Reform (1968–1971). During the third phase, a capital-intensive agricultural economy based on a highly mechanized cash-crop system of production was implemented in Iran, whereby many independent peasants were forced to exchange their land with paper shares in farm corporations. This led to the concentration of land ownership in the hands of large corporations, and in turn created a new breed of landless peasants. According to some estimates, after a decade of reform, by 1972 the absentee landowners including the Royal family, big landholders, multinational corporations and religious foundations still controlled nearly 20 percent of Iran's cultivated lands (Garzuel and Skolka, 1976).

**Rural Classes after the Land Reform**

Land Reform policies to certain extent introduced capitalist economic relations in rural Iran, but the planners' political objectives were not completely met. The Land Reform laws were envisioned based on at least two political objectives: 1) to destroy the power base of the major landowning families in rural areas; and 2) to gain the support and allegiance of peasants and hence forestall a mass-based uprising and possible revolution in the countryside. The first objective was achieved as many landlords with large holdings lost their political support and to some extent their economic base in the countryside. However, the second objective faced major structural obstacles during the implementation phase. In general, only former sharecroppers benefited from land redistribution, while rural agricultural laborers and wage-earners were in most part left out of the scheme. This resulted in a rapid deterioration of economic conditions for the already dispossessed agricultural *proletariat* and added to their resentment about reform policies (Kazemi, 1980: 35). In fact, the majority of the poor rural migrants who went to principal cities of Iran came from among the disenchanted landless peasants.

There are indications that land reform policies increased the number of landless peasants: by the early 1970s they comprised about 2.4 million households, up by 400,000 from a decade earlier (Khosrovi, 1973). These landless farm workers who were employed by landowners for carrying out work on irrigation, road building and other rural infrastructural projects lost that source of employment after the land reform. Intensive work on the land by farmers who benefited from the reform policies increased participation of their own family members and reduced employment of the landless peasants for obvious economic reasons. Thus between 1966 and 1969 the category of "unpaid family workers" rose from 9.9 to 16.9 percent and "wage and salary earners" dropped from 38.6 to 27.3 percent within the rural labor force (ILO, 1974).

Another rural class that was affected by the land reform policies was the independent petty producer. Since the direction of development thrust was toward reorganization of agricultural production and not rural manufacturing activities, petty commodity producers and artisans not only found they could not benefit from governmental plans, but also realized that industrial goods produced in urban centers were taking away their clientele in the countryside. The quality of consumer goods and appealing packaging of commodities produced in urban centers such as soap, shoes, garments, etc. was attracting the rural population who were willing to pay a higher price for these goods. Furthermore, due to an increase in prices of raw materials, the self-employed rural artisans also had to ask higher prices for their wares. This left rural producers with no alternative but to accept reduced earnings in order to compete with the often higher quality but lower priced urban industrial commodities (Dhamija, 1976: 23–26).

### Urban Classes in Post-Land Reform Era

Introduction of capitalism and gradual elimination of pre-capitalist relations as well as implementation of the Land Reform laws not only changed the class structure in rural areas, but it also greatly affected the class composition of urban population. Four major urban classes can be identified after the land reform. First, totaling no more than one-thousand individuals, the *comprador class* consisted of: 1) members of the Shah's family; 2) previous feudal families that had turned their interests to capitalist ventures in urban areas; 3) high ranking civil servants and military officers who sat in managerial boards and facilitated lucrative government contracts; and 4) the well-established class of businessmen who were attached to and benefited from the world capitalist economy after the Second World War commercial boom in Iran. Overall, the comprador class owned about 85 percent of major industrial, commercial, and banking institutions (Halliday, 1979: 151).

The second urban-based class was the *Petty Bourgeoisie*, increasingly becoming dependent upon the world capitalist markets for raw materials, credit requirements and even marketing its products. The urban petty bourgeoisie comprised of two sub-classes: 1) the "bazaar" community comprised of about half a million merchants, shopkeepers, traders and workshop owners; and 2) other petty entrepreneurs who operated outside the bazaar community, and had investments in neighborhood stores or medium-sized workshops. Through retaining their independent craft and trade guilds, the Iranian petty bourgeoisie, particularly the bazaar community successfully controlled about half of Iran's handicraft production, two-thirds of retail trade, and three-quarters of its wholesale trade. In addition, initial modernization efforts in the 1920s also created a *new middle class* comprised of non-propertied and salaried employees, who particularly found a fertile ground for growth after the 1960s reforms and gradual domination of a dependent capitalist economy. Consequently, this class doubled in size, from 310,000 in 1956 to over 630,000 in 1977, and included 304,404 civil servants, 208,241 teachers and school administrators, and 61,066 white collar workers. A substantial increase in industrial activities during the Fourth and Fifth economic Development Plans also contributed to a substantial growth of the Iran's urban *working class*. By 1977 Iran's working class totaled 880,000, including 600,000 factory workers in plants with more than 10 employees; 20,000 electrical, gas and power workers; 150,000 transport network employees; 80,000 mines, fishery/forestry workers and 30,000 oil industry workers (Abrahamian, 1982: 434).

In addition to the above-mentioned social classes, a growing army of the *urban poor* became an inseparable part of urban stratification system in Iran. The urban poor were mostly comprised of the impoverished rural immigrants and squatter settlers, who in most cases found seasonal and temporary employment in construction industry and similar activities. In desperation, many of them became self-employed petty retailers as peddlers, street hawkers and the like, and according to one estimate during the 1970s the urban poor numbered 1,500,000 (ibid., 435). Like many other developing societies, the urban poor represented the dark side of a dependent capitalist economic development in Iran. Later on in Chapter 9 a closer look at the urban employment structure for Tehran and entire country will reveal an increase in importance and size of this social class.

## Land Reform's Effects on Rural-Urban Migration and Rural Spatial Hierarchy

After the implementation of land reform policies, the high rate of migration from rural areas to major urban centers such as Tehran, Tabriz, Isfahan, Kermanshah, Shiraz, Mashhad, Abadan and Ahwaz produced anxiety among planners. The pattern of seasonal migration was particularly alarming, as 66 percent of seasonal migrants were peasants having farmland less than one and half hectares. Besides seasonal migration there was also a substantial permanent migration between1966 and 1971. Different rural classes had different incentives to give up their rural lifestyle and leave for urban centers. The landless peasants were attracted to urban employment because it offered higher pay with less working hours; beside the fact that they had little or no opportunities for work in the countryside. On the other hand, the independent peasants did not have enough land to subsist, let alone to prosper. Added to this, was the government's aggressive policy of importing the basic foodstuffs which were mostly subsidized and hence cheaper compared to domestic produce, which gradually pushed independent peasants out of the already squeezed rural markets. Finally, the well-off independent peasant producers were also confronted with a shortage of farm wage-laborers, since most of them had already migrated to cities in search of jobs (Riyahi, 1976: 6–7). An interesting pattern of migration was that while in 1966 most peasants migrated because of rural unemployment or lack of better jobs in the countryside, by 1970 the main reason for migration appeared to be family reunion between peasants who worked in urban centers and their relatives who were left behind in the villages (see table 5.5). This also signaled the beginning phase for the breakdown of family structure and pre-capitalist social relations in rural Iran.

Another consequence of reform policies was stagnation of sub-regional village centers which served as pre-capitalist rural market towns and provided non-farm services for rural settlements. As I discussed earlier in Chapter 4, small villages with a population of 500 or less had been relatively self-sufficient but at the same time dependent upon sub-regional village centers or regional urban centers that served as an outlet for their produce and a source of supplies for their needs. With the introduction of large-scale farming and consequent increased produce, sub-regional village centers did not have the means to handle the marketing of mass-produced agricultural commodities. That is, the traders in these centers had neither the warehouses for stocking the produce nor available credit to purchase the produce. As a consequence, they were being bypassed in many cases and the produce was being sold directly to merchants in regional urban centers. Hence the sub-regional village centers' prime function of being a local marketing and distribution center of agricultural produce was gradually undermined. To say the least, the implementation of the Land Reform policies destroyed the existing rural spatial hierarchy without creating a viable alternative spatial network.

**Table 5.5:  Reasons for Rural-Urban Migration, 1966 and 1970**

| Reasons | 1964 (%) | 1970 (%) |
| --- | --- | --- |
| Seeking work | 11.2 | 4.2 |
| Seeking better jobs | 49.2 | 17.2 |
| Joining the family | 8.8 | 61.0 |
| Marriage | 10.9 | 9.9 |
| Education | 1.3 | 0.9 |
| Transfer | 7.7 | 3.7 |
| Other | 10.9 | 3.2 |

Source: Dhamija (1976:52)

## The Effects of Oil Industry on Urban Development

We can evaluate the significance of the oil industry as the leading economic sector on urban development through an examination of its indirect and direct effects on Iran's economy. Earlier in the chapter I discussed in detail the direct effects of oil revenues on the state's budget and planning, namely, an increased earning capacity for government spending. With regard to direct effects of oil industry on other economic sectors and its role in rural and urban development I have identified four important factors. First, Iran's economy became increasingly dependent on revenues generated by the production and export of crude oil, which in turn contributed to the underdevelopment of industrial and agricultural sectors in Iran. That is, by providing the state with excessive available foreign exchange and credit, oil revenues enabled the government to import agricultural and industrial products such as consumer goods, food items, machinery, spare parts and military equipment. As is demonstrated in table 5.6, nearly half the Gross Domestic Product (GDP) in 1977 came from the oil sector compared to only 13.8 percent for a decade earlier. On the other hand, during the same period contribution of agricultural sector fell substantially from 24.5 percent to 8 percent, an indication of Iran's nearly complete dependence on imported agricultural products.

**Table 5.6: Contribution to Iran's Gross National Product by Economic Sector, 1967-1977**

| Sector | 1967 (%) | 1972 (%) | 1977 (%) |
|---|---|---|---|
| Oil | 13.8 | 19.5 | 48.7 |
| Agriculture | 24.5 | 18.1 | 8.0 |
| Industry and mining | 21.3 | 22.0 | 16.0 |

Source: Plan and Budget Organization (1975: 37).

Second, the oil industry in Iran had no backward linkages, as it had small or practically no demand for goods produced and services provided by domestic economy (Fesharaki, 1976: 143). For instance, in order to build the new port city of Abadan as the site of Iran's first oil refinery and the main oil export terminal, the British imported virtually all construction materials including the bricks. In addition, in the absence of a viable industrial sector, Iran's highly capital-intensive oil industry required the government to virtually import all the machinery, equipment, parts and even the know how from core countries.[4] Third, the capital-intensive nature of the oil industry had another disadvantage for Iranian workers in that it only employed a tiny labor force. With an increase in oil production capacity the situation became even worse due to the installation and introduction of highly automated machinery. While the work force employed in the oil industrial sector in the 1958–1972 period was reduced by half, the oil production was increased almost six-fold during the same period. Finally, the oil industry did not provide considerable forward linkages in Iran in that almost all the extracted crude oil was exported to Western industrial nations and the flow of low-cost fuel to the domestic market was minimal (ibid.: 173; Halliday, 1979: 139). This was manifested in the lack of an extensive network of roads and other transportation networks which were essential and vital for a viable and sustainable process of economic development (see table 5.7).

In general, although oil revenues in the hands of the state planning authorities could have been utilized for urban development, the industry itself had little or no direct effect on urbanization in Iran. For one thing, extraction of crude oil in isolated and remote areas and its wholesale export through pipelines only required port cities and few enclave communities to support the small contingent of workers. The oil industry's only major contribution to urban development was the establishment of the port city of Abadan in southwestern Iran. Lying on a large mudflat island situated in the estuary of the Tigris-Euphrates (Arvand) and Karun Rivers at the mouth of the Persian Gulf, Abadan was developed as an oil city in 1909 when the

Anglo-Iranian Oil Company (AIOC) established its pipeline terminus and refinery there.

**Table 5.7: Employment and Productivity in the Iranian Oil Industry, 1958–1972**

| Year | Manual Labor | Production (In cubic meters) | Cubic meters/Worker |
|------|-----------|-----------|-----------|
| 1958 | 48,477 | 47,767 | 0.98 |
| 1961 | 39,638 | 68,581 | 1.73 |
| 1964 | 31,564 | 98,343 | 3.11 |
| 1967 | 29,426 | 150,681 | 5.12 |
| 1970 | 26,952 | 222,180 | 8.24 |
| 1972 | 24,931 | 294,100 | 11.80 |

Source: Table constructed based on Fesharaki (1976: 145, Table 6.8)

Abadan might be considered as the prototype of a colonial "company town" in Iran, where the importance of the oil refinery as the dominant economic activity and the superior class position of the British colonial functionaries were clearly spelled out for its residents. In fact, the British built Abadan and Masjed-Soleyman, another company town where the first oil reserves were discovered in 1908 "(W)ith the sole purpose of exploration, extraction, transport, refining, storage, and export of oil" (Ehsani, 2003:  372). Similar to Cairo, but in a much smaller scale Abadan also evolved as a "dual city." In spatial terms, Abadan comprised a pre-modern, "unofficial" pre-capitalist section that housed Iranian residents indigenous to the region and related economic activites (Abadan Town), and a modern, "official" colonial section that catered to the needs of oil industry executives, functionaries and workers employed by the Anglo-Iranian Oil Company (Lahsaeizadeh, 2006: 176–77) (see plate 5.1).

The city was consisted of a series of well planned, well built, and strictly stratified compounds for the company's staff. An interesting feature of Abadan's layout was the spatial segregation of foreign staff and Iranian workers based on their perceived social class position. For example, spacious detached houses were provided for the British managers and high ranking officials; attached middle-class town houses for the British and Indian officials, clerks, technicians and petty bureaucrats; and attached row houses for both Iranian and foreign workers. This

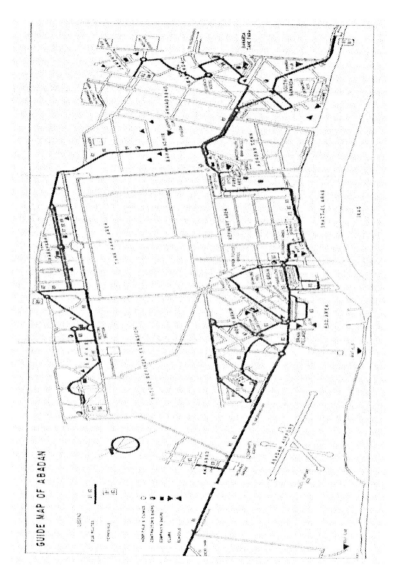

**Plate 5.1. Map of Abadan Highlighting Bus Routes (ca. 1958)**
 Source:  Paul Schroeder (2007):
 http: //www.iranian.com/Abadan/2007/July/Khuzestan/116.html

strict and deliberate stratification in housing was meant to minimize class, ethnic and racial contact. In the meantime, it emphasized each employee's social class as a means to control and contain possible class-based confrontations (Ehsani, 2003: 389-91). In his study of Abadan's planning and architectural design by the Anglo-Iranian Oil Company (AIOC) Crinson, (1997: 351) provides a vivid description of the city's stratified layout:

> For non-European staff Segoush-i-Braim and Amirabad were located to the north and Bawarda-i-Shemaili to the south. For non-European labour Bahar and Farahabad were sited beside the Bahmanshir River; Ahmedabad and Bahman-shir just east of the town; and Jamshid to the southeast. *To the northwest an extension of Braim was laid out for European staff.* (Italics mine)

An interesting insight on the lives of non-Iranian employees and their families is provided by the son of a former Exxon Mobil American employee who lived in Abadan from 1958–1960. In his memoirs as "an American boy" Paul Schroeder (2007) reminisces his childhood years in Abadan, where he lived with his parents in the posh neighborhood of Braim designed for European/British employees:

> I'll try to convey something of the uniqueness of Abadan, beyond these everyday arrangements. Foremost was the intensity of the physical environment. The blazing sun and baking pavements were most memorable. As a product of the frozen northlands, I truly loved the relentless heat—but of course I had a home and the pool for retreat, and didn't have to work in it. Bluer skies than Abadan's are impossible. The ever-flowing river was a constant presence, and the canal-watered date groves and irrigated neighbor-hoods of Braim provided a striking contrast with the surrounding parched tan earth, on which as far as I could see nothing grew except prickly camel thorns.

After the oil nationalization in 1950 by Dr. Mosaddeq, Abadan's foreign population was almost eliminated, from 30,000 foreign technicians and workers in the late 1940s to a meager 50 in 1950 (Ashraf, 1974: 50–56). Once considered as the largest oil refinery in the world, the city of Abadan and its refinery were bombed by Iraqi forces in 1980 during the Iran-Iraq war, both reduced to rubbles. After the war's end and cease fire in 1988 the refinery was reconstructed and became operational by 1990, but to this date neither the refinery nor residential neighborhoods have returned to their original pre-war conditions.

## Notes

1. For a detailed account of the historical events that led to the nationalization of the oil industry see Fesharaki (1976, Chapter 2); Elwell-Sutton (1955); and Ashraf (1971: 100–116).

2. It is worth mentioning that the promulgation of the United Nations' Resolution coincided with Washington's first economic aid program (Point IV) to Iran. The Point IV Program was then accompanied by a joint American-Iranian defense agreement in which the former agreed to supply Iran with arms in 1950 as a part of "Alliance for Progress" plan, which was initiated for suppressing any progressive (anti-colonialist/socialist) movement in peripheral countries.

3. There are some spill-over effects from the import of this machinery from abroad, insofar as the installation of this machinery would require the building of new plants (from domestic resources) and employment of domestic labor force. However, such spill-over effects are generally irrelevant to the issue of capital investments.

4. For a comprehensive study of the British colonial interests in using "social engineering" in the design of Abadan see Ehsani (2003). Visit the following web pages for two examples of stratified housing in Abadan:

http: //www.iranian.com/Abadan/2007/April/1958/92.html (attached housing units for Iranian and Indian company workers, Indian Quarters), accessed 11-12-2007. Image source: Paul Schroeder (2007).

http: //www.iranian.com/Abadan/2007/April/1958/80.html (house for European (British) staff, Braim neighborhood), accessed 11-12-2007. Image Source: Paul Schroeder (2007).

# Chapter Six

# Uneven Urban Development and Hyper-Urbanization in Iran: The Case of Tehran

As a small and relatively unimportant village during the 16th and 17th centuries, Tehran owed its existence to its military function by serving as a garrison for various regional and local rulers. Proximity to the city of Rey and being on the trade routes that connected central Iranian cities to those of the northeast and northwestern regions gradually increased Tehran's importance in the 18th century. Tehran's history as a city starts at the end of the 18th century when in 1796 it was selected as the government seat by Agha-Mohammad Khan, the founder of Qajar Dynasty. At that time, Tehran had an estimated population of 15,000, of whom about 3,000 were soldiers (Bahrambeygui, 1977: 11).

Tehran of late 18th and early 19th century was a sleepy town surrounded by 16th century gated walls. Even its new status as the capital city appeared to have no significant effect on its growth. There were few developments during the first decade of the 19th century, the main one being the construction of a new royal palace and an influx of tribal chiefs and their families who were close to the monarch (ibid.: 19). Later on, Russia's aggression in northwestern parts of Iran during the 1820s and 1830s led to population displacement, and Tehran's population increased considerably as a result of emigration from that region (Kinneir, 1813: 77). However, in the first half of the 19th century Tehran lagged behind Tabriz, the main trading post in northwest Iran both in terms of population growth and commercial importance. A British foreign office report in 1841 put Tehran as the "second or third city of the empire in respect to commerce" (Abbott, cf. Issawi, 1971: 118). Even by the late 1860s Tehran's population was estimated as 85,000 compared to 110,000 for Tabriz (Thompson, cf. Issawi, 1971: 28)(see figure 6.1).[1]

Tehran's increasing importance in the second half of the 19th century was related to two factors: 1) the presence of the Royal Court, the central government bureaucracy and accompanying support services; and 2) its central location for

95

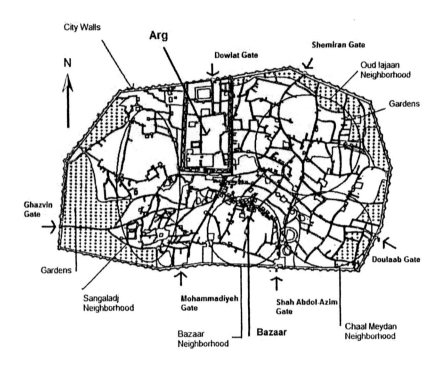

**Figure 6.1. The First Map of Tehran Surrounded by its 16th Century Walls (1852)**
Source: Map generated by author after "Town Plan of Tehran" by Berzin (1852).

trade with Khorasan to the northeast and east, and Qom, Kashan, Isfahan, and Shiraz to the southeast. Handled by Iranian merchants, commodities, mostlyEuropean-made goods, were purchased in Tabriz and Constantinople, brought to Tehran and re-routed to Mazandaran, Astarabad, Qom, Arak, Mashhad and other centers of trade in the country (Abbott, cf. Issawi, 1971: 118). The increasing economic and political relations between Iran and the European colonial powers also affected Tehran's spatial development. Impressed by the splendor of European cities, the Qajar ruler Nasser-od din Shah (1848–1896) was determined to improve Tehran's "urbanity." To give Tehran a more modern face, the King established several factories, a hospital, a power station, a horse-drawn tramway, a post office and other "urban amenities" (Hekamy, 1964: 14).

An interesting phenomenon during the second half of the 19th century, is the concentration of new industries in and around the capital city despite its unfavorable location for the import and transportation of machinery and needed equipment. This location preference, both by foreign and domestic entrepreneurs may be attributed to their proximity to the ruling elite, central government and foreign consulates for further protection on the one hand, and the availability of a potential consumer class (such as the Court contingent, government officials and merchants) for manufactured products on the other. Concentration of industrial activities in Tehran has to be regarded as the early signs of a nascent uneven urban development in Iran. However, as I discussed in Chapter 3 the 19th century Iranian economy was predominantly pre-capitalist and was not receptive to capital investments in industrial activities.

The effects of European technology and manufacturing activities on pre-capitalist Tehran's spatial development were mostly of superficial nature. Tehran's spatial development was not based on industrial activities, capital accumulation or circulation and appropriation of generated profit in the forms of land and real estate development. Rather, in the absence of a genuine urban development in a capitalist sense, the only visible signs of modernity were "shops with glass windows and European titles" and "street lamp-posts built for gas, but accommodating dubious oil lamps" (Curzon, cf. Shearman, 1961: 570). By 1900 Tehran had acquired the only railway in Iran spanning a total of eight miles, boasting the only electric power generating plant in the entire country (Bharier, 1971: 16). As late as 1920, Tehran was a walled city surrounded by a dry moat. The only entrances to the capital were through the city gates, which were closed at night to keep out robbers and cutthroats (Graham, 1979: 24). At the close of the 19th century, however, Tehran had expanded sufficiently to have outstripped any other city in the country, and by early 20th century Tehran's population was estimated at 250,000.

Following the Constitutional Revolution of 1906 and the subsequent establishment of the legislative assembly (*Majlis*), Tehran gained greater importance as a political and intellectual center. Later on, centralization of the state apparatus paved the way for capitalist development in the 1920s and led to rapid concentration of all governmental bureaucratic institutions in Tehran. With the concentration of administration and government bureaucracy under Reza Shah's ambitious modernization plans in the 1920s the city acquired a new growth pole: the new government administrative enclave which was built and expanded next to the old center of commerce, trade and pre-capitalist commercial activities, or the "bazaar." This new urban administrative core brought with it a new vitality, leading to rapid increase in the number of civil servants and government employees (Bahrambeygui, 1977: 23–24). As I stated in the previous chapter, one of the major developments in Iran toward the end of 19th century was the legal recognition of private property and especially that of land. This, along with the growth of a new government administration and the bureaucrats' increasing demand for new housing facilities prompted land speculation that contributed to Tehran's considerable urban expansion. As a result, Tehran witnessed an outward growth toward north, beyond boundaries of the old pre-capitalist city. It was in this period that urban development and urban renewal gained momentum, resulting in the clearance and reconstruction of slum areas in the center and northwestern parts of the city. But it was not until 1937 that the city walls surrounding and delineating Tehran's pre- capitalist era boundaries were pulled down. By 1940 the old walls were replaced with broad avenues, presumably a necessary step to be taken for urban development. This rather symbolic action of tearing down the traditional security walls signaled a new era for capital investment and urban development which required a secure and safe environment for industries and land speculators (see figure 6.2).[2] Katouzian (1996: 35) provides a vivid account of the prevalent mood related to the "modern" European facelift of the Capital:

> (T)he places that aroused the greatest interest were Meydãn-e Toupkhãne, Avenue Lãlezãr and Avenue Alã od-Dawle also known as Boulevard des Ambassadeurs. The Meydãn-e Toupkhãne (Cannon Square), was conceived as a great urban stage, where "modernity," the exalted enterprise undertaken by the ruling class of the country, was celebrated.

## Dependent Capitalist Development and Concentration of Economic Activities in Tehran (Post–1953 era)

Concentration of industrial and commercial activities in Tehran dates back to the late 19th century. But the 19th century efforts should be considered as an experimental anomaly, rather than a long-term plan to introduce capitalist measures in Iran. The unsuitable conditions for industrial activities and superiority of the European-made commodities to domestic goods forced most of the 19th century factories to close down. Table 6.1 demonstrates the nature and ownership status of the so-called "modern" Iranian industries during the second half of the 19th century.

The first serious efforts to invest in industries were made by Reza Shah during the 1930s as part of his modernization plans Iran. By the decade's end 20 percent of state's budget was allocated for industrial development, resulting in establish-ment of 64 factories (Bharier, 1971: 176–78). By imposing high tariffs on impor-ted goods and supporting state-owned industries Reza Shah increased the number of factories from 20 in 1925 to 346 in 1941 (Abrahamian, 1982: 146). A significant factor that contributed to uneven urban development in Iran was the magnitude of foreign capital investment especially after the land reform. With increasing interest and presence of multinational corporations industrial concentration in Tehran took

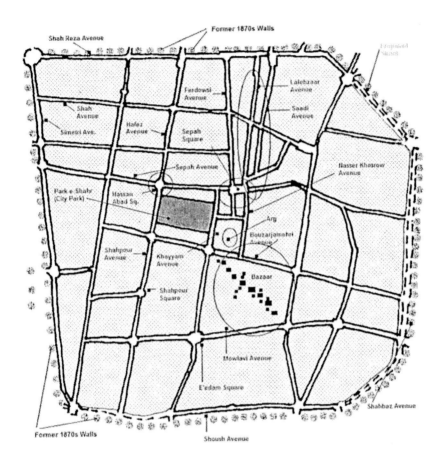

Figure 6.2. Map of Modernizing Tehran with Broad Avenues and Erased Pre-capitalist Era Walls (1937)

**Table 6.1:  Modern Factories in Iran, 1850-1900**

| Industrial Activity | Date Established | Location | Ownership | Remarks |
|---|---|---|---|---|
| Rifle factory | 1850/1851 | Tehran | state | |
| Spinning mill | 1858/1859 | Tehran | private | (a) |
| Paper factory | 1850s | Tehran | n.a. | (a) |
| Sugar factory | n.d. | Mazandaran | n.a. | |
| Calico weaving | n.d. | Tehran | n.a. | |
| Glass factory | 1868/1869 | Tehran | foreign | (b) |
| Glass factory | 1887/1888 | Tehran | private | (b) |
| Porcelain | n.d. | Tehran | private | (c) |
| Porcelain | n.d. | Tabriz | private | (c) |
| Candle making | 1850s | Tehran | n.a. | (b) |
| Linen weaving | n.d. | Isfahan | state | |
| Silk reeling | n.d. | Gilan | private | |
| Silk reeling | n.d. | near Rasht | Russian | (d) |
| Gasworks | 1881/1882 | Tehran | state | (b) |
| Beets processing | 1895/1896 | Kahrizak | Belgian | (e) |
| Spinning | 1894/1895 | n.a. | private | (e) |

Notes.    a: Ceased operation.
          b: Closed down due to lack of material.
          c: Closed down due to bankruptcy.
          d: Closed down due to poor management.
          e: Closed down, unable to compete with foreign goods.
          n.a.: information not available
Source:  Table constructed based on information in Jamalzadeh (1956: 93–96).

a new turn during the post-1952 period, particularly due to the provisions made for capitalist development in the Third Development Plan (1963-1968). In order to attract foreign investors, favorable terms for the repatriation of capital and earned interest and profits were conceived by the government. This led to an enormous increase in the volume of foreign investment in Iran particularly after 1963 (see table 6.2). The emergence of the United States as the new dominant player in the world capitalist economy and its increased influence and presence in Iran manifested itself in its share of Iran's foreign investments particularly during the Fourth Development Plan period (1968–1973). For instance, about 50 percent of all foreign investments in Iran during this period were made by American investors, followed by Germans (14 percent) and the British (10 percent) (Iranian-American Economic Survey, 1976: 86–87).

**Table 6.2: Share of Foreign Investment in Iran's Capitalist Development Plans, 1949–1973**

| Plan | Period | Foreign Investment (millions of dollars) |
|---|---|---|
| 1st seven-year | 1949–1956 | 68 |
| 2nd seven-year | 1956–1963 | 79 |
| 3rd five-year | 1963–1968 | 2,728 |
| 4th five-year | 1968–1973 | 7,700 |

Source: Iranian-American Economic Survey (1976: 131).

The second factor that indicates the degree of Tehran's vitality, especially for its nascent capitalist class, was concentration of company headquarters in the capital as a clear sign of management's preference for Tehran. For example, about 83 percent of all companies in 1972 were registered in Tehran (Plan and Budget Organization, 1973). By 1975, Tehran almost became the sole urban center for company headquarters, as 97 percent of them were housed in Tehran (Chaichian, 1997). Not surprisingly, American investors also preferred the capital for their wheeling and dealing activities, and all of the hundred or so American firms and corporations doing business in Iran had their headquarters in Tehran (Iranian-American Economic Survey, 1967: 151–162). Clearly, a decentralized model of economic development plan that would have better served Iran's national interests was not favored by the American policy makers and foreign investors. Table 6.3 illustrates the extreme uneven spatial location of company headquarters in Tehran vis-à-vis other major cities. This is a significant indicator of concentration of capital in one urban enclave, which in turn contributes to an uneven urban development (see figure 6.3).

In the absence of an adequate national infrastructure to support a decentralized economic and industrial development, Tehran emerged as the hub of new investments and industrial activities. According to a survey conducted by the Plan and Budget Organization in 1964 about 35 percent of national investments (excluding oil) and 66 percent of foreign investments were in industries located in Tehran or its immediate vicinity (Bahrambeygui, 1977: 106). By 1967, 29 percent of all industrial establishments, 46.1 percent of all large industrial establishments employing more than 10 workers, and 36.2 percent of industrial work force were also located in and around Tehran (Looney, 1973: 129).

**Figure 6.3. A view of Istanbul Avenue in downtown Tehran (1965). Note the new high rise "Aluminum Building" and the way it is Sandwiched between old pre-capitalist structures (sketch by author).**

**Table 6.3: Location of the Main Office Headquarters for Major Companies in Iran, 1975**

| City | Number of Companies |
|------|---------------------|
| Tehran | 649 |
| Tabriz | 4 |
| Isfahan | 4 |
| Shiraz | 2 |
| Khorramshahr | 2 |
| Zahidan | 2 |
| Gonbad Qabus | 1 |
| Abadan | 1 |
| Kashan | 1 |
| Mashhad | 1 |
| Ghuchan | 1 |
| Ahwaz | 1 |
| Total | 669 |

Source: Table constructed based on information in Bricault (1975: 87-175)

## The Effects of Rural-Urban and Inter-Urban Migration on Tehran's Growth

As I discussed in previous chapter the pattern of internal migration in Iran during the third period (1952-1979) particularly after the Land Reform was greatly affected by socio-economic changes taking place in rural Iran. For instance, during the 1900–1956 period about 61 percent of internal migration movements were inter-urban, with only 39 percent caused by rural-urban migration. But rural-urban migration during the 1956–1966 period alone comprised 64.6 percent of all migratory movements in Iran (Bharier, 1977: 331–341; Ministry of Labor and Social Affairs, 1964: 2476). In this particular period, Tehran became the leading urban center in absorbing the migrant population. For example, about 39 percent of approximately two million migrants whose birthplaces were enumerated in 1956 were living in Tehran, and by 1964 this ratio increased to 41 percent (Hemmasi, 1974: 37). On the other hand, while in 1966 about 74 percent of Iran's total urban populations were born in their hometowns, this proportion was much lower for the capital where only 49 percent of its residents were born in Tehran (Iranian Statistical Center, 1966: 4; Bahrambeygui, 1977: 59). This high ratio of migrant population for Tehran can be mainly attributed to the implementation of Land

Reform laws and consequent social transformation of many rural communities; as well as concentration of all economic, bureaucratic and administrative activities in Tehran. The pace of migration to Tehran seems to have slowed down by the mid-1970s, as alternative destinations for migrants were developed. This was mostly due to new planning strategies during the Fourth and Fifth Development Plans, which called for a certain degree of decentralization for new commercial and industrial activities.

One of the major issues of concern for both census enumerators and individual scholars for the 1956-1976 period has been an understanding of the reasons for people's mobility and migration. In Tehran's case, almost all the surveys conducted related to this matter indicate that unemployment at the place of origin was the prime factor for its migrant population. Obviously, those migrants who later joined their families who were already settled in Tehran have to be considered as an inseparable part of the first-wave migrants who came to the Capital in search of jobs (see table 6.4). If the two groups are perceived as victims of unemployment in their respective places of origin, it means that 86.4 percent of migrants in 1956 and 80.3 percent in 1966 came to Tehran in search of jobs. The unsettling fact, however, is that according to statistics few of those who came to find a job were actually successful. For example, in 1956 only 24 percent of migrants were able to get a job in Tehran. Unfortunately, available data do not indicate the average length of the time before a migrant was able to get employment in Tehran (ibid.: 49; Kazemi, 1980: 43–45).

**Table 6.4: Main Reasons for Migration to Tehran, 1956 and 1966 (%)**

| Date of Migration | Seeking Work | Joining their Families | Seeking a Better job | Other |
|---|---|---|---|---|
| 1956 | 25.6 | 59.0 | 7.2 | 8.2 |
| 1966 | 20.8 | 59.5 | 6.7 | 13.0 |

Source: Hemmasi (1974: 50).

The uneven nature of capitalist development not only manifested itself in spatial disparities among cities, but it was also visible within industrialized urban areas, particularly in the Capital. For example, as early as 1951, in a report on housing in Tehran *The New York Times* described the living conditions for 200,000 squatters as "living in underground caves and overcrowded mud huts that were like rabbit-hutches" (cf. Niroumand, 1969: 44). Two decades later, in a case study Bartsch (1971: 20–21) conducted a survey on the extent of unemployment in a model community (Ku-ye Nohom-e Aban District) established by the government to house the slum dwellers of Tehran. His findings indicate that most of the wage-laborers were in temporary employment and subjected to layoffs whenever the work assignment was completed or the short-term contract expired. In this particular community, over 70 percent of this community's labor force in 1971 was either unemployed or underemployed (see table 6.5).

**Table 6.5: Unemployment in the Ku-ye Nohom-e Aban, 1971**

| Category | % of Labor Force |
| --- | --- |
| Unemployed | 28.6 |
| Irregular wage-earners | 28.3 |
| Self-employed rejects of wage-earning market | 14.3 |
| Total | 71.2 |

Source: Bartsch (1971: 20–21).

## Petty Commodity Production and Urban Employment in Urban Iran and Tehran

Apart from prosperous traders and pre-capitalist money handlers who controlled the monetary exchange and wholesale trade in the bazaars, small merchants and artisans comprised a very important segment of urban population. The former owned small shops in the bazaars and worked with little or no help from hired workers; and the latter were master craftsmen who usually offered their wares for sale in front of their shops. Disintegration of pre-capitalist agrarian economy and increasing unemployment in the countryside caused by introduction of capitalist measures in Iran also created a new class of "semi-proletariat" in the cities, such as petty vendors, peddlers and haulers who offered all sorts of goods on the streets and in the bazaar itself (ibid.: 134–38). With the importation of European-made commodities and production of consumption goods under import- substitution industrialization policies Iranian markets were saturated with lower priced and in most cases better quality mass-produced manufactured products that effectively undermined the appeal of domestic pre-capitalist handicrafts to consumers. This gradually forced the bazaars into becoming distribution centers for foreign-made goods, and at the same time made petty commodity producers partially dependent on the world capitalist markets for obtaining raw materials needed for their products (Afshari, 1979: 393–94). In light of the magnitude of the unemployment rate among rural migrants, a clear examination of petty commodity production sector will signify the vitality of this peculiar form of urban economic activity both for the maintenance of the capitalist sector and creation of jobs for rural migrants.

Insufficient and inadequate data make it extremely difficult to portray an accurate picture of growth and development of the petty commodity sector. Available data are also often unreliable due to analytical and definitional differences in classifying various sectors of petty commodity production. For example, the official census data in most cases do not differentiate between the self-employed and the entrepreneur/employer. Wage-earners and artisans also come under one occupational category. Acknowledging these shortcomings, the following discussion is meant to provide a general framework for an analysis of several economic sectors that comprised petty commodity production in Iran. The discussion and classification of activities are based on the theoretical framework that I have outlined in Chapter 1.

## Small-Scale Industries (SSI)

In general, definition of small-scale industries is somewhat arbitrary and varies from one study to the other. But in order to provide a basis for comparison the SSI here refers to those establishments that employ less than ten workers and supply a range of consumption goods such as food, textiles, knitted goods and shoes, building materials, furniture and metal products (Hirsch, 1973: 56). A close look at available data for the number of small- and large-scale industries will indicate the absolute dominance of SSI in almost every single industrial activity. In 1963, for example, there were 88,114 small-scale and 2,429 large-scale industrial estab-lishments in Iran, indicating that 97 percent of total establishments were of a small-scale nature. For the same year, 94 percent of industrial establishments in Tehran were small-scale, employing less than ten workers in various industrial activities. Furthermore, the majority of industrial activities in Tehran were very small in size, employing only 1 to 4 workers (see table 6.6). Considering the primacy of Tehran as the center of economic and industrial activities as well as the main gateway to Western capitalist markets, this extraordinary dominance of small-scale industries in the Capital demonstrates that even in the mid-1960s large-scale industrial-capitalist operations were more of an exception rather than the rule in Iran's economy.

Although available data indicate the exact number of wage-earners/employees for industrial establishments, there is no distinction between one-owner/employer and multiple-owner/employer establishments (see table 6.7). Calculations in table 6.7 are based on the assumption that all establishments had only one owner/ employer. Thus the figures under the "average worker per firm" heading should be accepted by the reader with having the above interpretation in mind. Assuming the accuracy of data, the "shoes and made-up garments," "furniture," "leather pro-

**Table 6.6:  Industrial Classification of Small- and Large-Scale Establishments For Greater Tehran, 1963**

| Industry | Small-Scale (#) (1–9 employees) | Large-scale (10+ employees | % Small-scale to total |
|---|---|---|---|
| Food | 3,253 | 111 | 97 |
| Beverages | 90 | 9 | 91 |
| Textiles | 1,010 | 134 | 88 |
| Shoes and made-up Garment | 10,146 | 165 | 98 |
| Furniture | 2,602 | 45 | 98 |
| Leather products excl. shoes and clothing | 326 | 5 | 98 |
| Chemicals | 268 | 40 | 87 |
| Metal industries | 439 | 29 | 94 |
| Metal products except machinery & transp. | 4,429 | 120 | 97 |
| Transport equipment | 2,661 | 98 | 96 |
| Rubber products | 255 | 26 | 91 |
| Total | 25,479 | 782 | 94 |

Source:  Iran. Ministry of Interior (1964: 12, Table 7).

**Table 6.7: Employment and Average Size of Industrial Establishments for Greater Tehran, 1963**

| Industry | Owners/ employers | Wage-earners employees | Average wage-earner per firm |
|---|---|---|---|
| Food | 3,823 | 14,082 | 3.7 |
| Beverages | 117 | 945 | 8.0 |
| Textiles | 1,342 | 6,055 | 4.5 |
| Shoes & made-up garments | 10,804 | 14,943 | 1.4 |
| Furniture | 2,818 | 3,669 | 1.3 |
| Leather products except shoes and clothing | 340 | 642 | 1.9 |
| Chemicals | 363 | 1,831 | 5.0 |
| Metal industries | 531 | 1,177 | 2.2 |
| Metal products except machinery & transport | 5,096 | 8,357 | 1.6 |
| Transport equipment | 3,018 | 7,133 | 2.4 |
| Rubber products | 312 | 1,098 | 3.5 |
| Total | 28,564 | 59,932 | 2.1 |

Source: Iran. Ministry of Interior (1964: 13, Table 8).

ducts," and "metal products" industries are almost one- to two-person operations, an indication that they were operating exclusively at the artisanal level within the petty commodity production sector.

At the national level, the SSI's significance for Iran's economy was its capacity to provide employment opportunities. A comparison of data for 1956 and 1966 indicates that the SSI employed 91 percent and 85 percent of the industrial labor force, respectively (see table 6.8). Along with the introduction of capitalist measures and establishment of large-scale industrial plants in the post-WWII era, the small-scale industrial sector experienced a relative decline in its employment creation capacity. However, the SSI's continued importance for job creation and industrial production in Iran cannot be denied. The information in table 6.8 is worth a closer look. In terms of job creation capacity, despite the fact that the large-scale sector expanded rapidly during the 1956–1966 period as compared to a much slower growth pace for the SSI (164.3 and 48.8 percent, respectively), the former was still a relatively insignificant economic sector and employer, accounting for only 15 percent of the industrial work force. However, notwithstanding SSI's importance for employment creation, in terms of industrial value added it had a very low level of worker productivity compared to large-scale firms. This was due to the low level of capital investment and labor-intensive nature of production in the SSI sector (ILO, 1970: 12). As related to Tehran, in the late 1960s about 33 percent of the SSI were located in the capital employing 33.4 percent of the SSI work force for the entire country (Iran: Ministry of Interior, 1968: xix). This refers to both Tehran's importance in terms of centralization of the SSI and the SSI's importance for provision of urban employment in the Capital.

**Table 6.8: Selected Characteristics of Manufacturing Industries (Excluding Oil) by Large- and Small-Scale Sectors in Iran, 1956 and 1966**

| Sector | Employment 1956 | 1966 | Average Value Added/Worker (Rials) | % Change (1956-1966) |
|---|---|---|---|---|
| Large-scale[1] | 70,000 | 185,000 | 222,000 | 164.3 |
| Small-scale[2] | 703,000 | 1,046,000 | 24,000 | 48.8 |

1) Capitalist and mechanized units employing 10 or more workers.
2.) Capitalist/mechanized and pre-capitalist units employing 1-9 workers.

Source: Table constructed based on information in ILO (1970: 13, Table 7).

The degree to which industrial establishments and workshops utilized mechanized machinery and power tools in their daily operations is another factor that reveals the significance of pre-capitalist forms of production for Iran's economy. A 1963 survey of industrial, commercial and service establishments in Tehran indicated that only 11 percent of all establishments had prime movers (machines that converted any form of energy other than electrical into mechanical energy), power equipments or generators (Iran. Ministry of Interior, 1964: 14, Table 11). This is clearly an indication of the backward nature of industrial activities in Iran as late as the 1960s.

## Self-employed Petty Commodity Producers

This sector includes artisans who operate outside establishments, are self-employed and perform a variety of tasks within the production sphere. The self-employed petty commodity producers include carpenters, masons, tailors, plumbers, shoe repairers and the like. While in the case of Egypt there exist at least partially detailed data for artisanal and craft production activities in the mid-1970s, one has to scramble for comparable data for Iran and Tehran. Given the constraints, it is still possible to evaluate and compare the changes in the overall structure of employment for the self-employed in Iran. Here, my concern is with the self-employed that are operating within the production sphere, such as various industrial activities, technical and managerial occupations and transportation; as insofar it is related to handling the commodities and making them available for distribution and final consumption in the market. Available data for 1956 indicate that 24 percent of carpet making, 28 percent of garment and leather products and 17 percent of metal works within the industrial sector were produced by the self-employed artisans (see table 6.9).

    Furthermore, over 18 percent of the tasks within professional and technical occupations were also performed by the self-employed. Related to transportation; the census data make no distinction between mechanized people-movers and mechanized cargo-handlers, hence making an assessment of the share of self-employed in this sector almost impossible. But as is shown in table 6.9 about 40 percent of nonmechanized, animal-driven transportation was handled by the self-employed, a rather high share of the market in an important occupation within the production sphere. The role of self-employed artisans in Tehran's employment structure in 1956 was far less significant as compared to that for the entire country. Clearly, the high percentage of wage-earners for Tehran is supportive of the uneven nature of a dependent capitalist development even in its early stages of consolidation during the 1950s. If we add up the salaried government employees to wage-earners, the occupational disparity between Tehran and the entire country will be spelled out. That is, while in 1956 about 77 percent of male workers in Tehran were wage-earners and salaried workers, the figure for Iran as a whole was only about 45 percent (see table 6.10).

**Table 6.9: Employment Conditions for the Population 10 Years and Older in Selected Occupations for the Greater Tehran Census District, 1956**

| Occupation | Private Employee | State Employee | Self-employed | Unpaid Family Worker | % Self-employed to Total |
|---|---|---|---|---|---|
| Professional/ technical/ managerial | 3,564 | 16,557 | 4,519 | 11 | 18.3 |
| Administrative And clinical | 10,065 | 47,964 | 1,350 | 8 | 2.3 |
| *Transport:* | | | | | |
| Mechanized | 7,628 | 6,824 | 3,479 | 4 | 19.4 |
| Non-mechanized | 1,785 | 13 | 1,120 | 8 | 38.2 |
| *Industries:* | | | | | |
| Textile | 5,106 | 234 | 633 | 18 | 10.6 |
| Carpet making | 400 | 5 | 130 | 7 | 24.0 |
| Garment and Leather | 20,727 | 440 | 8,194 | 89 | 28.0 |
| Metal works | 18,118 | 3,193 | 4,434 | 60 | 17.1 |
| Construction | 56,296 | 654 | 2,712 | 9 | 4.5 |
| Food/tobacco | 15,804 | 2,818 | 1,865 | 39 | 9.1 |

Source: Table based on information in "Iran. Ministry of Interior" (1966: 38–39, Table 12).

**Table 6.10: Distribution of Male Worker Categories for Iran and Greater Tehran, 1956 (%)**

| | Self-employed | Wage-earner | Government Employee | Unpaid Worker |
|---|---|---|---|---|
| Iran Total | 44.1 | 37.2 | 8.1 | 9.4 |
| Greater Tehran | 20.1 | 54.8 | 21.9 | 0.5 |

Source: Iran. Ministry of Interior (1962: 397).

## Employment Structure in Service and Distribution Activities

In general, related to employment in service and distribution activities two groups can be identified: 1) the self-employed who operate within the distributive structure of the economy with little or no skills or craftsmanship, such as petty traders, street peddlers and the like; and 2) those wage-earners who are not engaged in productive activities and hence do not contribute to the creation of surplus value. Related to distribution of commodities, analysis of the data for Greater Tehran indicates that in 1956 retail activities both within and outside registered establishments were the monopoly of the self-employed who comprised 62.6 percent and 89.5 percent of total employment for this category, respectively (see table 6.11).

**Table 6.11: Employment Conditions for the Population 10 Years and Older in Retail Activities for the Greater Tehran Census District, 1956**

| Sales | Private Sector | State Sector | Self-Employed | Unpaid Family Worker | % Self-Employed to Total |
|---|---|---|---|---|---|
| Retail within establishments | 21,170 | 447 | 36,859 | 377 | 62.6 |
| Retail outside establishments | 967 | 91 | 9,067 | 17 | 89.5 |
| Total | 22,137 | 38 | 45,926 | 394 | 66.6 |

Source: Table based on information in "Iran. Ministry of Interior" (1966: 38–39, Table 12).

A comparison of nonagricultural employment levels for 1956 and 1966 between wage-earners and self-employed also indicates the latter group's relative significance for the Iranian economy, as within the "sales" occupational group, the self-employed had almost the monopoly over the market (see table 6.12). But in terms of growth, they somewhat lagged behind the wage-earning group during the 1956–1966 period. On the other hand, while within the services and petty commodity production sectors the wage-earners out-numbered the self- employed, the latter nonetheless had a much higher growth rate for the same period. In fact, with a meager 3 percent growth, the wage-earning employment within the service sector almost stagnated between 1956 and 1966; while the self-employed had a healthy growth rate of 86 percent. Due to lack of comprehensive data, it is difficult to identify various occupations within each occupational group. As a consequence, street peddlers, hawkers and petty traders may fall either under the "sales" or "petty commodity production and crafts" category. But the overall growth rates for wage-earners and the self-employed between 1956 and 1966 are an indication of a remarkable excess in growth for the latter category (36.0 and 58.2 percent, respectively). This is an interesting pattern within an emerging capitalist economy that under normal circumstances should promote the growth of a wage-earning working class.

**Table 6.12: Distribution of Non-agricultural Employment for Wage-Earners and Self-Employed for Iran, 1966-1976**

| | Employment Condition (000s) | | Employment Condition (000s) | | % Change | |
|---|---|---|---|---|---|---|
| | 1956 | | 1966 | | | |
| Occupation | Wage-Earner | Self-empld. | Wage-Earner | Self-empld. | Wage-Earner | Self-empld. |
| Sales | 63 | 281 | 104 | 400 | 65.1 | 42.3 |
| Services | 401 | 52 | 413 | 97 | 3.0 | 86.5 |
| Petty commodity production & crafts | 977 | 351 | 1,443 | 585 | 47.7 | 66.7 |
| Total | 1,441 | 684 | 1,960 | 1,082 | 36.0 | 58.2 |

Source: Table constructed based on information in ILO (1970: 18, Table 11).

The high percentage of self-employed in sales (distribution of finished goods) also suggests the importance of this employment sector for capitalist producers of certain consumer goods as a possible efficient means to speed up the distribution of their products, and hence a quicker realization of profit. Related to this issue, certain types of distributive activities within the petty commodity sector appear to have experienced a considerable growth. For instance, between 1966 and 1976 the street peddlers, hawkers and news vendors in the Greater Tehran area grew by 155 percent. Related to service activities, during the same period, housekeeping and related services and cooks also had growth rates of 63 and 127 percent, respectively (see table 6.13).

**Table 6.13: Employment in the Service and Distribution Activities within the Petty Commodity Sector in Greater Tehran Census District, 1966 and 1976**

| Occupational Category | Total Employed | | | % Tehran to Iran in 1976[3] |
|---|---|---|---|---|
| | 1966[1] | 1976[2] | % change | |
| Hawkers, news vendors and peddlers | 23,662 | 60,237 | 154.6 | 36.2 |
| Cooks | 5,326 | 12,104 | 127.3 | 32.6 |
| Bartenders, waiters, etc. | 9,741 | 8,511 | 32.7 | 35.1 |
| Housekeeping & related service workers | 35,551 | 57,995 | 63.1 | 38.3 |
| Launderers, dry cleaners and pressers | 5,415 | 5,124 | –5.4 | 39.5 |

Sources:
1) Iran. Plan Organization (1966: 214-17, Table 26)
2) Plan & Budget Organization (1980: 282-89, Table 28).
3) Iran. Plan & Budget Organization (1976: 94-109, Table 28).

What is significant here is the degree of concentration of such activities in Tehran compared to the rest of the nation, as about 40 percent of all petty commodity production and service-related activities took place in Tehran. However, the utility of street peddlers and hawkers for the capitalist sector should not be considered as a conscious marketing strategy on the latter's part. Rather, as much as this category of petty commodity production might be useful for a dependent capitalist economy, it is nothing more than a disguised unemployment in a massive scale.

## Conclusion

Although by the end of 18th century Tehran became the designated capital for the feudal Qajar rulers, its prominence as the most important city was only achieved in the second half of the 19th century. This was due to the presence of the Royal Court and central government, as well as Tehran's suitable location as a redistribution and trade center for the entire nation. Like Cairo in Egypt, Tehran also became a preferred center for industrial activities. Tehran's uneven urban development did not start until the 1920s, as centralization of the state apparatus led to concentration of all governmental and bureaucratic institutions in Tehran. Later in the 1930s, the ground was also laid for industrial-capitalist production in Iran with Tehran being a preferred if not an ideal site. The deposition of Dr. Mosaddeq, the eventual demise of the nationalist movement in 1953 and consequent events which reinstated the Shah led to the development of a dependent capitalist economy and the inevitable uneven urban/spatial development with Tehran being the preferred center of capital investment and urban growth. Tehran's unusual population and spatial growth can be attributed to four factors: 1) concentration of almost all the headquarters of commercial and industrial enterprises; 2) concentration of major industrial activities with a sizeable work force; 3) concentration of foreign as well as domestic capital investments; and 4) massive rural-urban migration with Tehran being the main destination point especially after the Land Reform. Related to the last factor, the majority of rural migrants came to Tehran in search of employment opportunities but the overgrown capital was not capable of absorbing all the new rural immigrants. This led to the emergence of a growing class of the urban poor comprised of landless peasants and small landowner/peasants who joined the ranks of the urban unemployed and underemployed. This proletarianization of the rural migrant population in Tehran greatly affected the urban employment structure in the capital and the entire country.[3]

As I will discuss in the following chapters, similar to Egypt, ascendance of capitalism and its increasing dominance as a mode of production along with structural changes in rural areas affected the urban class composition and employment structure in Iran. First, a careful reading of data on industrial establishments in Iran and Tehran indicates the absolute dominance of small-scale industries (SSI) in most industrial activities. What is more, within the SSI itself most of the establishments only employed between one and four workers. Some industries such as shoes and made-up garments, furniture, and metal products were even smaller in size, employing only one or two workers. Second, despite a rapid expansion of large-scale industries, the SSI maintained their importance as the main source of employment. However, the SSI remained underdeveloped with regard to the use of modern equipments. Third, a reading of data for Tehran indicates the increasing importance of the self-employed and artisans both in terms of sheer numbers and their vitality for retail activities. This clearly indicates the importance of petty traders and street peddlers in selling commodities produced by the capitalist sector, hence facilitating a quick return of profits for producers. Finally, the service sector and domestic work became an important source of employment in urban areas, with Tehran being the main urban locality for employment creation in this sector.

## Notes

1. Estimates of Tehran's population in the 19th century are mostly unreliable and hard to verify. For example, the first government enumeration in 1867 put the city's population at about 160,000 (ibid.).

2. For a historical analysis of Tehran's growth and development see Habibi (1996, Part 3: 107–199).

3. A recent experimental documentary film by Massoud Bakhshi entitled "Tehran Has No More Pomegranates!" (2006) is an excellent historical juxtaposition of the old and new Tehran. Using rare 19th and early 20th century footages of old Tehran and contemporary images of this megalopolis, Bakhshi's mesmerizing film documents the city's growth within the context of a dependent political economy; and would be an excellent companion to this chapter.

# PART 3

# Dependent Urbanization in Egypt

# Chapter Seven

# Urbanization in Pre-capitalist Egypt (1798-1882)

In contrast to the Iranian situation whereby external colonial interests did not play a significant role up until late 19th century, in examining the pre-capitalist Egyptian society one has to take into account the dynamics of interaction between the external forces of domination and exploitation on the one hand, and internal destabilizing factors on the other: the former being the Ottoman Empire and its bureaucracy for collection of taxes, and the latter being different factions of the ruling strata whose interests were threatened by imperialist interests of the Ottomans. The introduction of the Turkish element into the Egyptian politics dates back to the Ottoman conquest in 1517, A.D., when Egypt was nominally reduced to the rank of an Ottoman province for the next two hundred and forty years (McLoan, 1882: 28). By the end of the 18th century Egypt was ruled by the Mamelukes who formed a ruling stratum composed of former slaves. But the Mamelukes in turn were subjected to the central authority and control of the Ottomans. Under the Ottoman rule Egypt was divided into twenty four provinces, each being ruled by a Mameluke "Bey" or provincial governor and all being under nominal control of a Turkish "Pasha" or head administrator. The fiscal crisis of the Ottoman state in the late 16th and early 17th centuries necessitated the decentralization of provincial administration. As a consequence, provincial lands were granted to Turkish treasury officials who in most cases were unable to do the work themselves. They in turn appointed local agents who were drawn from the Mameluke rank and file.

The nature and inner dynamics of pre-capitalist Egyptian society have rarely been studied extensively. The descriptive accounts of various aspects of the Egyptian society mostly fit into the modernization schemes that simply refer to pre-capitalist Egypt as a "traditional society." These studies consider pre-capitalist Egypt as an entity based on subsistence agriculture in which the mass of peasantry did not own the land they tilled and land was mainly owned by the tax farmers (Baer, 1969; Issawi, 1963). Among historical studies of pre-capitalist Egypt only Amin's analysis (1978, 1980) provides an insight on the exact nature and dynamics of interaction among various socioeconomic forces. In his discussion of pre-capitalist "social formations" Amin (1976, 1980) argues that the "Asiatic mode of production" was in fact a "tributary mode" as a prevalent socioeconomic and political entity. The main characteristics of the tributary mode were: 1) extraction of surplus product by non-economic means; 2) organization of production based on use value rather than exchange value; and 3) the dominance of the superstructure, particularly religious institutions in extracting the social surplus (Amin, 1980: 50–54). According to this analysis, the tributary system was merely a different mode of production as compared with feudalism. For instance, related to property rights while the feudal forms of landownership were established out of a weak and decentralized political power, a centralized state in the tributary mode resulted in more advanced forms of landholding (ibid.: 48-62). Amin further considers the composition of the Egyptian pre-capitalist "social formation" as an articulation of the tributary mode of production with other forms of economic activities such as petty trading, small-scale craft production and long-distance trade (Amin, 1978: 97–98).

Another significant difference between pre-capitalist Iran and Egypt was the role of tribal forces and pastoral-nomadic relations in each nation's politics. While in the former the pastoral- nomadic mode of production played a significant role both at the economic and political levels, the evidence indicate the insignificance and historical subordination of pastoral-nomads to other socioeconomic and political forces in Egypt. However, the tribute-paying method of extracting the social surplus by the Ottomans resembles the practice of *iqta* in Iran. The only difference being that the Ottomans controlled Egypt's economy from outside, while the pastoral-nomadic rulers in Iran did it from within. Egypt was of interest to the Ottomans mainly as a source of tribute derived from the land (Marlow, 1965: 10). Hence, under a system of tax collection called "*iltizam*," the Mamelukes were held accountable for supervising tax collection, paying a fixed sum to the Ottoman treasury, and eventually pocketing what was left out of the surplus (Richards, 1982: 9–10; Baer, 1969: 62). Since iltizam was technically the property of the Ottoman imperial state, the Mamelukes held only the usufruct rights but with significant power and authority at the local level. It is estimated that out of 6,000 "*multazims*" or landholders only 300 were Mamelukes, but they held more than two-thirds of the cultivated land in Egypt.

## Disintegration of the Pre-Capitalist Egyptian Economy

The reinforcement of the Mamelukes' authority by the end of the 18th century and relaxation of the Ottoman control due to the Court's reluctant recognition of the Mamelukes put Egypt on the verge of political and economic disintegration (Little, 1958: 50–51). With the decline of the Ottomans' central power, there also was a marked tendency for the usufruct of the land to become hereditary and hence the evolution of private property rights in Egypt (Richards, 1982: 10). Thus the only source of influence left to the Ottomans was the policy of "divide and rule" and taking advantage of existing discord among the Mameluke rulers (Marlowe, 1965: 11–12).

At the time of the French expedition in 1798 Egypt was a poor, neglected agrarian society operating within the Ottoman dominion. Internally, under the Mameluke regime Egypt was parceled out by regional rulers, each controlling a group of village communities with most of the land consisting of communal land subject to tax. Externally, the diversion of Europe's long-distance trade routes from the Mediterranean to the Atlantic and the establishment of direct naval link with southern and eastern Asia that by-passed the Arab world left many trading centers behind. Among Arab nations Egypt in particular suffered immensely as she lost her hold on long-distance trade in the region. Napoleon Bonaparte's Egyptian expedition in 1798 and the defeat of the Mameluke army at the Battle of the Pyramids forced the latter contingent to flee to the Upper Egypt. However, in a show of colonial rivalry an alliance of the Anglo-Turkish armies eventually compelled the French to withdraw from Egypt in 1801. After the departure of the French forces, Egypt once again relapsed into anarchy as the Mameluke regional rulers tried to regain control over the land and agricultural production while the Ottoman Government tried to establish a centralized governing apparatus in Egypt subservient to its colonial interests.

It was during these years of anarchy that Mohammad Ali, a commander of the Albanian troops stationed in Cairo came into prominence by taking side with the Mamelukes and opposing the Turkish governor to whom he was serving. The popular support of Mohammad Ali by the citizens of Cairo in 1805 was instrumental in bringing him to power. This localized support prevented Mohammad Ali to extend his power beyond the province of Cairo. However, under pressure by Cairo's notables and religious leaders the Ottoman Court was forced to endorse his governorship for Egypt. Despite his non-Egyptian origin Mohammad Ali's attempts for centralization of the state apparatus have to be considered as a pro-Egyptian endeavor which conflicted in times with the interests of the Ottoman Court.

Following the withdrawal of the French in 1801 and re-entry of the Ottomans to Egypt, the Mamelukes' right to seize land for themselves was challenged by laws introduced by a newly created civil government in Cairo. But it was left to Mohammad Ali to carry out a real revolution in the land tenure system. At the time, the dominant tributary mode of production dictated Egypt's socioeconomic and political landscape—division of population into working peasants and landholding masters; the division of the social product into peasant means of subsistence and tribute in kind drawn by the ruling class; and centralization of state power in the hands of the appropriating class (Amin, 1978: 18, 97).[1] Under *iltizam* peasants had no property rights and were tied to the land, but were mostly left undisturbed as long as they met their taxes and worked on the tax farmer's estate and irrigation works (Issawi, 1963: 20). During the 1809-1818 period, Mohammad Ali abolished the system of iltizam, brought about the creation of the first Egyptian land register, and distributed in life tenancy, two million feddans among military leaders, members of the ruling family, the bedouin and some of the former tax farmers (Abdel_Malek, 1968: 6). This was the beginning of the disintegration of Egypt's tributary mode of production as the dominant economic and political system and gradual introduction of feudal relations of production.

Apart from reforms in the land tenure system, another change which occurred in rural Egypt during Mohammad Ali's reign (1805–1848) was his campaign to crush and settle the pastoral-nomadic population or the "Bedouin," who were considered both as a threat to the security of urban and rural communities and an obstacle to Egypt's agricultural development (Baer, 1969: 214). The Bedouin lived in camp units varying in size from 20 to 70 people. The grazing land and wells were owned communally, but the cultivated land in most cases was divided among the unit members. The life-style of the Bedouin in the coastal and inland areas was significantly different. Burja (1973: 146–47) gives two examples of coastal and inland camp units. While in the former 75 percent were engaged in cultivation and 8 percent in animal husbandry, in the latter only 7.5 percent were cultivators while 70 percent engaged entirely in animal husbandry. Estimates for the Egyptian nomadic population in the beginning of the 19th century are contradictory and ambiguous. Based on one estimate, in the 1880s the bedouin comprised about 6 percent of total population (McLoan, 1882: 22–23). This is believed to be an inflated figure for the Bedouin population, the main reason being certain privileges given to the nomads by Mohammad Ali, when in the 1830s he exempted the Bedouin from enlistment for their earlier services to his Syrian and Arabian expeditions. This led to repeated false claims by the peasants belonging to certain tribes in order to escape from conscription, which in turn inflated the number of the Bedouin in official and unofficial statistics (see table 7.1).

**Table 7.1:  Break-up of the Egyptian Population in 1882**

| Category | Population |
|---|---|
| Settled Arab peasants (fellahin) | 4,500,000 |
| Bedouin | 300,000 |
| Turks | 10,000 |
| Copts (Christian Egyptians) | 500,000 |
| Foreign Residents | 290,000 |
| Total population | 5,600,000 |
| % Bedouin to total | 5.45 |

Source:  McLoan (1882: 22–23)

Unlike their Iranian counterparts the Egyptian Bedouin were not strong political players, lacking both numbers and economic strength. This prompted Mohammad Ali to settle the Bedouin in the first decades of 19th century, almost hundred years earlier than Reza Shah's sedantarization plans in Iran, mainly by breaking up the tribal-communal unity and granting large tracts of land to tribal heads. In general, most of the Egyptian tribes were composed of associations of families as clans. Each subsection of a tribe had its own petty-chief or "*shaykh*," who were under the authority of the head shaykh who represented the tribe in all its transactions with other tribes, or with the external powers in general (Murray, 1950: 41).

The growing importance of Egypt's cotton production for the world capitalist markets probably was the main incentive for Mohammad Ali's government to settle the Bedouin, whose lifestyle was considered a threat to the security of roads and a hindrance to the free flow of goods and especially a safe transportation of cotton to the main ports for export to European markets. Furthermore, the profitability of cotton production as compared to pastoralism gave the Bedouin shaykhs a powerful incentive to acquire large tracts of land (Baer, 1969: 5–7). Later on, Mohammad Ali facilitated the break up of the tribal unity by appointing prominent shaykhs to government offices. It is important to make note that this was not done because of the pressures put by the tribal leaders upon Mohammad Ali. Rather, it was the policy of a government determined for sedentarization of the pastoral-nomadic population. As a result, while until 1833 all offices higher than the village head were held by non-Egyptians, many tribal chiefs and native Egyptians were appointed to be district officers or "*nazir qisms*" after 1833. Gradually, the tribal shaykhs moved to towns, acquired large mansions, intermarried with the ruling class and became government officials, while the rank and file Bedouin immersed in the peasant population or later on moved to cities and joined wage-laborers in railway construction and other urban-based activities. Thus as a result of conscious government policy of sedantarization in the 19th century the Bedouin population became subjugated to the state authority, and played no significant role in the politics of pre-capitalist Egypt. In his memoirs, a late nineteenth century observer of the Egyptian society claimed that "the desert on both sides of the Nile is as safe for caravans or even private travelers as are the streets of Alexandria and Cairo" (McLoan, 1882: 27).

There is no historical evidence to indicate that the measures taken by Mohammad Ali were dictated by foreign interests. However, legalization of private property, especially landownership rights, and forced sedentarization of the Bedouin undoubtedly served the interests of colonial powers in general and the British in particular. Mohammad Ali's attempts to build up modern industry in the first half of the 19th century is also one of the most debated and controversial issues among scholars of nineteenth century Egypt. By importing machinery and technicians, training and recruiting indigenous skilled workers and hiring unskilled workers at low wages, Mohammad Ali tried to carry out a program of "forced industrialization" in Egypt. This is praised by some scholars who acknowledge the imported nature of technology but at the same time argue that this technology was quickly assimilated by young Egyptians (Amin, 1978). Others give credit to Mohammad Ali's attempts for laying the foundations for a diversified economy but also argue that his prime interest was to build up a modern army and navy in order to safeguard his position and influence (Issawi, 1963: 23–24).

From 1848 to 1882 those who succeeded Mohammad Ali abandoned his autonomous position and direction for Egypt's development, and looked for European capital, knowledge and expertise in order to "modernize" Egypt. But what they actually did was to facilitate Egypt's integration into the world capitalist markets by opening up the country to colonial intervention. During this period Egypt experienced a structural transformation of her economy which led to the disintegration of the tributary mode of production and eventually prepared the country for piece-meal integration into the world capitalist system. There seem to be two historical reasons for this change. First, following Mohammad Ali's efforts to reform the structure of land ownership the 1850–1880 period witnessed the removal of restrictions on private land ownership, such as affirmation of the right of inheritance; the right to sell and mortgage land; and authorization of foreigners to acquire land in Egypt. Changes in property ownership rights also coincided with a rapid intensification of the cultivation of cotton under Ismail Pasha's rule (1863–1879). In order to supply the British textile factories that were deprived of American cotton imports in the aftermath of the American Civil War (1861–1865), Egypt's cotton output rose from 501,000 kantars in 1860 to 3,124,000 kantars in 1879 (Abdel-Malek, 1968: 7). Thus Egypt became more and more involved in a "one-crop" economy and the cultivated lands devoted to cotton increased from 4,160,000 feddan in 1862 to 4,743,000 in 1877.[2] With cotton becoming the major export commodity comprising more than 70 percent of the total value of exports in 1880, Egypt's foreign trade value also had a significant increase from LE 1.5 million in 1805 to LE 21.8 million in 1880. Hand-in-hand with the development of a one-crop, export-oriented economy, transportation and communication networks were also improved and expanded during the 1850–1880 period. The construction and consequent opening of the Suez Canal in 1869 increased Egypt's link to the outside world and channeled a vast flow of international traffic through the country (Issawi, 1963: 18–31; Abdel-Malek, 1968: 6–9). By 1877, there were 1,519 kilometers of standard gauge railways and 13,500 kilometers of irrigation canals, many of them navigable throughout the year. During the thirty years between Mohammad Ali's death and the beginning of direct British rule in Egypt in 1882 substantial investment was devoted to public works. During Ismail Pasha's reign alone (1863–1878) about LE 40 million were spent just for the improvement of the infrastructure. Often on highly unfavorable terms, a sizable proportion of this expenditure came from foreign investment. The borrowed money for the 1862–1873 period is estimated at about LE 68,500,000 (Barbour, 1972: 45). This was followed by the strengthening of Egypt's links to Western financial institutions. A spectacular growth of banking activity took place in the 1850s, and by 1877 eight banks were providing telegraph exchange in Paris and London and in 1880 two foreign-owned mortgage banks were opened in Egypt (Crouchley, 1936: 29–37) (see table 7.2).

**Table 7.2: Capital Investment in the Egyptian Infrastructure, 1863-78**

| Purpose | Investment (LE million) |
| --- | --- |
| Railways | 13,361 |
| Nile canals | 12,600 |
| Suez Canal | 6,700 |
| Alexandria harbors | 2,742 |
| Bridges | 2,150 |
| Suez dockyard | 1,400 |
| Telegraph | 0.853 |
| Lighthouses | 0.188 |

Source: Crouchley, 1936: 16; 1938: 117)

Often on highly unfavorable terms, a sizable proportion of this expenditure came from foreign investments. As an example, Barbour (1972: 45) estimates the borrowed money for the 1862–1873 period at about LE 68,500,000. This was followed by the strengthening of Egypt's links to Western financial institutions. A spectacular growth of banking activity took place in the 1850s, and by 1877 eight banks were providing telegraph exchange in Paris and London; and in 1880 two foreign-owned mortgage banks were opened in Egypt (Crouchley, 1936: 29–37).

## Colonial Penetration and Urbanization in Egypt

Historically speaking, Egypt's rural and urban settlements have evolved and developed within a peculiar geography and physical landscape. In General, the Egyptian territory is comprised of four regions, each having its own unique characteristics. First, the Western and Southern Deserts which in most parts are inhospitable even for the bedouin, except for several oases such as Kharijah, Bahriyah, Dakhilah, Farafirah, and Siwah. The oasis communities in the nineteenth century were relatively self-sufficient, but still dependent on the "outside world" for manufactured goods and commodities. Second, the Western Desert which is dissected by narrow and deep oases with sparse vegetation, where cultivation is practically impossible and few thousand residents lived in the villages along the Red Sea coast. Third, the Sinai Peninsula which is now separated from Egypt by the Suez Canal, has a low amount of rainfall, and is in most parts inhabitable. The sparse population mostly resided in the northern provinces with pockets of cultivation around wells at Al Arish, An Nakhle and Al Awja. Finally, the Nile Valley and the Delta which comprise only 3.5 percent of Egyptian land, but contain most of Egypt's population. The 550 mile narrow trench of the Nile River from Aswan to Cairo is also called the "Upper Egypt" and is one of the most densely populated agricultural lands in the world. Villages huddle together every one or two miles, surrounded by a mosaic of small plots. The delta, also known as "Lower Egypt" fans out from Cairo to the Mediterranean and resembles the back of a leaf, with the Nile and canals "obtruding like veins above the lowlands." All the major towns, the bulk of Egypt's industrial activities, and two-thirds of population are located in this area (Mountjoy, 1971: Vol. 8, 30–31). In fact, the Nile River has to be considered as an important unifying factor that has shaped Egypt's spatial configuration.

Egypt has been frequently cited as an example *par excellence* of an over-urbanized society (Davis and Golden, 1954). Some believe that Egypt's concentrated water supply is partially responsible for the location of its cities since, away from water resources there is little or no settlement of any kind. Thus population centers are located in the Delta or along the Nile above Cairo. It has been estimated that around 1800 about 10 percent of Egypt's population or nearly 300,000 people lived in towns with 10,000 or more inhabitants (Issawi, 1965: 102). This is rather a high ratio for an urban population. But Egypt's "over-urbanization" is not as extreme as others have claimed. In fact, the limited cultivable land and access to water supplies requires concentration of population in all settlements. Some argue that a "cultural preference" for concentrated rural settlements makes them look like urban centers (Abu-Loghud, 1965: 313–314). But as was the case for Iran, in the absence of a clear-cut division of labor, town and country in pre-capitalist Egypt also were indistinguishable from each other. This seems to be a plausible argument especially in the early 19th century when the tributary mode of production was dominant and industrialization had not yet taken place. Similar to Iran, one of the major difficulties in the study of urbanization in Egypt is the lack of reliable data. The first reliable census in Egypt was taken in 1897, but its results must be accepted by caution. Studies by Baer (1969) and McCarthy (1976) are probably the most reliable sources of information for the 19th and early 20th century.[3] Table 7.3 presents population changes for towns having over 20,000 inhabitants for the 1821–1907 period.[4]

Assuming the accuracy of data in table 7.3, during the first half of the 19th century Egypt appears to have witnessed a great increase in its urban population, with growth rate of 68.7 percent for 23 important towns compared to 25 percent for the total population. However, only few cities were accountable for this excessive growth in urban population: while between 1821 and 1846 the total population had a negligible growth of 0.04 percent, cities of Alexandria, Damietta, Tanta, Rosetta, and Suez had average annual growth rates of 10.3, 4.0, 2.6, 1.2, and 1.4 percent, respectively. Almost all of these cities were port cities and perhaps the simplest way to put it is that Egypt's economy "began to be oriented outward, toward the export of its primary products, that transport was developed accordingly, with railway lines or steamboat services pointing to the coasts, and that the alignment of towns shifted in consequence" (Issawi, 1969: 108).

Available data also indicate the enormous growth of the seaports and relative stagnation of "inland" cities. This can be attributed to two factors. First, despite Mohammad Ali's reforms in the land tenure system and abolition of iltizam the peasants continued to remain attached to the land. The main structural change was a shift from a more or less decentralized mode of appropriation of taxes and tributes during the Mameluke's reign to Mohammad Ali's efforts to collect taxes by means of a centralized state apparatus. Still under the Ottoman domain, from 1821 onward Mohammad Ali sought to improve agricultural production and particularly cotton for export to the ready European markets. This resulted in creation of sufficient employment opportunities in the primary sector in order to absorb the rural work force that was still tied to the land by traditional bonds. Production of cash crops for export also enhanced the growth of port cities such as Alexandria, which served as the main port for conducting Egypt's foreign trade. In fact, Alexandria's growth was one of the main reasons for Egypt's increase in urban population. The diversion and considerable elimination of foreign trade at the regional level and concentration of trade activities in Alexandria marked the beginning of a new era of dependent

# Table 7.3 Population of Selected Important Cities and Towns in Egypt (1821-1907)

| | 1821-1826 | Av. Annual Gr. rate (%) (1821-1846) | 1846 | Av. annual Gr. rate (%) (1846-1882) | 1882 Census | Av. annual Gr. rate(%) (1882-1897) | 1897 Census | 1907 Census | Av. annual Gr. rate (%) (1897-1907) |
|---|---|---|---|---|---|---|---|---|---|
| *Lower Egypt - inland* | | | | | | | | | |
| Cairo | 218,560 | + 0.65 | 256,679 | + 1.0 | 374,838 | + 2.8 | 570,062 | 654,476 | + 1.3 |
| Tanta | 10,000 | + 2.60 | 19,500 | + 1.5 | 33,750 | + 3.5 | 57,289 | 54,437 | – 0.5 |
| Al-Mahalla al-Kubra | 17,000 | + 0.65 | 20,000 | + 0.9 | 27,823 | + 0.7 | 31,100 | 33,547 | + 0.7 |
| Mansura | 8,500 | + 0.60 | 9,886 | + 2.8 | 26,942 | + 2.0 | 36,131 | 40,279 | + 1.0 |
| Damanhur | — | — | 8,000 | + 2.5 | 19,624 | + 3.3 | 32,122 | 38,752 | + 1.9 |
| Bilqas | — | — | — | — | — | — | 19,469 | 25,473 | + 2.7 |
| Minuf | — | — | — | — | 16,293 | + 1.3 | 19,726 | 22,316 | + 1.2 |
| *Lower Egypt - coastal* | | | | | | | | | |
| Alexandria | 12,528 | + 10.3 | 164,359 | + 0.95 | 231,396 | + 2.1 | 319,766 | 332,247 | + 0.3 |
| Damietta | 13,600 | + 4.0 | 37,089 | – 0.20 | 34,044 | – 0.5 | 31,515 | 29,354 | – 0.7 |
| Rosetta | 13,400 | + 1.2 | 18,360 | – 0.26 | 16,666 | – 1.0 | 14,286 | 16,810 | + 1.6 |
| Suez | 2,900 | + 1.4 | 4,160 | + 2.6 | 10,559 | + 3.2 | 17,133 | 18,374 | + 0.7 |
| Port Said | — | — | — | — | 16,560 | + 6.2 | 42,095 | 49,884 | + 1.7 |
| *Middle Egypt* | | | | | | | | | |
| Madinat al-Fayyum | — | — | — | — | 25,799 | + 1.2 | 31,262 | 37,320 | + 1.8 |
| Minya | — | — | — | — | 15,900 | + 1.7 | 20,404 | 27,221 | + 2.9 |
| Bani Suwayf | — | — | — | — | 10,085 | + 2.8 | 15,297 | 23,357 | + 4.2 |
| Mallawi | — | — | — | — | 10,777 | + 2.4 | 15,471 | 20,249 | + 2.8 |
| *Upper Egypt* | | | | | | | | | |
| Girga | — | — | 7,500 | + 1.9 | 14,819 | + 1.0 | 17,271 | 19,893 | + 1.4 |
| Total Population | 4,423,396 | + 0.04 | 4,476,439 | + 1.6 | 7,840,271 | + 1.4 | 9,734,405 | 11,287,359 | + 1.5 |

Sources: Baer (1969: 34–35); McCarthy (1976:33–34).

economic relations between Egypt and the European markets. For instance, once the main port of foreign trade in the Western Delta, the city of Rosetta suffered from the transfer of most of its commercial activities to Alexandria. The growth of Damietta, the only port city in the Eastern Delta was also impeded by a substantial decrease in the regional trade between Egypt, Greece and Syria (Baer, 1969: 137–138).

Second, Mohammad Ali's industrialization schemes partially contributed to an increase in the urban population. The nature and scale of his "forced industrialization" cannot be quantitatively described in detail, beside the fact that factories were dispersed all over the country and in conjunction with rural communities. However, there were a few towns with a greater concentration of industries and related economic activities. For example, Alexandria with glass, ropes and military industries; Rosetta with rice milling and hide factories; Cairo with its military, iron, paper and cotton textile industries; and Boulaq in the Lower Egypt with cotton textiles, woolen fabrics, printing and armaments seemed to have the highest share in industrial production and employment (Mabro and Radwan, 1976: 13–16).[5] There are several estimates for the total number of industrial workers in Egypt, and according to one account industrial work force may have involved more than 30 percent of the active population (Barbour, 1972: 39). A more conservative estimate puts the total number at 260,000 workers or 25 percent of the work force (Fahmy, 1954: 845). Yet others argue that even if workers in the arsenals and other military establishments are included the number of industrial workers has probably never exceeded 60,000 to 70,000 or some 6 to 7 percent of total employment in Egypt (Mabro and Radwan, 1976: 16). Even if we accept the latter estimate, this by all accounts is a high ratio for a predominantly pre-capitalist economy in the first half of the 19th century. Related to urban industrial workforce there are no reliable data, but Baer (1969: 136) attributes Alexandria's considerable growth during the 1821–1846 period to Mohammad Ali's industrial and maritime enterprises in this port city.

During the 1850–1880 period Egypt's population growth rate was unusually higher compared to that for the 1821–1846 period (1.6 and 0.04, respectively), while at the same time there was a decline in the overall growth rate of urban population.[6] In particular, the growth rate for Cairo and Alexandria was about the same as that of total population, indicating the nonexistence of immigration to these two major urban centers from other areas. The only urban centers that had higher growth rates than that of the overall population fall into two categories: a) the agricultural market towns and provincial centers of Mansura, Damanhour, Shibn Al-Kawn, and Girga with an average annual growth rates of 2.8, 2.5, 3.6, and 1.9 percent for the 1846–1882 period, respectively; and b) the port city of Suez with an average annual growth rate of 2.6 percent.

I attribute the aforementioned population movements and excessive rates of growth for certain urban localities to four factors. First, substantial improvements in transportation networks in turn helped some of the regional market towns to flourish

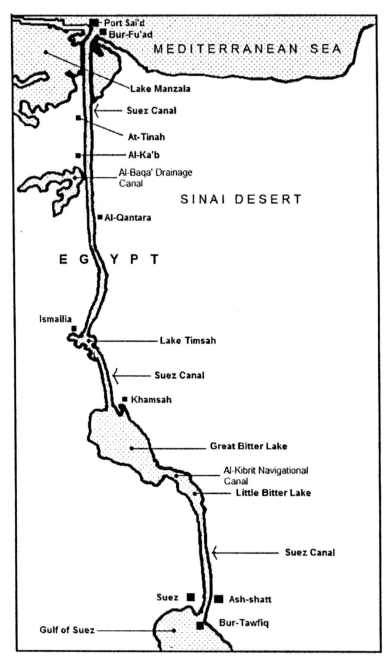

**Plate 7.1. Map of Suez Canal**

and hence experience population growth. For example, the connection of Mansura in 1855 and Tanta in 1856 to the railway network was primarily because of their importance for cotton production and its organized and timely export to the European markets. Thus, Mansura became one of the important market towns for the sale of cotton, wool, rice and oil seed in the Lower Egypt, while Tanta was known as the principal market for a vast area of cotton plantations.[7] This was the beginning of a trend in which small market towns gained some prominence as the export-oriented economy expanded its network of transport and communications for siphoning off the cotton production. But during the 1846–1882 period the growth of market towns had little impact upon the overall rate of urbanization in Egypt. In his assessment of the extent of urbanization in 19th century Egypt, Baer (1969: 140) concludes that "though all these mercantile centers of agricultural areas experienced a great relative expansion . . . none of them exceeded thirty five thousand, and most of them kept in the neighborhood of twenty thousand." Second, the digging of the Suez Canal and utilization of about 20,000 forced laborers or "*curvee's*" by the Suez Canal Company might have contributed to population increase in regional towns. Although the evidence is sketchy, there are indications that the terror caused by government agents and their recruitment efforts in rural areas resulted in abandonment of many villages; the breaking up of family relations; and eventual population movements and migration to nearby cities (Lacouture, 1958: 64). Third, the opening of the Suez Canal in 1869 affected the port city of Suez by the Gulf of Suez. In particular, the establishment of foreign commercial agencies and the influx of foreigners into the port of Suez accompanied by construction activities for building the Suez dockyard and other urban development projects more than doubled the town's population from 4,160 in 1840 to 10,559 in 1882. The newly established city of Port Said also benefited from trade activities because of the Canal. By 1882 Port Said had over 16,000 inhabitants, a 200 percent increase in thirteen years (see plate 7.1).

Despite a slower growth rate for the 1850–1882 period, Alexandria also continued to enjoy its supremacy and remained as the main center for imports and exports. Alexandria's relative decline can be attributed to the opening up of the Suez Canal and decline in industrial activities in the 1846–1882 period which kept its population in check. Finally, it is important to take into account the influx of Europeans to Egypt that greatly affected the growth of port cities of Suez, Port Said and Alexandria, as well as some inland cities like Mansura. For instance, between 1836 and 1878 the total number of foreigners in Egypt rose from 3,000 to well over 68,000, with higher concentrations in Cairo, Alexandria, and Port Said (Heyworth-Dunn, 1938: 343).

The relative decline in Egypt's rate of urbanization during the 1846–1882 period can be related to the intensification of agricultural production and its role in providing more employment opportunities in rural areas. Despite structural changes that took place in the land tenure system, such as the recognition of a limited form of private ownership, the peasants remained tied to the land with communal bonds. Therefore, except for few port cities and urban centers which served as bridgeheads for the administration of foreign trade, urbanization and rural-urban migration in Egypt remained relatively insignificant.

## Notes

1. See Amin (1980: Chapter 3) for a detailed discussion of the main characteristics of the tributary mode of production.

2. One cantar is equal to 99 lb., and one feddan equals 1.038 acres.

3. Among others who have done extensive research on Egyptian urbanization in this period, the works of Abu-Lughod (1961, 1964, 1965), and Issawi (1969) are important. It must be stated that the purpose of this paper is a historical investigation of the urbanization process in Egypt with regard to socioeconomic and political changes, and not a "demographic" study. Thus, available data have been utilized by assuming their relative accuracy.

4. Baer (1969: 134–36) cautions the reader about possible flaws in the figures presented in the table:

> According to these figures, the average annual rate of increase of Egypt's population was 3.0 percent between 1821 and 1846 and 2.8 percent between 1882 and 1897. Because of the high mortality rate in 19th century Egypt, population increase was certainly much lower.

5. For the range of industries under Mohammad Ali's rule see an interesting table in Mabro and Radwan (1976: 14-15).

6. Calling a center of population concentration of 10,000 people or more "urban" is an ambiguous definition any way. But in the absence of reliable information for the 19th century Egypt I accept it for the sake of our overall historical analysis of socioeconomic changes and hence, "urbanization" in that century. Later in Chapter 9 I will discuss the matter in more detail as it relates to 20th century development.

7. My conclusions on urban growth are in most part based on Gabriel Baer's analysis of urbanization in Egypt. See Baer (1969, especially pp. 133–148).

# Chapter Eight

# British Colonialism and Dependent Urbanization in Egypt (1882–1952)

By the 1870s Egypt had acquired an infrastructure comparable to that of European countries. But this was achieved through securing foreign loans with high interest rates. With the financial collapse of the Ottoman Empire being imminent and following the collapse of the Egyptian stock in 1875, Khedive Ismail, Egyptian ruler at the time asked the British for help in remedying Egypt's financial problems. This in fact was an open invitation for European intervention in Egypt's internal affairs. In response, the British Government sent a high level mission to Egypt which in turn forced France, the rival colonial power to make a counter-offer of aid by sending a French financial advisor to Cairo. Despite opposition from some Egyptian politicians, the above events in 1876 culminated in the formation of an Anglo-French dual control body, under which the British representative was placed in charge of the Ministry of Finance and the French counterpart of the Ministry of Public Works. This policy of dual control was in fact much to the advantage of the British government and bondholders who were anxious to retrieve their delayed dividends. Although the dual control was successful in increasing government revenues, this was done mostly at the expense of increasing pressure on peasants by taxing them beyond their ability to pay. Increasing control by colonial powers over Egypt's financial affairs also necessitated elimination of the ruling Khedive's authority, which at the time resided with Ismail, Mohammad Ali's grand son. Following the inquiries of an Anglo-French commission into his revenues and expenditures, the commission decided that the Khedive must delegate his power to the ministers; distinguish between the state public revenues and his private income; and cede all his personal estates which comprised about 20 percent of Egypt's cultivable land. This was the final blow to the political power of a centralized pre-capitalist state, and a necessary step to be taken for paving the way for a complete colonial control. Because of the colonial powers' presence the weakening of Khedive Ismail's authority did not lead to a decentralization of political power in the hands of regional governors of Egyptian origin. Rather, it was followed by an influx of foreigners into Egypt who were then appointed to serve in senior administrative posts throughout Egypt. As a consequence, while between 1871 and 1875 there were 201 European civil servants in Egypt, by 1879 their number more than doubled to 534 (Mansfield, 1971: 7–16).

Despite persisting rivalry between European colonial powers in North Africa, Egypt was not considered as an immediate target for the installation of a colonial administration. Even in the late 1870s neither the British nor the French were yet willing to contemplate strategies for direct intervention. The British still hoped to manage Egyptian affairs through reforms in the government structure and run the country by Egyptian functionaries who were subordinate to the British Crown. But the events leading to the outbreak of the nationalist-patriotic and anti-colonial movement led by Colonel Ahmed Orabi (Arabi in common Transliteration) in 1881–1882 left no alternative for the British except direct military intervention. The anti-colonial movement consisted of three disparate and incompatible groups which were temporarily united against foreign intervention. The first group was represented by a religious reformer, Jamal ed-Din al Afghani and his followers who were supported by petty commodity producers, merchants, peasants and intellectuals. They believed that a national "Islamic unity" must be maintained as a defense against European colonialism. The second group was the "Constitutional Party" which represented the interests of big landowners who were opposed to both Khedive's absolute power and British colonial domination. The third element was comprised of a group of Egyptian officers with peasant origins. Led by Colonel Arabi, this faction of Egyptian officers was discontented with the current recruitment procedures in the army; as by 1880 virtually all the military posts were held by Turco-Circassians.[1] This exclusionist policy prevented Egyptian officers of peasant origins to enter the Military Academy. Arabi's appeal to the masses and also support from within the army made him the undisputed leader of the anti- colonial movement.

When all efforts by the Ottoman Court and Khedive to arrest and subdue Colonel Arabi had failed, in 1881 the government bowed to the public's demands for a written constitution and implementation of drastic social reforms. Although the Khedive's position and power was reinstated, a new nationalist government was nonetheless established in Cairo. Some historical documents indicate that the French and British were optimistic about the new developments in Egypt. But a change in the French government's leadership in late 1881 led to a new political stand taken by the French which favored quick military action in support of the Khedive. Apprehended about France's unilateral military intervention in Egypt and following a riot in Alexandria in which about 50 Europeans were killed, the British made the final decision in order to invade and occupy Egypt as a preemptive action against the French. Subsequently, following a brief confrontation between Arabi's army and British forces, the former surrendered and the national movement was promptly defeated (Mansfield, 1971: 17–50).

Internally, at the time of the British invasion and consequent occupation of Egypt in 1882 Egypt's pre-capitalist economy was still dominated by a tribute paying mode of production. The peasants were still tied to the land and there was no viable industrial development and/or significant industrial labor force. Under increasing pressure by the European advisors whose intention was to synchronize Egypt's economy with the needs of an expanding world capitalist economy, the Egyptian government implemented one major policy that changed the nature of land holding in rural areas: on the one hand structural changes in the land tenure system laid the ground for reinforcement of feudal relations in the countryside, and on the other hand introduction of private ownership rights paved the way for concentration of land in the hands of of Turko-Circassian large landowners. The new landowners were also joined by the village Shaykhs (former heads of tribes) who owned lands as well and functioned as prominent political intermediaries between the government and the peasants (Richards, 1982: 31–37). On the other end of the spectrum was a class of oppressed peasants (*fellahin*) who were confronted with a steady rise in the land tax rates, leading to their loss of rural land use rights. The fellahin's detachment from agricultural lands was caused by various factors, such as an outright seizure of the land by the government such as the land grants during Mohammad Ali's reign; flight from the land to escape forced public work (*Curveé*) for the government; fear of conscription; failure to pay excessive taxes; and property foreclosures due to the nonpayment of private debts (Richards, 1982: 37–38).

Immediately after the occupation, the British colonial administration established a set of economic objectives in Egypt that further perpetuated the country's dependence on agriculture. Lord Cromer, the British Consul General and the true power-holder in Egypt from 1883 to 1907 clearly defined Egypt's vital role within the context of British colonial economy in the following statement of policy:

> 1) Export of cotton to Europe subject to 1% export duty; 2) imports of textile products manufactured abroad subject to 8% import duty; nothing else enters into the government's intentions, nor will it protect the Egyptian cotton industry, because of the danger and evils that arise from such measures, since Egypt is by her nature an agricultural country, it follows logically that

industrial training could lead only to the neglect of agriculture while
diverting the Egyptians from the land, both these things would be disastrous
for the nation (cf. Abdel-Malek, 1968: 7).

This blunt policy statement clearly demonstrates the British colonial
interests which favored the dominance of British industries and protected the
commodities produced in the core by favorable tariffs and tax measures. For
instance, the British colonial administration blocked any serious attempts at
industrial development, especially in textiles and manufacture of commodities
that could undermine the imported products manufactured by British factories.
Later on, by legalizing the private ownership of tax-exempt land in 1883 and of
land under cultivation in 1891 the last barriers for the recognition of full private
property were also removed. However, because of peasant unrest and discontent
the British colonial administration was forced to reduce tax rates by bringing
them more in line with the cultivators' ability to pay. This in turn reduced the
power of the village Shaykhs and big landholders who usually thrived through
excessive exploitation of peasants in the countryside (Richards,1982: 56-57;
Abdel-Malek, 1968: 7). In this context, an Egyptian land owning class closely
tied to the British cotton markets and British predominance and interests
emerged in Egypt. Gradually, the proportion of land held as private property
(*mulk*) increased from one-seventh of the total area in the 1850s to one-third in
the 1890s. At the same time, by 1896 all the lands subjected to tax and tribute
(*kharajiya*) were fully assimilated to mulk (Baer, 1969: 85). During this period,
Egypt witnessed further polarization of two classes of landholders with unequal
access to agricultural land: a shrinking class of large landholders owning more
than 50 feddans and with increasing power and wealth; and a growing class of
small landowners owning less than 5 feddans with a decreasing power and
wealth (see table 8.1).

**Table 8.1: Polarization of Landowning Classes and Concentration of Land
Ownership in Egypt, 1897–1913**

|  | 1897 | | 1913 | |
|---|---|---|---|---|
|  | Large[1] | Small[2] | Large | Small |
| % of total Proprietors | 1.5 | 80.4 | 0.8 | 90.7 |
| % of total agricultural land | | | | |
| held by each group | 44 | 20.2 | 44.2 | 25.9 |

1. Landowners holding more than 50 feddans.
2. Landowners holding less than 5 feddans.
Source: Table constructed based on information in Mabro and Radwan (1976: 24–25).

As is shown in table 8.1, in 1913 the large landowners declined in size and represented only 0.8 percent of total proprietors yet still held 44.2 percent of the land (as compared to 44 percent in 1897). On the other hand, while small land-holders increased in numbers from 80.4 percent in 1897 to 90.7 percent in 1913, they held only 25.9 percent of agricultural land, a mere 5 percent increase in landholding. Since the large land-owning class did not have any interest in investing in industrial activities, their investments were concentrated almost exclusively on land and land speculation. For instance, between 1895 and 1909 agricultural output had a 16 percent increase, and land values also increased by 50 percent during the same period. This led to a peculiar process of capital accumulation that was mostly the result of land speculation and not investment in industrial activities (Mabro and Radwan, 1976: 24–26).

## Urban Development under British Colonial Rule

One common feature of colonial domination is concentration of commercial, administrative and political institutions in a few localities for the purpose of reducing the costs of running the colony. Egypt was no exception and Cairo became the center of British colonial administration. An expanding colonial administrative system provided working opportunities for many Egyptians especially at lower ranks of the government. This attracted rural immigrants to Cairo from all over the country and contributed to a considerable increase in the number of civil servants as well as construction workers and petty traders in the Capital (Baer, 1969: 143). As a consequence, Cairo's average annual growth rate of 12.5 percent far exceeded that of total population and all other major cities. In addition, an efficient handling of the export of raw materials also required an adequate system of internal transportation network and adequate port facilities. The expansion of the railway system during the second half of the 19th century fulfilled the former objective, and concentration of export and import activities in a few port cities and particularly Alexandria fulfilled the latter.

Finally, the majority of factories during the 1882-1900 period were established either in Alexandria or Cairo (see table 8.2). As can be seen in table 8.2, out of 14 major industrial enterprises seven were established in Alexandria alone and five in Cairo. With its efficient infrastructure, Alexandria continued to be the most important port city. But cities of Port Said and Suez also experienced considerable growth during the 1882–1907 period with growth rates of 3.2 and 6.2 percent, respectively.

One of the main reasons behind the British occupation of Egypt was to secure the Suez Canal and use it as the stepping stone on the road to India.

Owing their growth mainly to the Suez Canal, the two port cities of Suez and
Port Said became principal fuelling stations for European vessels on the
Europe-Asia sea route. Another distinct pattern of urbanization during this
period was the growth of local market towns with an average rate twice that of
total population. Thus, the provincial market towns of Tanta, Damanhur,
Zaqaziq, Mallawi, and Quena had growth rates of 3.5, 3.3, 3.9, 2.4, and 3.0
percent, respectively.

**Table 8.2: Principal Egyptian Factories Founded Between 1882 and 1900**

| Year | Locality | Product or Activity |
|------|----------|---------------------|
| 1884 | Alexandria | Alcoholic drinks |
| 1885 | Alexandria | Printing |
|      | Alexandria | Tanning |
|      | Cairo | Weaving, Knitting |
| 1890 | Cairo | Sweets |
|      | Cairo | Publishing/Printing |
| 1892 | Cairo | Publishing/Printing |
| 1894 | Alexandria | Cotton |
|      | Kefr al Zeyat | Cotton |
| 1895 | Cairo | Millers |
| 1896 | Sinai | Petroleum |
| 1897 | Alexandria | Brewers |
| 1899 | Alexandria | Tobacco |
|      | Alexandria | Mining and Refinery (3) |

Source: Barbour (1972: 59)

In general, the British colonization of Egypt contributed to an increase in
Egypt's urban population. First, legalization of private ownership of land and
abolition of slavery led to the emergence of a new class of laborers who were
detached from the land and therefore available to be exploited as wage-

laborers.[2] Second, during the 1882-1890 period the production of cotton did not increase significantly and thus the volume of Egyptian cotton exports remained almost the same (see table 8.3). This might have contributed to an increase in the rate of rural-urban migration and hence, an increase in urban population. Finally, British colonialism brought with it a new wave of immigrants, mostly of European origin, who came to Egypt either as functionaries of colonial administration or as speculators who in most part resided in Cairo, Alexandria, Port Said and Suez. By the turn of the 20th century foreign residents comprised a sizeable proportion of population in the main urban centers. According to Issawi (1963: 83), in 1907 the number of foreign citizens in Egypt totaled 221,000. This amounted to about 2 percent of total population, and represented about 16 percent of urban population in Cairo, 25 percent in Alexandria, and 28 percent in Port Said. In Cairo alone, the number of foreign residents almost doubled between 1897 and 1907, from 31,543 to 62,000 (Baer, 1969: 144). This considerable influx of foreigners actually divided the city into two parts in a peculiar way: a deteriorating pre-capitalist Cairo and a thriving colonial Cairo—the latter catering to a growing number of foreign-born, mostly European residents.

**Table 8.3: Volume of Egyptian Cotton Exports, 1800-1914**

| Year | Volume (000 qantars) |
|------|------|
| 1880 | 3,000 |
| 1885 | 3,540 (period of urban growth) |
| 1890 | 3,203 |
| 1895 | 4,840 |
| 1900 | 6,512 |
| 1905 | 6,376 (period of urban decline) |
| 1910 | 5,046 |
| 1914 | 7,369 |

Source: Table constructed based on Crouchley (1939: 263–65).

This increase in the rate of urban population, however, was short-lived, and by the end of 19th century Egypt witnessed a sharp decline in urban growth. Overall, while between 1897 and 1907 Egypt's population grew by 1.5 percent, most of the major urban centers had a lower rate of population growth. Baer (1969: 144) attributes this lack of urbanization or "de-urbanization" to a tremendous development of agriculture and particularly the cultivation of cotton. This was due to improvements in agricultural technology and a shift from three- year to two-year crop rotation. Thus, the volume of Egyptian cotton exports rose from 3,203,000 cantars in 1890 to 7,369,000 in 1914 (see table 8.3).

In the absence of viable industries and industrial development, many branches of local crafts which had previously flourished succumbed to European competition and an influx of European goods which were subjected to minimum import duties. Thus as a result of the British colonial policies by the early 20th century the guild system under which the artisans and merchants functioned in Egypt was virtually eliminated. The balance sheet of British colonial policy and consequent demise of pre-capitalist industries was clearly spelled out in a 1905 report by Lord Cromer, the British Consul General:

> The difference is apparent to any man whose recollection goes back some ten or fifteen years. Some quarters of Cairo that formerly used to be veritable centers of varied industries—spinning, weaving, ribbon making, dyeing, tent making, embriodery, shoe making, jewelry making, spice grinding, copper work, the manufacture of bottles out of animal skins, saddlry, locksmithing in wood and metal, etc., have shrunk considerably or completely vanished. Now there are coffee houses and European novelty shops where once there were prosperous workshops (cf. Abdel-Malek, 1968: 8).

**Introduction of Capitalist Measures**

By the turn of the 20th century Egypt was about to witness another fundamental change in her economic and political structure, marking the end of a long transitional period. Under British rule, Egypt's agricultural production was geared to satisfy the needs of an expanding European capitalist market. However, capitalist measures were not introduced into Egypt's pre-capitalist land tenure system. The only development during the 19th century was the subordination of tribute paying mode and reinforcement of feudal relations in the countryside. The increasing demand for Egyptian cotton in international markets forced the exploiting class of landholders to increase pressure on peasants in order to boost production, which in turn pushed the latter into debt and led to their further impoverishment. Consequently sharecropping became a dominant form of agricultural production with feudal landholders tightening their grip and control over the agricultural production process (Clawson, 1977: 19). Unable to pay their debts, many peasants were forced out of their assigned agricultural lands and gradually joined the already existing pool of day laborers and wage-workers in rural areas. An underdeveloped rural market economy that was neither capable of absorbing day laborers nor conducive to the development of independent producers therefore forced many of the desperate peasants to move to cities and urban centers in search of employment. Thus, a combination of several factors, including the British colonial policy of promoting an export-oriented, a mono-culture agricultural economy; concentration of cultivable lands in the hands of few landowners; and disenfranchisement of a sizeable portion of Egyptian peasantry who were traditionally tied to the land gradually prepared Egypt for the introduction of capitalist measures. In his discussion of primitive accumulation, Marx (1977: 713–14) identifies two major prerequisites in order to establish an economy based on capitalist relations: a mass of money that can be utilized as capital for investment, and a group of peasants who are detached from land and are forced to sell their labor in order to survive. With regard to the second prerequisite, based on some estimates by the end of 19th century wage-laborers comprised 37 percent of Egypt's agricultural work force (see table 8.4).

**Table 8.4: Egypt's Agricultural Work-Force by Occupation, 1907 (An Estimation)**

| Occupation | % of Categories |
| --- | --- |
| Small Peasant Proprietors | 23 |
| Renters (Cash Share Leasers) | 18 |
| Laborers on Family Land | 22 |
| Paid Laborer | 37 |
| Total | 100 |

Source: Richards (1982: 61, Table 3.3).

What was missing for a capitalist transformation in Egypt was the concentration of the excess generated profit (money capital) in the hands of non-producers. As a first step toward this goal, the National Bank of Egypt (NBE) was founded in 1898 in order to function as a central financial agency to hold state's receipts and large landowners' deposits. At the same time, foreign capital investment in Egypt rose from LE 21,280,000 in 1902 to LE 100,152,000 in 1914, with a high concentration on land speculation and mortgage financing (Abdel-Malek, 1968: 8–9).[3] At the global level, after a century of capital accumulation, concentration and centralization the European finance capital was beginning to dominate industrial capital in core countries and seeking new potential sites for investment and accumulation. Thus, at the conclusion of the First World War, developments within the world capitalist system was gradually leading core countries to export capital instead of investing in consumption goods industries for export. As a repercussion of international situation, two major developments took place in Egypt. The first was creation of a committee for commerce and industry in 1917 and establishment of the Bank of Egypt (Bank Misr) in 1920 by an emerging *bourgeoisie* in the cities. This new social class included merchants, businessmen and members of the professions representing the "modernist" wing of the rich landowners that was also supported by urban and rural middle classes, intellectuals and government employees. But influenced by nationalist sentiments and under the guidance of the Wafd Party, the Egyptian bourgeoisie favored a boycott of British products to support and reinforce its own collective class interests.[4] In response to the nationalist demands of the bourgeoisie in 1924 the Egyptian Federation of Industries (EFI) was created by a group of industrialists and financiers who were either European or pro-European Egyptian nationals. The EFI also represented the large landowning class who were in favor of top-down industrialization with the help of foreign capital (Abdel-Malek, 1968: 10). Obviously, pursuing two divergent paths in terms of Egypt's industrial development, the two factions were in sharp ideological conflict.[5]

The Egyptian revolution of 1919–1923 that concluded in a formal declaration of independence was in fact a process in which the newly emerging bourgeoisie in both rural and urban areas managed to share the state power with feudal landlords. But in reality, Egypt gained a "quasi-independent" status while economic and political systems continued to be dependent upon colonial interests and particularly those of the British. For instance, in order to protect British colonial interests, Egypt's sovereignty was heavily mortgaged by inclusion of four special protective clauses in the Egyptian Declaration of Independence: 1) the security of communication networks within the British Empire; 2) defense of Egypt against foreign aggression; 3) protection of foreign interests; and 4) control of the Sudan by the British (Abdel-Malek, 1968: 18).[6]

## Dependent Urbanization in Egypt:  The Beginnings

An intensified agricultural production and the absence of industrialization led to the decline in the growth rate of urban centers between 1897 and 1907. This was also the period in which a new ruling class emerged consisting of high-ranking government officials and feudal landowners who were consolidating their power by producing agricultural goods for capitalist markets. As a result, no "urban bourgeoisie" in the European sense emerged in Egypt, a social class that has historically been dependent on industrial production. By the same token, this new rural-based bourgeoisie had no vested interest in the promotion of urban centers (Baer, 1969: 224-25). As a consequence Egypt underwent a period of transformation that also affected the urbanization process. First, while Egypt's population rose from 9,714,000 in 1897 to 12,292,000 in 1914, the cultivated acreage increased negligibly from 5,327,000 to 5,652,000, at a time when approximately 80 percent of Egypt's population resided in the countryside.[7] This tightening population-land squeeze created by demographic pressures and declining agricultural productivity particularly between 1907 and 1916 created a process of rural-urban migration that was mainly directed toward few major urban centers (Clawson, 1977: 19). Second, during the First World War merchants and urban traders made fortunes by supplying British forces with goods and commodities and providing various services. Factories with fifty or more workers were also established as a result of increasing demand by the war economy. As a reflection of a thriving but short-lived war economy in urban areas while Egypt's population grew by 1.2 percent during 1907–1927 period, almost all major cities experienced a growth rate above 2 percent. In particular, port cities of Alexandria, Port Said, and Suez had considerable rates of growth (2.7, 3.7, and 4.1 percent, respectively), as well as Cairo and almost all major provincial agricultural market towns (see table 8.5). Although the growth rate of urban centers somewhat declined between 1927 and 1937, the pattern of rural-urban migration targeting Cairo, the three Canal zone cities, and Alexandria remained the same up until 1952. The very high rates of urban growth in the late 1930s, and later on during the Second World War period can be attributed to hundreds of thousands of Egyptians who had been mobilized by the war effort yet decided not to return to their villages (Waterbury, 1982: 310). As a result, the population of five urban governorates of Cairo, Alexandria, the Canal Zone, Damietta, and Suez rose from 2,249,000 in 1937 to 3,416,000 in 1947—an average growth rate of 4.3 percent compared to 0.9 percent for entire Egypt (Issawi, 1954: 59; and table 8.5).

At this juncture I have to emphasize the magnitude and nature of rural to urban migration and its effect on the growth and development of certain urban centers. In a study of Cairo's growth in the 20th century Abu-Lughod (1971: 174) argues that since 1917 only 3 percent of those who migrated to Cairo have come from other cities, while rural areas and especially the Nile Delta governorates in Lower Egypt have supplied most of its migrant population. Furthermore, with regard to Cairo's share of migration, between 1937 and 1947 its population increased by 779,000, of which only 179,000 was based on the city's natural population increase and the remaining 600,000 were migrants. Thus, while during the 1937–1947 period the city had a natural increase rate of 1.3 percent/annum; its net in-migration rate was 2.5 percent/annum (Waterbury, 1982: 310). What is more, 56 percent of total investment in principal Egyptian factories established between 1920 and 1952 was concentrated in and around two cities of Cairo and Alexandria, with 41 percent of total industrial capital invested in Cairo alone (see table 8.6).

**Table 8.5:   Average Annual Growth Rates for Selected Egyptian Cities Classified as Urban in 1947 (1907–1960)**

| City | 1907–1927 | 1927–1937 | 1937–1947 | 1947–1960 |
|------|-----------|-----------|-----------|-----------|
| | | (% Increase) | | |
| Cairo | 2.4 | 2.1 | 4.7 | 3.6 |
| Alexandria | 2.7 | 1.8 | 2.9 | 3.8 |
| Port Said | 3.7 | 1.8 | 3.5 | 2.4 |
| Suez | 4.1 | 2.0 | 7.6 | 4.9 |
| Tanta | 2.5 | 0.5 | 3.9 | 2.1 |
| Mehalla al-Kubra | 1.7 | 3.1 | 6.1 | 3.0 |
| al Mansura | 2.3 | 0.7 | 3.9 | 3.1 |
| Damanhur | 1.4 | 1.8 | 3.0 | 3.1 |
| Zaqaziq | 2.1 | 1.2 | 3.1 | 3.1 |
| Asyut | 1.9 | 0.5 | 4.0 | 2.3 |
| Fayoum | 1.8 | 1.9 | 1.4 | 2.5 |
| al Minya | 2.4 | 1.5 | 3.2 | 2.3 |
| Beni-Suef | 2.8 | 1.7 | 2.4 | 2.5 |
| Damietta | 0.9 | 1.3 | 3.0 | 2.2 |
| Quena | 11.7 | 1.9 | 2.3 | 2.3 |
| Shebin al Kom | 1.2 | 2.0 | 2.4 | 2.1 |
| Mallawi | 1.7 | 0.0 | 2.4 | 2.9 |
| Akhmim | 0.9 | 0.6 | 1.2 | 1.4 |
| Belqas | — | — | 3.0 | 0.6 |
| Rosetta | 1.5 | 1.2 | 1.4 | 0.4 |
| Guerga | 0.9 | 1.9 | 1.6 | 1.6 |
| Menuf | — | 0.3 | 1.4 | 2.3 |
| Aswan | 1.3 | 2.6 | 1.7 | 4.7 |
| Total | 1.2 | 1.2 | 0.9 | 2.4 |

Source:  Table Constructed based on information given in Abu-Lughod (1965: 334-336) and Baer (1969: 134-35).

**Table 8.6:  Principal Egyptian Factories Founded during the 1920–1951 Period**

| Location | Paid-up Capital (L) | Percent of Investment to Total |
|---|---|---|
| Greater Cairo (including Shubraal-Kheima and Mehella al-Kubra) | 25,467,295 | 40.9 |
| Alexandria | 9,268,000 | 15.5 |
| Kafr al Dowar | 7,000,000 | 11.3 |
| Other Localities | 20,222,000 | 32.3 |
| TOTAL | 62,317,295 | 100.0 |

Source:  Table based on information given in Barbour 1972: 66–67).

The period between the two World Wars marked the beginning of import-substitution industrialization in Egypt and its rapid and substantial progress. Needless to say, this process of dependent industrialization was made possible by the support of foreign capital, technology and expertise (Mabro and Radwan, 1976: 27; Clawson, 1977: 20; Issawi, 1963: 44). Although plans for import-substitution industrialization after 1937 offered employment to substantial numbers of urban workers, it was not sufficient enough to absorb the surplus agricultural labor force (Nassef, 1970: 103).[8] Instead, the service and petty commodity production sectors absorbed most of the rural migrants (Tignor, 1982: 35–36). To conclude, urbanization in Egypt during the second period can be summarized as the growth and development of port cities in response to the country's growing export-oriented and dependent economy, as well as the spectacular growth of the capital, Cairo, as the command center for the British colonial administration and the hub of both foreign and domestic capital investment. This peculiar pattern of urbanization was taking place against the backdrop of a stagnating pre-capitalist, mono-culture and export-oriented cash crop rural economy controlled by the British and their Egyptian allies, namely, the big landowning class.

## Notes

1. Also known as the *Mameluke,* Turko-Circassians were Egyptians who considered themselves (and perceived by other Egyptians) as part of the Ottoman governing class. They regarded ordinary Egyptian masses and their religious leaders with contempt, which in turn became a constant source of friction between the two entities.

2. For a detailed discussion of slavery in Egypt see Baer (1969: 161–189).

3. Figures for foreign capital investment do not include investments by the Suez Canal Company. On this issue, see the detailed analysis of Richards (1982: 69–77).

4. I will discuss the class origins of the Wafd Party in Chapter 9.

5. For a detailed discussion of various factions of the bourgeoisie and the question of a "nationalist bourgeoisie" in Egypt, see Abdel-Malek (1968: 17–20) and Clawson (1977: 20–22).

6. For an account of the events leading to Egypt's independence see Mansfield (1971: 203–263).

7. See Abdel-Malek (1968: 9–10).

8. According to Nassef (ibid.), import-substitution industrialization process created 577,000 jobs by 1945. For a detailed discussion on this issue see Anis (1950: 786).

# Chapter Nine

# Dependent Urbanization in Post-Revolution Egypt (1952–1970)

The Second World War weakened the European colonial powers' ability to exert political, economic and military pressure on their colonies. The European *center*'s reduced economic and political leverage in the *periphery* created a power vacuum and allowed the nationalist and anti-colonialist movements in the colonies to increase their activities and put pressure on colonialists in order to gain their independence throughout the world. The greatly increased strength and prestige of the socialist camp such as the victory of the Chinese Revolution and the role of the Soviet Union during the Second World War also provided new initiatives for popular movements to wage war against tyranny, oppression and colonial domination. The post-War period also gave rise to a new capitalist power, the United States, which gradually increased her power and influence in the old colonies once being off limits under the European colonial domination. In the years following the Second World War a mass-based patriotic movement took shape in Egypt that opposed all forms of foreign domination, including the newly established state of Israel. The sharp decline in power and prestige of Great Britain as an invincible colonial power in the world also allowed for more political participation by the Egyptian masses, and led to an increase in the level of political and national consciousness. Drastic developments in global geopolitics and an intensified class conflict in Egypt provided the social context for a revolutionary movement that brought Jamal Abdel-Nasser into power in 1952.

As has been the case for earlier periods, changes in the dynamics of town-country relations, displacement of population and migration, and the process of urbanization are all spatial manifestations of a changing political economy. A critical analysis of Egyptian urbanization in post-WWII period necessitates an understanding of the intricate nature of the 1952 Revolution and dynamics of social change during the transitional period from monarchy to the establishment of the new republic. In order to accomplish this task first we have to learn more about class composition of the Egyptian society on the eve of the 1952 Revolution. In general, four distinct classes can be identified which in various degrees were instrumental in shaping the course of events during the revolutionary period, namely, the ruling class, the working class, the petty bourgeoisie, and the working class/working poor urban and rural masses.

As a segmented and heterogeneous social entity, the Egyptian ruling class was torn between various political and ideological factions and tendencies. But its members had one thing in common: all were dependent on a colonial economy. We can distinguish three sub-categories within the Egyptian ruling class. First, the aristocratic faction with its roots in feudal relations and comprised of big landowners of Turkish origin. With close ties to the Palace, this faction was a strong advocate of British colonial presence and controlled the economy of rural Egypt as well as a portion of urban economy. The second faction comprised of members of the ruling class with Egyptian origins, both Muslim and Christian Coptic, who had a weaker political position and in most cases were subordinate to whims and wishes of the first faction. This sub-class represented a faction shaped out of an alliance between the commercial bourgeoisie and a segment of the big landowners mostly of Turkish origin. Politically, the second faction was represented by the Wafd (literally meaning "delegation") Party leadership which claimed to represent the nation as a whole. As a reformist bourgeois-nationalist organization, the Wafd Party emerged during the 1919 struggle for independence, and fought to gain an independent status for Egypt. But ideological, and to some extent economic dependency of its members to a capitalist system that operated beyond Egyptian political boundaries at a global level limited the party's capabilities as a viable nationalist political force. Finally, the industrial-capitalist faction comprised of influential Egyptian capitalists with heavy investments in urban industrial centers. This faction had close ties to the Misr Bank (Bank of Egypt) and the Federation of Egyptian Industry, both largely having been controlled by foreign capital interests. Due to its strong dependence on foreign capital and colonial support the industrial-capitalist faction was not devoid of anti-nationalist and anti-democratic tendencies (Hussein, 1973: 62–69). On the other end of the social class continuum, the Egyptian working class comprised about 10 percent of the urban population. However, due to Egypt's weak industrial base and its dependency to foreign capital the working class lacked a viable and established organization to provide a potentially effective and revolutionary leadership for a mass-based anti-colonial movement. This organizational and ideological weakness forced the working class movement to align itself with the Wafd reformist leadership. As a result, the post-war Egyptian political struggle evolved around an intra-class conflict within the ruling class, with the Wafd Party and its working class and petty bourgeois supporters on one side; and the big landowners supported by the King and the British on the other.[1]

Apart from the above-mentioned classes, an ascending capitalism within a disintegrating pre-capitalist economy created a new class of impoverished and disenfranchised masses in the countryside and eventually in the cities. This class was comprised of landless peasants who were deprived of the possibility of working for themselves in the countryside, and rural peasants owning a small but insufficient plot of land for subsistence farming. As I will discuss later in the chapter, many of the rural poor were driven to the cities where they joined the urban poor with little or no access to a regular and permanent work. The members of this new class had to perform low key and mostly non-productive jobs as waiters in small coffee houses, odd-jobbers, temporary laborers, itinerant peddlers, servants, caretakers and the like; and based on one estimate in the early 1950s they comprised about 56 percent of urban and 79 percent of rural population. This indicates their numerical significance as a potentially important social force in Egypt. But, because of their low economic status they were unable to mobilize as a viable political and ideological force. Two factors contributed to this inherent weakness. First, the transitional social position of this class separated them from both capitalist and pre-capitalist social relations, making them a fluctuating political force susceptible to political and ideological manipulation by dominant classes (Hussein, 1973: 45). Second, since their structural detachment from pre-capitalist relations of production in rural areas was not a class-conscious act, their undermined economic position did not lead to a class-based solidarity which could challenge the status quo.

Within the above context of social class relations the post-War anti-colonial and nationalist movement in Egypt further evolved in two stages. Spanning from 1945 to 1947 the first stage was marked by the formation of a militant alliance between students and workers who opposed British occupation and internal oppression. At the same time, The Palestinian struggle found its supporters among the militant Egyptians who sent volunteers to Palestine and connected the Palestinian cause with that of the Egyptian people. Repressed and crushed in 1939, the Palestinian liberation struggle flared up again and took new initiatives against the Zionist colonization and subsequent creation of the state of Israel in 1948. On the other side of the fence, the British saw the new state of Israel as the mainstay of rival American interests, but were also threatened by the increasing militancy of the popular movement in Egypt. This led to the second stage of struggle when the British supported Egypt's involvement in a classic war against Israel. As a clever colonial strategy, the war potentially would have served two objectives for the British: 1) to undermine the militant alliance of workers and students and their revolutionary goals in the Palestinian case; and 2) to strengthen the Egyptian King's position (as well as that of the British) as the major political power in the region.

The subsequent defeat of the regular Egyptian army not only undermined the dominant role of the King and his allies among the ruling class, but also marked the end of British colonial power and influence in Egypt. The technical inefficiency of the regular army and its consequent moral degradation led to expansion and rapid organization of a secret nationalist group known as the "Free Officers." This organization had its roots in the lower- and middle-rank army officers, largely of Egyptian descent. Because of their rural-based ethnic origin, the Free Officers were linked to the rural landowning class. But their position within military as middle-ranked officers also brought their class aspirations close to those of the petty bourgeoisie and middle class government bureaucrats. The Free Officers' political agenda was based on their deep resentment of a long- standing British occupation; the influence and important role of foreign capitalists in running Egypt's economy; feudal landlords with large holdings; and the Egyptian dependent (comprador) bourgeoisie.

The leadership of the Free Officers viewed the aspirations of the middle-rank military elites and the petty bourgeoisie as paralleling those of the entire nation. In order to fulfill their nationalist mission, the Free Officers planned for a coup d'état to oust the appointed military chiefs, seize all the strategically important command posts, and then present their program for national renovation to the entire army. They also wanted to make sure that should they be successful, the United States would not side with the British and the Court, and would give them a chance to consolidate the state apparatus and restore "national dignity." Since the Free Officers had the advantage of occupying positions within the military arm of the state apparatus, it made their presence in the political arena less threatening to the propertied class who were more apprehensive of the unpredictable outcomes of a popular movement developed and led from outside the confines of the "establishment." It was under these circumstances that the July 1952 coup d'état brought the Free Officers and Jamal Abdel-Nasser into power (Hussein, 1973: 72–86).

## The 1952 Revolution: Removing the Obstacles to the Development of Dependent Capitalism

Transition from a pre-capitalist economy to one based on capitalist principles was in the making in Egypt after the Second World War, and the 1952 revolution was in fact a vehicle by which this transition was completed. Based on historical documentation of Egypt's post-1952 history, it is possible to identify three distinct stages of economic and political development during the reign of the Free Officers and consequent presidency of Jamal Abdel-Nasser.[2] The first stage of the military regime (1952–1956) was aimed at reforming the political power structure in order to create a modern nationalist, independent and industrialized society. The most important aspect of this period, the agrarian reform, sought to weaken the landed bourgeoisie, increase the number of small landowners, and redirect capital investment from agriculture to industry. On this matter, the United States played a crucial role not only in Egypt, but in the entire region including Iran. In brief, the post-War American foreign policy in the Middle East concentrated on modernization of the economy and political institutions in the region. Related to the agrarian question, in 1950 the U.S State Department declared the American policy in the Middle East as follows:

> It is clear that the urgent economic problem in the Middle East is the agrarian problem . . . it is essential to extend and improve irrigation, to reclaim the idle land, to modernize agricultural technology and to take reasonable steps to reform

the land ownership and insurance systems in the countryside (cf. Abdel-Malek, 1968: 67).

A year later, a U.S. Presidential advisory committee recommended that in certain countries the only way to combat "hunger" and "socialism" is through land reform. In fact, the Egyptian land reform was conceived and carried out from above in order to block any revolutionary effort by peasants and progressive elements. Thus, in response to internal class conflicts and international pressure, once in power the Revolutionary Command Council (RCC) initiated land reform in Egypt. The 1952 Egyptian Land Reform was aimed at the compulsion of the landed bourgeoisie (who managed to accumulate agrarian capital) to redirect their investment into the industrial-capitalist sector. This was not going to happen, however, unless the rural social bases of the landed bourgeoisie were also undermined.

The Land Reform was hailed by those members of the ruling class that represented Egypt's industrial and finance capital as one of the most fruitful policies for the future of industry. But the landed bourgeoisie was obviously greatly disappointed by, and apprehensive of the consequences of land reform. Gradually, the big land-holders understood the nature of the reform, especially its implicit objectives, which was to avoid peasant upheavals and the outbreak of a socialist revolution. Later on, they also began to appreciate the Government's intentions and good will that protected their interest under the law and offered them attractive compensations for their loss of land (Abdel-Malek, 1968: 80–81). The main objectives of the agrarian reform in Egypt can be summarized as: 1) distribution of the expropriated land by the state to peasants within five years; 2) fixing the land ownership ceiling at 200 feddans; 3) appointment of a committee for fixing wages for farm workers; 4) establishment of agricultural cooperatives for small land-holders of up to 5 feddans; and 5) provision of farm loans, supplies, fertilizers, seed and machinery. In order to reduce the inefficiency of small holdings in agricultural production, the state gave considerable impetus to rural co-operatives. Based on some estimates, in 1953 there were 400 co-operative societies with 200,000 peasant members. Another outcome of land reform was the state's control over and utilization of the acreage not yet distributed to the peasants, known as "agrarian-reform land." This resulted in the State's appropriation of a net profit of LE 2,754,800 in 1955. By 1962, the state was claiming to have redistributed some 645,642 feddans out of 5,964,000 feddans of cultivable land. But overall, implementation of land reform policies in Egypt has to be considered as a failure, since at best the Land Reform affected only 10 percent of the agricultural land, and hence rendering its structural effects as negligible.

The second stage (1956–1961) started with the Suez crisis in 1954, and was followed by the nationalization of the Suez Canal Company, foreign aggression against Egypt and unexpected nationalization of 55 French and British-owned firms by the Egyptian government. The highlight of the second stage was a coalition between the military state apparatus and the financial/industrial section of the Egyptian bourgeoisie (Abdel-Malek, 1968: XIII–XVI). Ever since the 1952 coup, the main objective of the Revolutionary Command Council (RCC) has been to compel the landed bourgeoisie to redirect its capital investment into the industrial sector. This strategy did not work, however, as wealthy landowners preferred to deposit their excess capital in banks rather than investing in Egyptian industries. As a consequence, of LE 45 million taken out of the land, only LE 6 million was invested in industry.

The third stage (1961–1967) started with nationalization laws based on the principles set by "Arab Socialism" in Egypt. By early 1962, all banks, heavy industries and medium-sized economic units had to accept 51 percent state participation in their capital ownership and administration.[3] Nationalization of banks and basic industries was portrayed by the government as a major step toward Arab Socialism. But a careful look at the actual outcome of these measures will reveal the precarious nature of Egyptian socialism. For one thing, it can be argued that even nationalization of the greater portion of privately owned industries and property is not synonymous with suppression of the rights to private property in the constitution of a given country. As has been the case in many colonized societies, nationalization by the government is often a means for reorganization of an underdeveloped dependent capitalist economy or an economic activity under colonizer's control. The state thus acts temporarily on behalf of the comprador class to revive the economy. A comparison of the nationalization process in Egypt with that of the former Soviet Union by Mandel (1979: 109) supports this interpretation and reveals the shortcomings of Arab Socialism in Egypt:

> In the former, much property was nationalized but the capitalist class was not expropriated and therefore, it was relatively easy to de-nationalize what had previously been nationalized. On the contrary, the right to private property is forbidden de facto in the Soviet Union and that means in turn forbidden by the law and the secular arm of the law: the state and all its institutions.

Despite its inherent shortcomings, Arab Socialism was nonetheless a remarkable social experience in Egypt that retarded a process of dependent capitalist development so endemic in many other developing countries. For instance, with the consolidation of multinational corporations in the post-War period, the capitalist countries in the core changed their policy of producing consumer goods commodity for colonial markets that greatly affected the economies of the colonies and countries in the periphery with dependent economies. That is, instead of producing commodities bound for peripheral markets in the center, Western companies established factories in the periphery which produced consumer goods for its internal markets (Dos Santos, 1970: 232). This was what Ewans (1979: 40) called a "triple alliance" between the peripheral state, indigenous capital and foreign capital investments by multinational corporations. In contrast to this general trend, Egypt offers an example of a peripheral society where for almost twenty years (1952–1972) Multinational corporations played no significant role in that nation's economy. Although a triple alliance was formed in Egypt between the state bourgeoisie, the military and the former Soviet Union up until 1972, the latter's presence in this partnership moved Egypt in a completely divergent path of economic development (Waterbury, 1983: 28–29). Thus Egypt continued to pursue her import-substitution industrialization plans, but because of her alliance with the former Soviet Union the economy did not become dependent upon capitalist markets (Abdel-Fadil, 1980: 107–112). This was mainly due to the Soviet Union's doctrine of "non-capitalist path of development" at the time that aimed at helping newly decolonized nations to develop economically while at the same time detach themselves from a long-established dependency to the global capitalist economy. Based on this doctrine, technological and manufacturing operations set up by the Soviets were to be paid for partially by export of Egyptian products to the former at "non-market" negotiated prices. However, despite its benign appearance this alternative path also had its own shortcomings, as it did not lead Egypt to an independent process of economic development and in fact created a situation of double dependency leading to "reliance upon the USSR for technological support of existing projects and the servicing of the debts; and reliance on Western capitalist markets to finance the growing trade deficit that emerged in the late 1960s" (Waterbury, 1983: 29).

The Egyptian Government's quasi-socialist measures proved to be disastrous, and by 1965 there was a savings crisis in Egypt with no easy solution at hand. Extreme government initiatives such as extending nationalization further down into middle and lower-middle class assets; increasing "forced savings;" and further manipulation of prices for agricultural products required a "sincere effort at socialist indoctrination and mobilization at all levels," which was too dangerous to be a viable solution for Nasser's military state (Waterbury, 1983: 428). This internal crisis was deepened by Egypt's devastating defeat in the 1967 Six-Day War with Israel that led the country into a power struggle between two major factions of the ruling class coalition. The outcome of this intra-class struggle between the advocates of state capitalism and those who favored unrestricted capitalist development proved to be costly for Egypt. As one chronicler of Egypt's modern history explains, the victory of the latter faction which "favored major retreat from state capitalism by advocating a much greater reliance on market forces and free enterprise and by asking for more concessions to foreign capital" clearly signaled the end of an important era in Egypt's contemporary history (Abdel-Fadil, 1980: 112). In fact, that the post-Nasser era was marked by Sadat's initiation of open door policies (*Infitah*) in order to attract Western capital investments is proof of the inadequacy of nationalization without abolition of the right to private property. Thus, despite measures taken to provide basic needs and to reduce social and economic inequality in Egypt, Nasser's "Arab Socialism" was nothing more than state capitalism, and as such was an attempt to concentrate and direct investments toward non-agricultural capitalist production.[4] After twenty or so years of isolation, by the early 1970s Egypt once again opened its doors unconditionally to multi-national corporations and foreign capital.

## The Effects of Land Reform on Dependent Urbanization

In an article on Egyptian urbanization, Abu-Lughod (1965: 315–22) argues that the most critical problem of contemporary Egypt is "over-concentration of population in relatively few cities," rather than "over-urbanization per se." She further argues that what appeared to be over-urbanization is nothing but reclassification of many rural settlements that exceeded the 20,000 threshold as "urban." Based on this argument, by redefining "urban" as a place with at least 20,000 inhabitants with densities greater than 1,500 persons per square kilometer, and having no more than one-third of its labor force engaged in agriculture, she concludes that Egypt is "less urbanized" as compared to the official classification. Abu-Lughod's concept of over-concentration of population in urban areas becomes important in analyzing the trends and patterns of urban growth and/or decline related to socioeconomic factors and historical events, as well as understanding underlying reasons for Egypt's massive rural-to-urban migration.

As I stated earlier, the Lower Egypt urban centers and port cities have always had a higher rate of growth as compared to those of middle and Upper Egypt. But in different periods the fluctuations of urban growth rates compared to those of total population growth were related to structural changes in the Egyptian economy. A comparison of the growth rates for the 1937–1947 and 1947–1960 periods reveals the fact that while in the former period both market towns and Lower Egypt urban centers had an enormous growth, there was a general slowdown of urban growth in the latter period (see table 8.5). Furthermore, as a comparison of data for 1952 (pre-Reform) and 1961 in table 9.1 demonstrates, this to a great extent can be attributed to the consequences of land reform; an increase in the number of small landowners in rural Egypt; and a steady fall in the absolute number of landless families in rural Egypt up to the mid 1960s. At the same time, the number of landless families decreased from 1,217,000 in 1952 to 970,000 in 1961 or from 44 percent of total number of rural families to 30 percent (Abdel-Fadil, 1975: 44).

Despite considerable changes in the structure of rural land ownership, a slowdown in the overall rate of urban growth, and absence of an intensified industrialization process the growth rate for major urban centers was still double that of the national population. There seems to be only one plausible explanation for this phenomenon, and that is the plight of small land holders prior to, and after the land reform. According to one estimate, about 70 percent of small holders (or about 2,000,000 peasants) in 1952 owned less than half a feddan each, so that they were virtually destitute (Ibrahim Amer, cf. Abdel-Malek, 1968: 58). In addition, the small landholders were obliged to pay about LE 50 per year for each feddan received from the state in payment of loan installments, irrigation facilities, farm supplies, etc (Abdel-Malek, 1968: 73). Abdel-Malek concludes that various disbursements incurred by peasants owning 3 feddans amounted to more than LE 125 per year, whereas their annual income was only LE 115. This resulted in the further impoverishment of small landholding peasantry and their inevitable inclination toward migration to the cities and finding new sources of survival in urban areas.

**Table 9.1: A Comparison of Landholding Patterns Before and After the Land Reform , 1952 and 1961**

| | 1952 | | | 1961 | | |
|---|---|---|---|---|---|---|
| | Owners (000s) | % of All Owners | % of Land | Owners (000s) | % of All Owners | % of Land |
| Small holdings (1–5 feddans) | 2,642 | 94.3 | 35.4 | 2,919 | 94.1 | 52.1 |
| Medium holdings (5–50 feddans) | 148 | 5.3 | 33.5 | 171 | 5.5 | 32.6 |
| Large holdings (50+ feddans) | 11 | 0.4 | 33.1 | 11 | 0.4 | 15.3 |

Source: Table constructed based on Waterbury (1983: 269).

## The Effects of Rural Poverty on Dependent Urbanization

Another important element in the study of over-concentration of population in urban areas is the position of landless peasants in rural Egypt and their eventual migration to the cities. Abdel-Fadil (1975: 44–46) identifies two types of landless peasants in Egypt. First were permanent agricultural wage-laborers who were mostly employed year-round on medium and large farms, and included all groups of specialized agricultural laborers such as tractor drivers, farm machine operators and the "kallaf" who looked after the livestock. They were also fully employed and enjoyed steady income all year round. Second were casual Farm Laborers or those landless peasants who entered into the labor force for short periods of time (as in the peak seasons) for harvesting and sowing and thus supplemented the permanent regular labor force. Ayrout (1963: 55) adds a third type, the "Tarahil" or casual laborers as the poorest of the rural poor, who comprised a substantial portion of landless peasants. Within a system called "Tarhila," these extremely mobile laborers were recruited for four to six weeks for the maintenance of canals and other rural public works.

Among landless peasants, those who benefited the least from agrarian reform in Egypt were the casual laborers. According to Abdel-Fadil (1975: 125), in redistributing the land preference was given to cultivators/tenants and permanent laborers, whereas not all casual laborers could receive a holding. In addition, the breakup of large estates that caused a reduction in demand for their labor further harmed the casual workers. Saab (1967: Chapter 8) and Abdel-Fadil (1975: 125–26) attribute this reduction in employment opportunities to three factors: 1) a tendency for utilizing self-employed family labor by the new medium-sized landholders; 2) a general slackening in agricultural investment by big landowners; and 3) a "voluntary" break-up of large holdings and their sale to small holders by the large-scale farmers. In short, Egyptian agrarian reform aggravated the landless peasants' problems of employment. Within this context, then, it is my contention that "over-concentration of population" in urban areas occurred because of the deterioration of employment opportunities and increasing poverty in rural Egypt, and not because it was "necessary and inevitable" (see Abu-Loghud, 1965: 315).[5] In the absence of a full-fledged industrialization process, what I theorize here is that urbanization in Egypt was in fact an intensification of rural-urban migration facilitated by the availability of a relatively cheap and abundant labor force in the countryside. Abu-Lughod (1961: 23) identifies two types of rural migrants: the "bright youths," who migrate to towns in search of education or wider opportunities, and the "village poor," who constitute the majority of the migrants. The fact that the larger portion of rural migrants come from the poorer strata is borne out by the findings of an ILO-INP sample survey, indicating that 26 percent of migrants came from families earning less than LE 50 per year; 40 percent from the LE 51-75 bracket; 22 percent from the LE 76-100; and only 6 percent from those with an income higher than LE 100 (cf. Abdel-Fadil, 1975: 113). Another ILO-INP rural employment survey (1968: 29-30) further illustrates that the strongest "push" factor for migration was peasants' state of landlessness (86 percent) and the lack of rented land in their region of origin (53 percent). This further reveals the fact that rural population displacement in Egypt is not urban-rural migration per se, but migration of the poorest of the rural strata to urban areas.

To conclude, the internal socio-economic forces following the Free Officers' coup in 1952 did in fact contribute and affect the course of events. Related to internal migration and population movement, for a brief period the implementation of the Land Reform policies increased the number of small landholders and slowed down the rural-urban migration. However, lack of structural support further led to the worsening living conditions of the rural population and their migration to the cities. Thus urbanization effectively became an over-concentration of population in urban centers because of increasing poverty in the countryside and migration of the poorest peasants, and not because of a general rural-urban migration.

### Notes

1. As an endangered class the Egyptian *Petty bourgeoisie* was made up of heterogeneous social strata including those who possessed a small amount of capital or a small plot of land, with their economic viability being undermined by an influx of cheap imported colonial goods. This relative economic independence enabled them to make a living

without having to sell their labor power and/or buying the labor power of others.

2. For the discussion of Nasser's era (1952–1970) I am indebted to the work of Abdel-Malek (1968, xiii–xvi, and Chapters 1 and 3).

3. For the extent of nationalization see Waterbury (1983, Chapter 4, especially pp. 74–79).

4. The common features of socialist construction that apply to all countries making the transition from capitalism to socialism can be defined as: guidance of the working masses by the working class; establishment of the dictatorship of the proletariat; the alliance of the working class and the peasantry; the abolition of capitalist ownership and the establishment of public ownership of basic means of production; gradual socialist reconstruction of agriculture; planned development of the national economy; and the carrying of the socialist revolution in the sphere of ideology and culture. However, despite Nasser's nationalization efforts, "Arab Socialism was not based on socialist principles since it repressed the working class and excluded them from political and economic decision-making processes. For a detailed analysis of the events leading to the nationalization efforts and Arab Socialism see Hussein (1973: Chapters 4–6, 134–241).

5. In fairness to professor Abu-Lughod I have to remind the readers that later on she had a paradigmatic shift in her approach and renounced her earlier analyses of urbanization process in Egypt. See for instance, Abu-Lughod (1989).

# Chapter Ten

# Uneven Urban Development:  The Case of Cairo

Some observers of Egyptian history regard the French expedition of 1798 as the beginnings of "modernization" for Egypt (Gibb and Bowen, 1950: 231). But in actual terms modernization process of Egyptian economy in terms of introduction of capitalist relations and its ensuing socioeconomic and cultural changes did not start until after Mohammad Ali's era (post-1848). Following the Ottoman reoccupation of Egypt under Mohammad Ali's command, Egypt experienced a period of social and political chaos and anarchy. With Mohammad Ali being in control of Upper Egypt, and parts of Lower Egypt including Alexandria being controlled by another Turkish faction Egypt faced a decentralized and bankrupt economy, and an increasing power of local feudal landlords and tribal chiefs who vied to have command over various regions, cities and villages.

Mohammad Ali captured Cairo at the time when three centuries of a deteriorating economy and decentralized political power had virtually eliminated the need for a capital city. As a result Cairo in the 1800s was in ruins, when "house after house in the older quarters had crumbled and been neither cleared nor rebuilt" (Abu-Lughod, 1971: 86). Spatially, Cairo changed little during the first half of the 19th century, and statistically her population increased negligibly during the 1798-1868 period. It was no historical accident that Cairo's physical and economic development remained contingent upon the restoration of political and economic stability and the centralization of power during Mohammad Ali's reign. Except for Mohammad Ali's projects for building palaces and connecting roads, the older Cairo on the coast of the Nile remained almost untouched during the 1800–1830 period.

Mohammad Ali's preference for Bulaq, the extreme northwest corner of the city was first demonstrated by building his palace there and later making it the site for his new industrial establishments. Among new industrial establishments were several textile factories, a wool factory (1808), Egypt's first iron foundry (1820), the first national press (1822), spinning mills and a bleaching plant (Government

Printing Office, 1956: 88–89). Although his efforts for industrialization eventually failed, Bulaq nonetheless established itself as Cairo's future industrial zone (Abu-Lughod, 1971: 91). But Cairo's growth actually did not take off until after Mohammad Ali's era (post-1848 period), and when it did, it was directly related to internal political developments, external political pressures, and economic constraints. Mohammad Ali's successor inherited a new export- oriented economy with a relatively organized and centralized state apparatus at the time when there was increasing foreign competition to control the Egyptian economy. Thus, while Alexandria continued to grow as the main port for exports and imports, Cairo started to gain momentum as the domestic administrative center as well as the center for political manipulation by rival colonial powers.

The spatial expansion and development of the communications and transportation networks is a strong indicator of uneven economic development in Egypt. Transportation networks under British colonial rule were developed not to connect centers of population concentration or facilitate economic development at the national level. Rather, they were expanded to serve colonial interests, from extracting and exporting raw materials and agricultural products to connecting locations deemed strategically important for colonial interests. The fact that railway networks in Egypt were initially conceived as an efficient means of transportation for the export of cotton is manifested in Egypt's peculiar and rather illogical dual railroad system: a local/regional narrow gauge network to bring the product from cotton fields to provincial centers; and the standard gauge trans-Egyptian railway that connected provincial centers to Cairo, and Cairo to the rest of the country. In one instance of the conflict of interests among colonial powers Cairo benefited the most, when during the1850s the French pressed for a seaway canal through the Isthmus of Suez. Concerned about losing their sea trade monopoly around the Cape of Good Hope in the southern tip of the African Continent the British government vehemently opposed the French-proposed plan. Instead, it advocated construction of a railway network to carry passengers and cargo between Europe and India by connecting Alexandria to Suez via Cairo. Under British pressure the second scheme was approved and in 1854 Cairo was connected to Alexandria by rail.[1] The railroad affected Cairo's growth in two ways: 1) its port of entry to Cairo stimulated further spatial development and absorbed many of the later immigrants; and 2) by connecting it to Alexandria, the once isolated city during Mohammad Ali's reign Cairo was directly linked to the outside world especially the European capitalist markets (Abu-Lughod, 1965: 432–34). During the 1863–1882 period Cairo's population growth lagged behind that of Egypt, but there were some developments that drastically changed the physical character of the city. Similar to the efforts made by Qajar kings in Tehran's case, Initial changes took place under Mohammad Ali's grandson Khadive Ismail, Egypt's ruler from 1863 to 1879, who attempted to give a modern look to Cairo. Thus by hiring a famous French city planner, the "modern Cairo" but not yet the "colonial Cairo" was born west of the old, pre-capitalist city. Ismail's plan included "the construction of parks, open squares, roads, bridges, villas, an opera house, a theatre, a library, and residential palaces for his European guests" (Ibrahim, 1987; Rodenbeck, 1998, cf. Ghannam, 2002: 27). However, his efforts should not be regarded as a genuine plan for Cairo's urban development but merely a superficial imitation of the European city planning ideals of the time sponsored by an Asiatic state.[2]

## Cairo's Growth under British Colonial Administration (1882–1952)

Cairo's spatial composition and the state of the economy in Egypt are closely linked. As I explained in Chapter 8, although Egypt's agricultural production was directed toward capitalist markets, one cannot talk about the existence of capitalist relations of production during this period. The British involvement was also aimed at reorganization of production in a pre-capitalist setting, meaning that their reorganization efforts initially took place only at the political level. The British needed the help of indigenous administrators to extract agricultural surplus from the rural population, and while Egypt remained as a nominal member of the Ottoman Empire, its ruler Khedive Tawfiq (1879–1892) was reinstated by the British as the ceremonial head of the state. But in reality the decisions were made by Lord Cromer, the British Consul General and the chief colonial administrator for Egypt from 1883 to 1907. Thus, in the absence of industrial-capitalist production, control over pre-capitalist means of production was shared by the British and domestic rulers.

After Colonel Arabi's defeat and the consequent British invasion in 1882 Cairo entered a new phase of development. With its European-style subdivisions, the western Cairo district of Bulaq which had remained mostly as an empty shell since Mohammad Ali's early modernization efforts finally found its *raison d'être* by serving as the headquarters of the British colonial administration. Aside from an intensive rural-urban migration during the 1882–1890 period mainly caused by an stagnating agricultural economy, Cairo's population increase resulted from the influx of a new wave of foreign immigrants. Cairo's foreign residents were housed in West Cairo (modern quarters) and were comprised of three distinct groups: 1) Italians who came to staff small-scale industries and machine shops; 2) the Greek, French, Swiss, Swede, Belgian and English entrepreneurs and adventurers who were attracted by new business opportunities under British protection; and 3) the British military and civil servants who were sent in to administer and protect the newly acquired colony (Abu-Lughod, 1965: 454–55). The increasing demand for housing for both foreign residents and high ranking indigenous officials, along with the final steps taken for legalization of private land ownership opened up a new era of land speculation in the capital. By the turn of the 20th century Cairo had developed a dual spatial character: the old, pre-capitalist Cairo with a growing rural migrant population; and "colonial Cairo" as the seat of the new colonial administration and a residential area for more than 60,000 foreign residents and local elites (see table 10.1). As is illustrated in table 10.1, Cairo of the late 19th century was in fact the spatial manifestation of two divergent socioeconomic systems juxtaposed at one locality.

**Table 10.1: The Dual Nature of Cairo's Spatial Formation at the End of 19th Century**

|  | Eastern Cairo (pre-capitalist city) | Western Cairo (colonial city) |
|---|---|---|
| Technology | Pre-capitalist, Handicraft industries | Steam-powered technology |
| Street Patterns | Labyrinth, not influenced by the grid iron pattern resulting from land registration; unpaved streets | Wide, straight streets paved with macadam |
| Water Supply | Itinerant water peddlers | Conduits connected with the steam pumping stations |
| Lighting | None | Gas lights |
| Transportation | Foot or animal-back | Railroad, horse-drawn carriages |

Source: Abu-Lughod (1965: 430).

In time, several urban developments characterized the core of "colonial Cairo": a Garden City along the banks of the Nile River that connected colonial Cairo to the old, pre-capitalist section via a wide boulevard; the residential city of Heliopolis on the eastern suburbs of the old city core modeled after the British New Towns; residential suburbs of Ma'adi and Helvan south of Cairo on the banks of the Nile River; and a palace and residential villas on Gezira Island located on the Nile. In addition, several bridges connected Cairo to the west bank of the Nile. Cairo became an example of the spatial translation of this transitional period, as pre-capitalist quarters and modern (colonial) Cairo coexisted and contributed to the city's uneven spatial development.

During the opening decades of the 20th century the promise of lucrative commercial gains attracted a large number of foreign immigrants not only from other parts of the Ottoman Empire, but also from Southern and (to a lesser extent) Northern Europe. One urban scholar attributes 70 percent of Cairo's growth during this period to in-migration, two-thirds of which was due to the influx of foreigners (Abu-Lughod, 1971: 122). However, this pattern was short-lived and the crash of the European stock market in 1907 and subsequent foreclosures and mortgage defaults discouraged foreign immigration to Egypt. At the outbreak of the First World War, the British unilaterally declared Egypt as a protectorate, designating her as an important base for Britain's Middle East operations. The presence of the British army in Egypt generated a new demand for service and supplies, drawing a portion of rural population to major urban areas such as Cairo, Alexandria and the Canal cities.[3] Meanwhile, new industries were established in cities to meet shortages created by a crippled wartime European economy. The revived industrial activities in major Egyptian cities coupled by a deteriorating agricultural economy created a new wave of rural-urban migration. The post-War years also witnessed a booming construction industry in Egypt. This is attributable to the beginnings of capital accumulation in the hands of Egyptian landowners, who, in a predominantly pre-capitalist society did not have any other outlet for investment. In Cairo's case, increasing population and serious housing shortages provided a fertile ground for construction activities and hence, the urgent need for construction workers and wage-laborers. Like Tehran but several decades earlier, rural-urban migration played a significant role in shaping Cairo's economic and spatial development. For example, in 1926 Egypt experienced a severe recession due to a drop in the price of cotton in the world markets followed by the world-wide recession of the 1930s. This negatively affected the rural labor market and inevitably forced large number of peasants into the cities, particularly Cairo and Alexandria.

## The Effect of Rural-Urban Migration on Cairo's Growth after the 1952 Revolution

Rural-urban migration and especially migration to major urban centers like Cairo and Alexandria continued with a steady pace during the years immediately after the conclusion of the Second World War. Although land reform policies in Egypt offset the rate of rural-urban migration in general, there was a slight increase in migration from the Upper-Egypt rural provinces during the 1947–1960 period, while migration from the Delta provinces to Cairo remained steady. As the seat of a highly centralized government the public sector employment witnessed a three-fold increase, from 325,000 in 1952 to more than 1,000,000 in 1967. In order to house

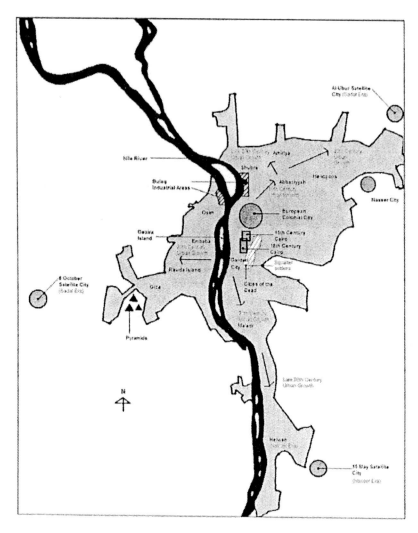

**Figure 10.1. Various phases of Cairo's urban development. Map created by author based on information from Hadwin (n.d.) and Freund (2007: 150–52).**

the new influx of immigrants and government employees, many new public housing complexes, mostly high rise, were built in and around Cairo, including in poor areas of Helwan, Shubra, Amiriya and in areas on the west bank of the Nile such as Embaba & Osim (see figure 10.1).

During the same period, migration from urban governorates to Cairo comprised only 3 percent of its migrant population. In the absence of growth in industrial activities, and along with structural developments in rural areas considerable investment efforts by large landholders took place in the construction industry, almost all of them concentrated in Cairo and Alexandria (Abdel-Malek, 1968: 81). As an example, by 1956 investment in construction industry comprised 47.3 percent of the total investments and 75.8 percent of all private investments (see table 10.2).

**Table 10.2: Percentage of Egyptian-born Migrants from Different Localities to Cairo's Total Population, 1947–1960**

| Migrants' Place of Origination | 1947 (%) | 1960 (%) |
|---|---|---|
| From Urban Governorates | 3 | 3 |
| From Upper Egyptian Provinces | 12 | 15 |
| From Delta Provinces | 19 | 18 |

Source: Abu-Lughod (1971: 174, Table 5).

The years 1961–1967 were marked by nationalization laws and initiation of the First Five Year Plan (1960–1965). The previous reductions in employment opportunities in rural areas were offset by the new demand for casual labor generated by the construction of the High Dam and the new land reclamation schemes in Upper Egypt whereby the work force grew by nearly 22 percent or from 6 to 7.3 million (Abdel-Fadil, 1975: 125). In absolute terms, 40 percent of the increase occurred in agriculture, 17 percent in industry, and 43 percent in the service or tertiary sector. As a consequence, in this brief but exceptional period there was a relative improvement in the living conditions of the rural population, when the landless families as a proportion of total rural families were further reduced in size from 30 percent to 28 percent. In addition, in spite of undeniable presence and persistent poverty in rural areas, there was a slight increase in rural per capita income and living conditions for poor peasants, while in the cities the tertiary sector provided the rural migrants with new employment opportunities (Waterbury,

1983: 90-92, 208-209). The last three years of Nasser's regime (1967-1970) were a period of no growth and a slow down in rural land distribution. As a result the landless families once again increased in absolute numbers from 28 percent to 33 percent. This reversal of the trend is attributed to the growing population pressure on land and the government's freeze on agrarian reforms in the late 1960s (Abdel-Fadil, 1975: 43).

## Dependent Capitalism, Uneven Development and Centralization of Economic Activities

The early industrialists looked for a site where they could expect to maximize their profits by relying on local and regional raw materials, a readily available skilled labor force and the proximity to the would-be customers who usually resided in major urban areas. To this end, Alexandria was favored by industrialists for its reputation as a cosmopolitan community; its convenient access to supplies of raw materials and imported machinery; and its superior port facilities for the export of cotton. On the other hand, three major factors helped Cairo to gain its prominent status as an important urban center of commerce and industry. First, concentration of pre-capitalist crafts and hence access to a potential pool of skilled workers made Cairo a preferred industrial site. Second, Cairo's strategic location made it an ideal center of trade by receiving imports from Alexandria, Port Said and Suez, while redistributing goods and commodities throughout the country. Finally, Cairo served as the national headquarters for government bureaucracy, commercial activities and the Egyptian ruling class (Barbour, 1972: 120–122). Thus Gamal Abdel Nasser's government inherited an economy which had long been experiencing an uneven and lopsided growth. Prior to 1952 the import-substitution and metal-working industries had been concentrated in or near Cairo and Alexandria. After 1952, the above-mentioned industries along with mining activities became the fastest growing sectors of the economy which also received the most encouragement for new investments. The decisions made by the post-1952 regime of the Free Officers in Egypt were aimed at economic and industrial restructuring and redirecting the Egyptian Capital toward capitalist- industrial activities. But while policy makers focused on economic development, they remained less concerned with correcting the striking regional imbalances of the location and distribution of industrial and commercial activities.

The new revolutionary government's emphasis on industrial development did not take effect until after 1956. A comparison between pre- and post-1956 characteristics of industries with regard to capital investment, labor force, and number of establishments will reveal the nature of the new government's industrial policy. Yet a careful reading of available data strongly suggests the continued dominance of Cairo and Alexandria as clear favorite sites for industrial investments, indicating the new government's inability to decentralize the Egyptian economy (see table 10.3). For example, in 1958 over half of the labor force in establishments employing 10 or more workers were in Alexandria or Cairo (28 percent and 23 percent, respectively), while only 5 percent were employed in Upper Egypt (Issawi, 1963: 174). As is shown in table 10.3, in terms of the number of factories Cairo clearly remained as the leading industrial center. But in terms of workers employed and the volume of capital investment during the 1959–1965 period Alexandria achieved an almost equal status to that of Cairo.

**Table 10.3: A Comparison of Work force, Capital Investment and Industries Established Before and After 1956 in Major Egyptian Provinces (%)**

| Province | Factories | | Work force | | Capital | |
|---|---|---|---|---|---|---|
| | 1865-1956 | 1957-1963 | 1865-1956 | 1957-1963 | 1865-1956 | 1957-1963 |
| Cairo | 47.5 | 48.9 | 28.0 | 27.9 | 17.1 | 15.4 |
| Alexandria | 19.6 | 17.9 | 27.8 | 23.6 | 18.6 | 18.7 |
| Canal | 1.6 | 2.0 | 0.5 | 3.4 | 0.3 | 1.8 |
| Damietta | 1.5 | 1.4 | 0.3 | 1.7 | 0.1 | 1.4 |
| Suez | 0.8 | 0.5 | 2.1 | 0.5 | 3.2 | 1.2 |
| Sinai | 0.2 | 0.2 | 0.5 | 4.0 | 4.6 | 9.1 |
| Red Sea | 0.2 | 0.6 | 0.9 | 4.6 | 0.3 | 10.6 |
| Kafr el Sheikh | 0.9 | 0.9 | 0.3 | 0.3 | 0.3 | 0.3 |
| Buheira | 11.8 | 1.4 | 4.7 | 3.1 | 12.5 | 0.2 |
| Gharbia | 6.7 | 6.4 | 5.0 | 3.9 | 7.4 | 1.9 |
| Daqahlia | 2.6 | 2.3 | 0.9 | 2.5 | 0.9 | 1.2 |
| Sharqia | 1.3 | 1.2 | 1.2 | 0.3 | 1.1 | 0.5 |
| Minufia | 1.1 | 0.8 | 0.4 | 3.6 | 0.2 | 5.9 |
| Qalyubia | 5.3 | 8.9 | 11.2 | 10.5 | 7.4 | 12.1 |
| Giza | 3.3 | 3.2 | 10.3 | 3.2 | 14.8 | 1.9 |
| Beni Suef | 1.0 | 0.5 | 0.4 | 0.2 | 0.3 | 0.2 |
| Minia | 1.3 | 0.9 | 1.1 | 0.4 | 1.1 | 0.5 |
| Sohag | 0.9 | 0.5 | 0.3 | 1.4 | 0.1 | 0.7 |
| Asyut | 1.1 | 0.8 | 0.6 | 0.4 | 0.3 | 0.1 |
| Qena | 0.3 | 0.2 | 1.5 | 1.3 | 1.4 | 0.9 |
| Aswan | 0.3 | 0.5 | 1.9 | 2.9 | 8.0 | 15.3 |

Source: Table based on Barbour (1972: 129) and *Guide to Industries* (Cairo, 1963).

There are no conclusive data available on the total value added by manufacturing activities in each city for this time period, and the only alternative to
measure each urban locality's degree of industrial importance would be their size of
labor force involved and the volume of capital investment. A reading of data in
table 10.4 clearly indicates that during the 1960s Cairo and Alexandria were the
leading industrial metropolitan areas related to both variables within the capitalist
sector. Another indicator of urban concentration and uneven development is the
location of company headquarters for major commercial and industrial establishments in Egypt. Cairo and Alexandria also stand out as the most important urban
locales for company headquarters in 1975, with Cairo being the most preferred
locality for companies to have their headquarters (see table 10.5).

**Table 10.4: Share of National Labor Force and Capital Investment for
Cairo and Alexandria, 1963**

| Metropolitan Area | No. of Workers (% National) | Capital Investment (% National) |
|---|---|---|
| Greater Cairo | 39.6 | 34.5 |
| Greater Alexandria | 28.9 | 26.4 |
| Total for Cairo and Alexandria | 68.5 | 60.9 |

Source: Based on data in Tables 7.4 and 7.5 in Barbour (1972: 193–94).

**Table 10.5: Location of Major Company Headquarters in Egypt, 1975**

| City | No. of Companies | % National |
|---|---|---|
| Cairo | 231 | 75.24 |
| Alexandria | 44 | 14.33 |
| Helwan | 13 | 4.23 |
| Giza | 2 | 0.65 |
| Kafr el Dawar | 2 | 0.65 |
| Tanta | 2 | 0.65 |
| Other Cities (Total) | 13 | 4.25 |
| Total | 307 | 100.00 |

Source: Table constructed based on Bricault (1975: 41–85).

## Petty Commodity Production and Urban Employment Structure in Urban Egypt and Cairo

In studying the employment structure of urban areas in the periphery one noticeable feature in all the analyses concerning "urban informal economy" is the alleged structural duality of the size composition of establishments or number of persons employed. That is, large and medium-sized factories within the capitalist sector are surrounded by a large fringe of small-sized workshops engaged in petty commodity production, handicrafts, services and repair activities (Abdel-Fadil, 1980, 1983; Mabro and Radwan, 1976; World Bank, 1977). Similar to the Iranian case, my main concern here is to understand the dynamics of petty commodity production and its role in terms of production and distribution of commodities as well as job creation related to Egypt's dependent capitalist economy.

### I. Small-Scale Industry (SSI)

Similar to Iran, definitions for small-scale industries vary from one study to the other. But this sector of the Egyptian economy is simply defined as a group of manufacturing establishments in which one to nine persons are employed.[4] For a number of technical reasons the number and contribution of SSIs tend to be underestimated in official statistics of many countries in the periphery. For instance, enumeration of SSIs always tends to be incomplete because a sizeable portion of operations take place within farms or individual households (Mabro and Radwan, 1976: 115). In Egypt's case, a comparison of employment data for 1947 and 1960 indicates that the 1–9 size class dominated the industrial sector even if the SSI's share of created jobs declined considerably from 62 percent in 1947 to 51.2 percent in 1964. On the other hand, while during the same period the 10–49 size class remained unchanged (12.7 percent), increase in size and number of workers in the 50–499 and 500+ size classes compensated for the decline in smaller firms' employment capacity (from 12.5 to 14.5 percent, and 14.1 to 21.7 percent, respectively). Lack of comparable data for longer intervals makes any definitive judgment about SSI's employment structure impossible. But results of two separate studies indicate that the ratio of industrial labor force employed in the 1–4 size class dropped from 55 percent in 1957 to 35 percent in 1972 (Abu-Lughod, 1971: 162; Abdel-Fadil, 1980: 91). Generally speaking, despite a steady decline in sheer size, small scale industries played a significant role in Egypt's post-1952 economy and maintained a virtual control over certain areas of industrial activities (see table 10.6).

The SSI employed about one-third of the labor force in the manufacturing sector, yet they had a low level of productivity and generated less than 16 percent of total value added. For instance, based on the 1967 data a majority of the garment, wood, and furniture industries were small-scale with a share of 90.1, 81.9, and 75.8 percent of total employment in each manufacturing activity, respectively (see table 10.7). Furthermore, over half of all jobs created by small-scale leather processing, metallic products (such as doors, windows, furniture and other items for construction industry) and transport equipments and parts industries were small-scale. Yet small-scale textile establishments employed only 11 percent of the sector's work force, an indication of the monopoly of big capital over this branch of industrial activity.

**Table 10.6: Size Distribution of Establishments and Employees According to the Number of Persons Employed in Egypt, 1960 and 1964 (000s)**

|  | 1960 Number of Employees | % | 1964 Number of Employees | % |
|---|---|---|---|---|
| One Employee | 262 | 20.0 | 294 | 18.5 |
| 2–4 | 400 | 31.0 | 387 | 24.4 |
| 5–9 | 140 | 11.0 | 132 | 8.3 |
| 1–9 size class | 802 | 62.0 | 813 | 51.2 |
| 10–49 | 158 | 12.7 | 200 | 12.7 |
| 50–499 | 163 | 12.5 | 229 | 14.5 |
| 500+ | 182 | 14.1 | 244 | 21.7 |
| Total | 1,305 | 100.0 | 1,586 | 100.0 |

Source: Table constructed based on Abdel-Fadil (1980: 91, Table 6.3).

Industries that supply basic consumer goods such as clothes, shoes and bread, provide yet another picture in terms of their ranking based on employment capacity and added value. For instance, tailors constituted the largest group among small-scale industries with their establishments spread all over the country. Not being affected by competition from capitalist industries, they have thrived by mass production of suits and *gallabya* (the traditional Egyptian garment) (ibid.: 122). Another significant small-scale industry was bread-making. While lagging behind other industries in terms of numbers of employees, it ranked third in terms of its share of added value. Bread-making is a uniquely urban industrial enterprise in Egypt, since in most rural areas bread is produced by households for domestic consumption and not as a commodity (see table 10.8).

Aside from basic consumer goods industries, the most important small-scale industrial activity both in terms of the gross added value and number of jobs created is the furniture and fixture industry with its estimated share of total value added at

72 percent in the late 1960s. Products in this branch of the SSI ranged from beds and benches for rural houses to the rudimentary wooden tables, chairs and coffers as well as doors and window frames (ibid.: 123–124). Lack of sufficient data makes a comparative analysis of the SSI and its historical developments in Egypt almost impossible.

**Table 10.7: Shares of the Egyptian Small-Scale Industries in Total Value Added and Employment by Branch of Activity, 1967**

| | Gross Value-Added | | Employment |
|---|---|---|---|
| Industry | % Share in Total Manufacturing | Numbers | % Share in Total Manufacturing |
| Food | 25.7 | 38,385 | 37.8 |
| Beverages | 2.8 | 257 | 4.3 |
| Tobacco | 1.8 | 216 | 1.7 |
| Textiles | 3.5 | 31,659 | 11.3 |
| Wearing Apparel | 78.4 | 90,709 | 90.1 |
| Wood | 71.1 | 16,148 | 81.9 |
| Furniture | 72.1 | 27,849 | 75.8 |
| Paper | 4.7 | 1,067 | 7.3 |
| Printing | 13.8 | 3,312 | 19.6 |
| Leather | 56.4 | 3,366 | 53.4 |
| Rubber | 2.6 | 293 | 6.6 |
| Chemicals | 1.1 | 921 | 1.9 |
| Petroleum | 0.0 | 10 | 0.1 |
| Non-metallic products | 17.5 | 8,846 | 21.3 |
| Basic metals | 2.9 | 1,186 | 4.9 |
| Metallic Products | 35.4 | 27,706 | 52.1 |
| Non-electric machinery | 13.7 | 2,441 | 21.4 |
| Electric machinery | 8.7 | 3,825 | 25.4 |
| Transport equipment | 33.6 | 18,790 | 49.6 |
| Miscellaneous | 31.3 | 6,914 | 50.8 |
| TOTAL SSI | 15.7 | 283,900 | 32.7 |

Source: CAPMAS, Census of Industrial Production, 1967, Parts I and II. Table constructed based on data in Mabro and Radwan (1976: 121, Table 7.3).

**Table 10.8: Ranking of Six Branches of SSI Based on Employment, Establishments and Gross Value-Added in Egypt, 1967**

| Industry | Employment Numbers | Rank | Establishments Numbers | Rank | Value-Added Rank |
|---|---|---|---|---|---|
| Clothes and Garments | 63,623 | 1 | 42,926 | 1 | 1 |
| Furniture and Fixtures | 27,849 | 2 | 15,447 | 2 | 2 |
| Metal products | 27,706 | 3 | 13,404 | 3 | 4 |
| Spinning and weaving | 20,835 | 4 | 9,685 | 4 | 6 |
| Shoes | 18,874 | 5 | 9,693 | 5 | 5 |
| Bakeries | 14,258 | 6 | 2,955 | 6 | 3 |

Source: table constructed based on information in Mabro and Radwan (1976: 123, Table 7.4).

A survey of the SSI was conducted in 1974 by the Handicraft Industries and Productive Cooperatives Organization (HIPCO), but its coverage of activities was much narrower compared to the 1967 survey. In addition, by excluding the unskilled workers and emphasizing on crafts, the 1974 survey created a set of data incompatible and incomparable with those of the 1967 survey (World Bank, 1977: 10–13). According to the 1967 data the SSI also were predominantly located in urban areas (63 percent), with the two metropolitan areas of Cairo and Alexandria accounting for 30 percent of all small-scale industries and 35 percent of its labor force (see table 10.9).

**Table 10.9: Spatial Distribution of Small-scale Industry in Egypt, 1967**

| | Establishments No | % | Employment No. | % |
|---|---|---|---|---|
| Cairo & Alexandria | 42,768 | 29.6 | 98,132 | 34.5 |
| All urban areas | 91,316 | 63.3 | 196,620 | 69.0 |
| All rural areas | 53,027 | 36.7 | 88,060 | 31.0 |
| Total | 144,343 | 100.0 | 284,680 | 100.0 |

Source: CAPMAS, Census of Industrial Production, 1967, Part I, Tables 5 and 12.

## II. The Structure of Employment in the Service and Distribution Activities

This sector of the petty commodity production economy is comprised of two groups: 1) the self-employed who are operating within the distributive structure of the economy and usually do not have any skills or craftsmanship, such as petty traders, street peddlers and people operating within the pre-capitalist transportation systems; and 2) those who work as wage-earners in nonproductive activities such as paid domestic servants, porters and the like. A comparison of data for 1947 and 1960 (pre- and post-revolution periods) indicates that domestic servants were the most important occupational category, but their functional utility declined after the Revolution. For one thing, following the 1952 revolution, large number of servants, maids and other service employees of the pre-1952 Egyptian ruling class were laid off (see table 10.10). But it is more likely that economic factors rather than ideological shifts have contributed to this change in the employment structure. For instance, previously considered as a status symbol for the middle class families to employ full-time, live-in domestic servants, after the revolution the former could no longer afford this luxury due to a sharp increase in living expenses (Abdel-Fadil, 1980: 17-18). Of note, is a sharp rise in the number of petty traders such as street hawkers and peddlers during this period, which can be both an indication of a rising unemployment in disguise, and increasing importance of this segment of the petty commodity sector in offering and distributing certain commodities produced by the capitalist sector.

**Table 10.10: Employment in Service and Distribution Activities within the Egyptian Petty Commodity Production Economy, 1947 and 1960.**

| Type of Activity (or Occupation) | ( Numbers Employed) | | | | % Change |
|---|---|---|---|---|---|
| | 1947 (000s) | % | 1960 (000s) | % | |
| Pre-capitalist transportation [1] | 57 | 13 | 67 | 12.2 | 17.5 |
| Petty traders (street hawkers and peddlers) | 82 | 18.8 | 188 | 34.2 | 129.3 |
| Paid domestic servants | 235 | 53.9 | 192 | 35.0 | -18.3 |
| Waiters, porters and caretakers [2] | 62 | 14.3 | 102 | 18.6 | 64.5 |

1. Includes those engaged in nonmechanized transport (i.e., animal and cart transport, as well as porters working in railway stations and the big wholesale markets).
2. Includes those employed in hotels, bars, cafes and restaurants.

Source: Table constructed based on information in Abdel-Fadil (1980: 18).

## Conclusion

The origins of Cairo's growth as a domestic administrative center and a political arena for various colonial functionaries date back to Mohammad Ali's reign and his attempts to establish a new export-oriented economy. During the 1882–1952 period Cairo served as the main headquarters for the British colonial administration and developed a dual spatial character: the pre-colonial Cairo which maintained its pre-capitalist identity; and colonial Cairo with its European style planned neighborhoods and a display of Western urban amenities such as broad avenues, street gas lights and water conduits. Cairo's population and spatial growth during this period was also greatly affected by an influence of European immigrants who came to Egypt to take advantage of new investment opportunities under the British rule.

After the 1952 revolution, Cairo along with Alexandria entered a new phase of spatial development and expansion. Particularly for Cairo, this was mainly due to rural-urban migration, industrialization, and concentration of construction activities in the two urban centers. Although uneven urban development in Egypt started with British colonialism, it was intensified after the 1952 revolution when domestic measures were taken by the government to redirect capital investments toward industrial production. Uneven spatial development took a peculiar path in the enormous growth of Cairo and Alexandria: the former became the preferred center for companies to have their headquarters, while as the main port city the latter gained an almost equal status in terms of concentration of capital and the size of industrial work force. As another sign of uneven urban development, Cairo enjoyed its strategic central location as communication and transportation networks branched out from the capital connecting Cairo to the rest of Egypt.

Reinforcement of capitalist relations of production after 1952 also affected the class composition in Egypt, particularly in urban areas. First, independent artisans and shop keepers declined in numbers while white collar workers and civil servants assumed more significance. Second, small-scale industries (SSI) employing one to nine workers also declined drastically while industries employing 50 or more workers compensated for the decline in the former. None-theless, the SSI maintained a clear monopoly over certain areas of industrial activities such as garment, food and furniture industries. Third, almost half the SSI in urban areas were located either in Cairo or Alexandria. Finally, within the petty commodity production sector the self-employed petty traders and street peddlers had a considerable growth due to their importance and function as a cheap and efficient network for the distribution of consumer goods produced by the capitalist sector.

## Notes

1. Although the Cairo-Suez railway was opened in 1858, because of its poor design it was abandoned ten years later. See Abu-Lughod (1965: 473).

2. The interested reader is referred to the work of Ali Mubarak, the Minister of Public Works during Ismail's reign. See Mubarak (1888) *Khitat al-Tawfiqiyah al-Jadidah* (Arabic). Cairo: Bulaq Press.

3. For an account of the economic effects of WWI on Egypt see Crouchley (1938: 182–209).

4. Some studies like the World Bank's Report (1977) define this sector as "artisanal." However, since the majority of studies define the 1–9 size class as "small-scale," I adopted the latter definition for this study.

# PART 4

# Divergent Paths of Dependent Urbanization in Iran and Egypt

Chapter Eleven

# Dependent Urbanization and Development in Iran and Egypt: Comparing the Incomparable

In this chapter I will present a historical assessment and comparative analysis of the two qualitatively different processes of economic and political development in Iran and Egypt and their effects on spatial developments both in rural and urban localities. In comparing pre-capitalist Iran and Egypt, we have to appreciate the differences in physical settings and climatic conditions and their indirect and subtle effects upon sociopolitical and economic structures, state formations and urbanization. First, a closer look at Egypt's geography will reveal the fact that the Nile Valley and the Delta region functioned as a unifying element in providing the inhabitants with fertile land for cultivation and as the main means of their livelihood, to the extent that non-agricultural life became almost insignificant. As a consequence, more than two-thirds of inhabitants in Egypt have lived in the Valley and the Delta (Lower Egypt). In contrast, Iran's varied geographical regions and climatic conditions necessitated the existence of different pre-capitalist modes of production, with pastoral-nomadism and feudalism being the two most important players. Second, unlike Iran pastoral-nomadism has never played a significant role as a viable and important political and economic system in Egypt; and nomadic tribes (*Bedouin*) did not comprise more than five percent of population in pre-capitalist Egypt. In sharp contrast to Egypt, even up until the 1930s the pastoral-nomadic population comprised between one-fourth and one-third of total population in Iran. Furthermore, while for over a century Iran was ruled by pastoral-nomadic rulers (1796-1920), the Egyptian Bedouin always remained as marginal elements in the Egyptian politics. Finally, related to their involvement with the world capitalist economy while Egypt experienced a full-fledged colonial domination by various imperial entities Iran's dependency relations took a different path due to her semi-colonial status. In the following pages I will employ the same periodization model that I have used for each of the two nations in preceding chapters in order to compare two incomparable nations and their historical development.

## Social and Economic Conditions in Pre-capitalist Iran and Egypt during the First Period (1800-1880s)

It is difficult to provide a clear-cut and distinct spatial-territorial definition for pre-capitalist social formations. Societies with a centralized state were of precarious and unstable nature, as they often were challenged by local ruling strata and external invading forces. This made any attempt for creating a unified socioeconomic and political entity extremely difficult. An important aspect of the nature of most pre-capitalist states was that their means of controlling regional and local rulers as well as their efforts to exploit the masses were predominantly political—not only surplus products, both in kind and cash, were being extracted through political means, they were also distributed proportionate to each ruler's position and power within the political hierarchy. This later puts pre-capitalist states in a sharp contrast with their capitalist counterparts, who, through establishing a centralized monetary system exploit and control the population through economic means such as wages and taxes on commodities and income. Internally, the political structure of the 19th century pre-capitalist Iran was characterized by a centralized state that was controlled by rulers of pastoral-nomadic origins. Operating under pastoral-nomadic and tribal socio-economic relations and cultural values the central government and the court were always in conflict with regional and local feudal rulers whose *modus operandi* was within the context of an agrarian feudal economy, and yet were subordinated to pastoral-nomadic laws for land holding and methods for the extraction of surplus product and taxes. This was possible through the practice of *iqta* under which the land was exclusively the state's property while local landlords had only usufruct rights and in turn exploited the peasants as a collective.[1] Although under different historical conditions and socio-economic relations, political control and extraction of taxes and surplus products in pre-capitalist Egypt had striking similarities with that of Iran. As subjects of the Ottoman Imperial Court the Egyptian masses were exploited under the system of tribute-paying or tax collection called *iltizam*. The Egyptian "iltizam" and Iranian "iqta" were in fact two identical systems of landholding that were utilized by two different forms of government. Unlike Iran which by the turn of the 19th century was governed by an emerging centralized state, Egypt was internally governed by local feudal rulers who were in turn subservient to the Ottoman Court as the external imperial power. This relationship was later changed, however, when Mohammad Ali established his centralized state apparatus in 1805.

Externally, Iran and Egypt had quantitatively different relationships and economic ties with other states. In the 1830s Iran lost considerable territories to Russia, but because of a relatively strong centralized state she never lost her sovereignty and was able to maintain her independence. In contrast, Egypt was formally a province within the Ottoman dominion for centuries, and establishment of a semi-independent centralized state by Mohammad Ali was quite a new experience for the Egyptians. It appears that in the early 19th century none of the European colonial powers had an immediate interest in colonizing Iran. The British were only interested in Iran in order to have access to India by land. The Russo-British rivalry in Iran thus served the latter's interests to keep Iran as a neutral zone. Egypt of the 19th century on the other hand provides a different picture compared to that of Iran. The rival colonial powers particularly the French and British were interested in getting trade concessions from Egyptian courts. But by the mid-19th century the cotton economy had become so vital for the British textile industry that losing Egypt could have been a disaster For the British economy. At the same time that colonial rivalries and interests over Egypt were fermenting, the internal developments during Mohammad Ali's reign prepared the country for the establishment of nascent forms of capitalist relations. Even if unsuccessful at the end, Mohammad Ali's attempts for industrialization, forced sedentarization of the Bedouin, abolition of iltizam and the consequent introduction of private ownership of land were all conducive to the development of capitalism in Egypt. All of this was happening at a time when Iran's development was taking place within the confines of a pre-capitalist economy that was mostly ignored by European colonialists.

Mohammad Ali's industrialization program in Egypt was carried on with the help of European technology and expertise, yet there is no historical evidence to support that any of the colonial powers were in favor of his plans. The 1848 Anglo-Turkish Treaty that limited his army and put an end to his ambitious economic and industrial schemes is supportive of this hypothesis. But what the British in particular did not like about Mohammad Ali's plans, was his independent and autonomous course of action that was considered a serious threat to their vested interests. Within this context, some scholars have praised Mohammad Ali's ambitious economic development plans and claim that Egypt was historically forced to abandon an independent path of development because of an abrupt colonial intervention. For example, Amin (1978: 30) puts Egypt on a par with countries like Japan, and does not rule out the possibility of an emerging independent capitalist Egypt during Mohammad Ali's reign:

No one can say what Egypt might have become without this European intervention. The analogy with Japan springs immediately to mind, and not without reason. The material progress achieved during the first forty years of the century was prodigious . . . the state workshops and manufactories employed hundreds of thousands of workers . . . all this was achieved by indigenous national managers in national industries.

Egypt's importance for the world capitalist economy began with Mohammad Ali's introduction of long-staple cotton and its production for the world markets, especially the British textile industries. At the time, the British were not eager to directly intervene in order to supervise and control the production process. Rather, they much preferred to have the Egyptians run the Egyptian affairs as long as they were able to get the needed raw materials. Later, the outbreak of the American Civil War that deprived the British textiles industry from American cotton forced Britain to seriously reconsider its policy toward Egypt, which clearly emerged as a prized territory particularly for its agricultural production. In addition, colonial rivalry between the British and the French coupled with the economic crisis of the Ottoman Empire and its consequent negative effects on the Egyptian economy led to a change in the British colonial policies and a gradual shift from indirect rule to direct intervention in the region and sub-sequent occupation of Egypt in 1882.

## Urbanization during the First Period (1800–1880s)

The main difficulty in studying urban development during the first period is the lack of reliable data for both Iran and Egypt. The need for reliable statistics stems from the fact that having fairly accurate data could have helped us to see how the historical processes of spatial development both in town and countryside corresponded to numerical changes and movements of population in space. By analyzing the scanty data on Iran's population, it appears that there existed little or no spatial displacement and migration between tribal, rural, and urban areas. This seems to be a plausible possibility since there were no radical structural changes within the Iranian socioeconomic relations. Thus the spatial displacement of population was mostly resulted from intra-unit movements, i.e., within rural and/or urban areas. However, in spite of differences between pastoral-nomadic and sedentary rural-agricultural lifestyles, population movement between tribal and rural communities during the times of crisis seemed also imminent.

Likewise, there are no available statistics or studies on this subject for Egypt, making any comparative analysis impossible. But based on historical events and sporadic data I will argue that the Egyptian case was somewhat different from that of Iran. First, although the Egyptian Bedouin population never exceeded 5 percent of total population (compared to 25-30 percent for

Iran) Mohammad Ali's sedentarization schemes forced many of the tribal people to settle in rural areas. In contrast, the forced sedentarization of nomads and tribal population took place almost a century later under Reza Shah's modernization policies in Iran. Second, unlike Iran there were structural changes in social relations of production in Egypt during the first period, especially in property ownership rights and the nature of agricultural production, causing considerable spatial displacements between rural and urban areas.

In the absence of a clear-cut division of labor between town and country in 19th century Iran, and by considering places with more than 10,000 inhabitants as "urban"; we can then conclude that urbanization in Iran during the first period was limited to the growth of cities located on the regional and international trade routes. The cities of Tabriz, Shiraz, Barfroosh, Rasht, Kashan and Khoi which served as regional and international trade centers and outposts had the highest growth rates. Many other regional and provincial urban centers such as Mashhad, Isfahan, Yazd, Kerman, Kermanshah and Hamadan either stagnated or had a lower rate of growth than that of the total population.[2] On the other hand, Egypt's urban growth was mostly due to the growth of port cities, particularly that of Alexandria. The only explanation for this phenomenon is Egypt's status in the world capitalist system as an emerging export-oriented nation that required efficient port facilities as well as transportation networks. Alexandria's growth was both due to its being the main urban center for Mohammad Ali's industrialization efforts, as well as the main depot for the export of cotton and the import of European goods. This is in sharp contrast with the Iranian situation where no port cities ever gained prominence beyond their significance as local trade centers, with the port cities of Bushehr by the Persian Gulf and Anzali by the Caspian Sea being prime examples.

The growth, stagnation and/or decline of Egyptian inland cities, all serving as provincial centers and regional market towns, was dependent on the fluctuations in agricultural production and its subsequent effects on the rest of the economy. For example, most of Egypt's inland cities during the 1821–1846 period stagnated since cotton cultivation provided enough employment in rural areas. However, removal of financial and legal restrictions on private ownership of land which even allowed foreigners to purchase land in Egypt paved the way for further concentration of land in fewer hands particularly in rural Egypt. Hence, despite an increase in cotton cultivation during the 1846–1882 period the aforementioned factor led to gradual detachment of many peasants who were previously tied to the land through pre-capitalist bondage systems. There are no available data on this issue, but it is likely that this might have caused an increase in the number of landless peasants and their eventual flight to the cities in search of employment.

Although in different ways, urbanization in Iran and Egypt during the first period was also greatly affected by foreign trade. For instance, the most important urban center in Iran was the city of Tabriz in the northern province of Azarbayejan which served as the headquarters for handling regional and foreign trade. Likewise, urbanization in Egypt was in fact limited to the phenomenal growth of Alexandria as the main port city, also for handling foreign trade. The only difference between Egypt and Iran was the degree of significance of foreign immigrants related to urban growth. That is, while the number of foreign residents in the former rose from 3,000 in 1836 to over 68,000 in 1878, there were only 161 foreign residents in Iran as late as the 1860s. Finally, a common pattern of urban growth in Iran and Egypt during the first period is the relatively insignificant growth of political capitals as compared to urban centers for commerce and trade. For example, even if Cairo remained as the most populated urban center in Egypt, its growth lagged far behind that of Alexandria in the first half of the 19th century (see table 11.1). Likewise, despite Tehran's remarkable growth since 1786, the year it was designated as the capital city, it nonetheless lagged behind Tabriz in both population and commercial importance throughout the 19th century.

**Table 11.1:  Growth of Cairo and Alexandria during the First Period**

| City | Average Annual Growth Rate (%) 1821–1846 | 1846–1882 |
|---|---|---|
| Cairo | 0.65 | 1.0 |
| Alexandria | 10.3 | 0.95 |
| Total Population | 0.04 | 1.6 |

## Disintegration of Pre-capitalist Economies in Iran and Egypt during the Second Period (1880–1950)

A reading of historical events during the first and second periods will indicate that Iran and Egypt's involvement with international trade and their consequent integration into the world capitalist economy took two divergent paths. First, Egypt entered the world market, underwent drastic structural changes in its socioeconomic and political structure and experienced rural-urban migration much earlier than Iran. Although the effect of external factors such as foreign trade and colonial powers' interests in Egypt cannot be denied, internal social forces and class alliances were definitely decisive in changing or delaying the course of events. For example, the events leading to the defeat of Colonel Arabi and his supporters in 1882 and eventual British invasion and occupation of

Egypt was in fact the defeat of petty commodity producers, merchants and intellectuals who were emerging as new forces of social change and were eager to get a share of the state power through parliamentary participation. Likewise, introduction of parliamentary democracy in pre-capitalist Egypt was also a sign of a weakened centralized state and the increasing power of local feudal rulers whose participation in the national politics would have served their narrow localized interests. However, the nationalist, uncompromising and anti-colonial nature of the Arabi revolt threatened the British investments and interests in Egypt, which in turn necessitated their direct military and political intervention. Thus instead of supporting the pro-capitalist, albeit nationalist faction represented by Arabi, the British supported the ruling Khedive who represented the pre-capitalist faction, big landowners and feudal landlords.

Twenty five years later, and under a more or less similar situation the British took a quite different stance in Iran. Similar to Egypt, the disenchanted petty commodity producers and merchants who were adversely affected by unfair foreign concessions and trade monopolies and supported by the clergy and the intellectuals, revolted against a pre-capitalist state in order to establish parliamentary democracy. Contrary to the Egyptian case, during the Iranian Constitutional Revolution, the British took sides with the Constitutionalists against the Asiatic state and the Court which at the time was supported by Russians, a rival colonial power in Iran. This clearly demonstrates the opportunistic nature of the British colonial policy, as the British were ready to form alliances and support any class or faction in the two countries as long as their long-term colonial interests in the region were secured.

The newly installed British colonial administration in Egypt eventually disarmed the weakened central government and its system of tribute collection and direct taxation of the peasants. The measures previously taken for private ownership of land paved the way for local feudal rulers to take charge of agricultural production under the new colonial administration. Gradually, the old landholding class in Egypt was transformed into an "agrarian bourgeoisie," as Egypt's agricultural production was being reorganized and becoming increasingly dependent on the world capitalist markets. This newly emerging class had a complex and combined pre-capitalist and capitalist characteristics:

> On the one hand, it produced for the capitalist market; employed wage-laborers; and took part in investments. On the other hand, it resorted to, and reinforced pre-capitalist methods of exploitation based on pre- capitalist social relations. Thus the new "agrarian bourgeoisie" was neither a feudal nor a capitalist, a clear manifestation of class formation in pre-capitalist Egypt during the transitional period of the 19th century (Amin, 1978: 27–28).

The British colonial policy in Egypt was not intended to introduce a full-fledged capitalist economy—the fact that the British prevented industrialization and instead promoted agricultural development is supportive of this argument. For instance, while the institution of feudalism remained intact, capital accumulation in the form of land speculation and concentration of money capital in the newly established banks took place in Egypt. In the meantime, in the absence of any viable industrialization plans a new class of wage-laborers was on the rise in the countryside, and by 1900 it represented 37 percent of rural labor force. Compared to Egypt, pre-capitalist Iran was historically less developed and hence less prone to the introduction of capitalist measures. First, while Egypt had the first land register during the 1809–1818 period, it was not until 1907 that the pre-capitalist system of landholding (iqta) in Iran was abolished and private landownership was introduced. Second, while banking (as a sign of concentration of capital in the hands of non-producers) started as early as 1850s in Egypt and was well developed by the 1870s, the first bank in Iran was not established until 1888. The centralization of banking activities in Egypt and Iran also took place with a thirty year lapse, in 1898 and 1927, respectively. Finally, unlike in Egypt, the Iranian peasants were attached to the land up until the 1930s and wage-labor was not a significant form of exploitation in the countryside. In addition, while Mohammad Ali's sedentarization attempts in the 1830s trans-formed many Bedouin into rural wage-laborers, this process was delayed for about a century in Iran and was finally accomplished by Reza Shah in the 1930s. Iran's backward pre-capitalist economy was not conducive to the introduction of capitalist relations. This backwardness was also perpetuated by a lack of interest on the part of colonial powers. In fact, Iran's importance as a producer and provider of raw materials was recognized only in 1908 by the discovery of oil reserves in southern provinces.

Later developments in the early decades of the 20th century further prepared the two nations' economies for their new role in Europe's expanding capitalist economy. The 1906 Constitutional Revolution in Iran enabled the urban petty bourgeoisie and merchants to exert their influence upon the state through their strong presence in the newly established parliament (*Majlis*). At the same time, a weakened central government provided an opportunity for feudal landholders in the provinces to strengthen their power and position. This was done especially through an effective control of the Majlis by feudal elements in 1908 amidst political disintegration of the central authority.

At a time when the prospects of oil production were so vital for the British economy, a weakened central state and a divided country was not conducive to their colonial interests. Thus, unable to establish their protectorate in Iran due to internal opposition the British helped to overthrow the *ancien regime* in 1921 and install Reza Khan, an obscure lower-ranked member of the Iranian army as the head of the new government. A more or less similar process of political change took place in Egypt. While the 1919–1923 social upheaval culminated in a formal declaration of independence in Egypt, as the dominant colonial power the British managed to impose their will in writing the Declaration of Independence document in order to safeguard their interests in the region. Thus in spite of internal pressure and opposition to colonial domination, the British also succeeded in setting the stage for the continuation of dependency relations in Egypt.

In comparing Iran and Egypt during the 1920s and afterwards, I can draw two conclusions. First, through foreign intervention and participation of the comprador bourgeoisie in Egypt and pro-capitalist elements in Iran both societies were set up for further integration into the world economy. Attempts for import-substitution industrialization and further steps taken to control the state apparatus in the 1930s are indicative of this process.[3] Second, despite similarities in timing of the two nation's integration, historically speaking Iran lagged far behind Egypt in acquiring the prerequisites for the introduction of capitalist measures into her economy. In clear terms, with a half a century delay of accumulation of money capital in the hands of non-producers; separation of direct producers from their means of production; and provision of an adequate infrastructure Iran in the 1930s reached a more or less similar level of development that Egypt had already achieved in the 1880s.

## Urbanization during the Second Period (1880–1950)

Before comparing the processes of urbanization in Iran and Egypt during the second period, two concepts need further clarification. First, as I have stated throughout the study, by "urbanization" I mostly mean the process of spatial displacement of population primarily due to structural changes in the countryside. Therefore, the growth and development of the built environment in "urban" places is secondary in my analysis. Second, "dependent urbanization" refers to a process of spatial displacement of population in a country where its political economy has become an integral part of the world capitalist system. Based on these definitions, one may speak of "dependent urbanization" in Egypt from the 1880s onward even if "capitalism" per se was not present. But dependent urbani-zation in Iran was delayed until the 1920s-1930s, when Iran's economy became fully incorporated into the world capitalist system and conscious measures were taken for capitalist development by the newly installed government.

In the last two decades of the 19th century, Egypt under British colonial administration witnessed unusually high rates of urban population growth as compared to previous decades. The most spectacular growth was that of Cairo which had an average annual growth rate of 12.5 percent for the 1882–1897 period, as compared to only 1.5 percent for total population. This can clearly be called a *dependent urbanization* as a result of concentration of all colonial administrative and governmental activities in the capital. In the absence of reliable statistics or a historical analysis, the only viable method is to look for socioeconomic reasons for the growth and/or decline of urban population. I consider dependent urbanization in Egypt during the second period as the outcome of three socioeconomic factors: 1) stagnation of agricultural production and hence lack of adequate rural employment; 2) an increase in the number of landless and wage-laborer peasants who were forced to migrate to urban areas in search of employment; and 3) an increase in the number of foreign residents who mostly resided in Cairo, Alexandria and Port Said. This influx of urban population happened at a time when no industrial development was allowed under British colonial policy in Egypt. Compared to a simultaneous period of urban decay and decline in the rest of Egypt during the 1846–1882 period, Cairo's growth rate along with those of all port cities and provincial centers demonstrates the clear impact of colonial penetration on urbanization process.

On the other front, in a period when all the symptoms of dependent urbanization were discernible in Egypt, Iran was experiencing a period of slow growth within the confines of a pre-capitalist economy. Almost all population movements in Iran between 1880 and 1920 were either of intra-rural or intra-urban nature. This means that there existed neither internal nor external factors to induce structural changes within Iran's predominantly agricultural and pre-capitalist economy that in turn may have led to dependent urbanization.

The post-WWI economic depression of the late 1920s in the center had its repercussions on the economic development of peripheries. Along with many other peripheral societies import-substitution industrialization (ISI) was imposed upon Iran and Egypt, which, despite its provisions for job creation proved to be quite inadequate in absorbing the increasing number of rural immigrants. First, in a country where 80 percent of population was rural, a stagnating agricultural economy was incapable of providing enough jobs for Egypt's growing rural population. Thus in the absence of an urban-based industrial bourgeoisie, urban expansion in Egypt continued to be mostly a result of land speculation and construction activities and not industrialization. Dependent urbanization in Egypt was also continuation of a process which started in the 1880s, with its ups and downs being in line with fluctuations in the country's agricultural production and output. Second, unlike Egypt that experienced an internal process of socioeconomic change conducive to capitalist development during Mohammad Ali's reign, Iran's dependent urbanization process was induced by external pressures in the 1920s. Measures such as sedentarization of pastoral-nomads, heavy taxation of rural population, construction of roads, railways and other infrastructures, and establishment of private property rights all took place after the First World War. Like Cairo but with a historical delay, concentration of economic, political and administrative activities in Tehran gained momentum in the 1940s. As a consequence, while the old centers of trade such as Tabriz, Khoi, Yazd and Kerman stagnated, as the major urban growth pole the Capital absorbed 60 percent of rural migrants. At the same time, the oil cities of Ahwaz and Abadan in the southern Khuzestan Province developed as the two major urban centers catering to the needs of a flourishing but dependent oil industry, and absorbed 22 percent of rural immigrants. Finally, like Egypt in the second half of the 19th century, the post-1940 Iran also witnessed the growth of towns that were located on the railway routes. In brief, a comparison of the historical events and political economy of Iran and Egypt during the second period indicates that dependent urbanization took place in both countries but with a time-lag of about half a century.

## Dependent Urbanization in the Third Period (1950–1970)

The 1950s are crucial years related to my historical analysis of dependent urbanization in Iran and Egypt, as significant socioeconomic changes took place at the global level as well as in the two countries. In particular, the emergence of the United States as a new world power in the post-WWII era changed the balance of forces within the world capitalist system. For instance, American-based corporations challenged the old colonial economic structure and the United States became actively involved in the peripheries in order to increase her influence and secure her economic interests. Political and economic develop-ments that reshaped the dynamics of center-periphery relations during the third period were a pretext for second phase of the globalization process from the 1970s onward.[4] Therefore, the third period remains open-ended in my analysis, and the only rationale for periodization here is to delineate a crucial historical and socioeconomic turning point that facilitated the two nations' entry into the new global economy. At this juncture I will make the case that the third period for Iran started in 1953, marking the oil nationalization movement and Dr. Mosaddeq's eventual downfall; whereas 1952 marked the Egyptian Revolution and state takeover by the Free Officers. In line with my analyses in preceding chapters, in the following section I will discuss factors that have contributed to the development of dependent urbanization in the two countries during the third period, namely, removal of the obstacles to dependent capitalist development; implementation of land reform policies; unusual growth and spatial development of Tehran and Cairo; and proliferation of petty commodity production and small-scale industries.

## Removal of the Obstacles to a Dependent Capitalist Development

Historical events following the Second World War will suggest that class conflict and the degree to which various classes had access to state apparatus in the two countries became a decisive factor in the success or failure of colonial policies. For instance, the unsuccessful oil nationalization movement led by Dr. Mosaddeq in Iran and the Egyptian Revolution which brought the Free Officers into power are two examples of the decisive role internal forces of change play in the peripheries. An examination of the class background of those who supported the two social movements in Iran and Egypt will indicate a striking similarity. In Iran, the oil nationalization movement received most of its support from urban middle class; students; professionals such as doctors, lawyers and university professors; and petty commodity producers who were represented by leaders of various guilds. Similarly, the Free Officers in Egypt were supported by the urban middle class, students, petty commodity producers, a portion of the commercial bourgeoisie and industrial workers. But despite similarities, situational disparities in seizing the state apparatus resulted in two opposite outcomes in Iran and Egypt. For instance, although Dr. Mosaddeq was able to gain state control and challenge the Parliament controlled by the rural-feudal elite and the British-backed Royal Court, his radical nationalization plans and lack of effective control over the military led to his eventual defeat and downfall. Mosaddeq's platform for nationalization of all industries and establishment of state capitalism was not acceptable to both the indigenous ruling elite and Western capitalist interests. Unlike Iran, the Free Officers in Egypt managed to gain substantial support from within the army and had more appeal for the Egyptian bourgeoisie, since their initial platform for social change did not ask for radical reforms.

It is my contention that certain social classes such as the petty commodity producers and an emerging urban middle class comprised of intellectuals, professionals and university students played a decisive role in affecting the course of events of the two social movements. Similar to the 1882 Arabi Revolt in Egypt and the 1906 Constitutional Revolution in Iran, the nationalist movements of the 1950s were middle-class based movements. This happened at a time when the working classes in Iran and Egypt were historically incapable of leading a nationalist movement. Thus in the absence of a fully developed capitalist economy and a strong working class this was a logical outcome of specific historical conditions. Generally speaking, the nationalist and anti-colonial movements which aim at state takeover and complete control of the economy are not a desirable choice or alternative for Western colonial interests because of the danger of state takeover by the more radical elements of the middle- and working class origins. But under peculiar historical circumstances and based on the nature of colonial interests and rivalry in a particular region Western colonial powers have demonstrated considerable degree of flexibility in dealing with nationalist movements. Thus while through a joint U.S.-British operation Dr. Mosaddeq in Iran was overthrown and the nationalist movement was effectively repressed, in a clear show of a fierce colonial rivalry the Free Officers in Egypt were unilaterally supported by the United States, when the other alternative was a radical shift to the left or the continuation of British domination.[5]

While the defeat of the nationalist movement and reinstatement of the pro-American Shah in 1953 paved the way for implementation of capitalist economic development plans in Iran, promotion of "Arab Socialism" in Egypt had a semblance of a revolutionary movement that was determined to rid Egypt of foreign domination. Yet in reality Nasser's Arab Socialism eventually set the foundations of state capitalism in Egypt. That is, despite all measures taken to promote a populist ideology of socialism the government stopped short of the abolition of private property rights as the most crucial step to be taken for a socialist economy. This seems to be a common trait in the newly independent and decolonized societies when the state takeover is done by elements from within the middle-class. As a common trend, by inheriting a capitalist-oriented economy the new middle-class ruling elite try to achieve their aspirations for creation of an independent state while sympathizing with the working class and the poor. But the Egyptian case is a clear documentation of the failure of a middle-class initiated socialism, as anti-imperialist sentiments and socialist ideals are not compatible with a dependent economic infrastructure where it has remained intact.

The third period was also marked by the emergence of multinational corporations and the increasing influence and importance in controlling dependent capitalist economies in the peripheries. The defeat of the nationalist and anti-colonialist movement in Iran facilitated a smooth transition from monopoly control of oil production by the British to a consortium comprised of multinational corporations. But the victory of the Free Officers and their alliance with the socialist camp at least temporarily kept multinationals in check and out of the Egyptian political economy. Later on, the events leading to the state takeover by Anwar-el Sadat, a representative of the pro-capitalist faction of the ruling elite eventually opened up Egypt to foreign capitalist investments and multinational corporations in the early 1970s.

## The Effects of Land Reform on Dependent Urbanization

With no doubt in both Iran Egypt the land reform policies were implemented from above. Also, in both countries the main objective of the land reform was to undermine the rural class base of big landholders, namely, the landed bourgeoisie in Egypt and feudal landowners in Iran, in the hopes of redirecting capital investment from rural areas to urban-based industrial activities. In both countries lack of a long-term policy to support the newly emerging small landowner-peasant population eventually led to the demise of independent peasant producers. Since only the sharecroppers benefited from land reform policies, declining employment opportunities in the countryside for landless peasants and rural wage-earners gradually forced them to come to cities in search of employment. Even those peasants who benefited from land redistribution were not able to subsist, and eventually followed the wave of landless peasants and rural wage-earners to the cities. As the evidence for both Iran and Egypt indicate, rural-urban migration especially after the implementation of land reform laws was migration of the poorest and the most destitute strata of peasants in the countryside to urban centers. To be sure there were peasants who migrated to cities in search of "better jobs." But they always constituted a tiny and statistically insignificant minority among rural emigrants.

## Uneven Urban Growth: Comparing Tehran and Cairo

A historical investigation of spatial changes in Iran and Egypt is indicative of the diversity of the processes of socioeconomic development which led to different patterns of dependent urbanization. Uneven urban growth and over-concentration of population in few urban localities as an outcome of dependent urbanization was also not a universal pattern. A comparison of the growth and spatial development of Tehran and Cairo during the three periods since 1800 will make this assertion clear.

In the early 19th century Cairo was a sizeable city with about 200,000 inhabitants which dominated the Egyptian urban scene. But it had already lost its prominence as the seat of a centralized state since such a government no longer did exist. On the other hand, Tehran as the newly designated Capital with 50,000 inhabitants was second in importance to Tabriz, yet throughout the first period (1800-1880s) it lagged behind Tabriz both in terms of population growth and economic/commercial importance; with the latter remaining as the dominant urban center commanding regional and international trade activities (see table 11.2). Cairo also lagged behind Alexandria in terms of population growth. Compared to Cairo, Alexandria was a small port city in the early decades of the

19th century. But an emerging export-oriented economy and the need for efficient port facilities boosted the latter's growth with a rate far exceeding that of Cairo (see table 11.3). Later on, attempts to improve transport networks in Egypt and establishment of the Cairo-Alexandria railway during the 1848–1882 period accelerated urban growth in the stagnating capital city.

**Table 11.2: Population Changes and Average Annual Growth Rates for Tehran and Tabriz during the Three Historical Periods, 1800–1970.**

| Year | Population (000s) | | |
|------|--------|--------|------------------|
|      | Tehran | Tabriz | Total population |
| $1800^1$ | $50^6$ | $40^6$ | 5,000 |
| $1867^2$ | 85 | 110 | 4,400 |
| $1900^3$ | 200 | 200 | 9,860 |
| % Change, 1st period (1800-1900) | 1.3 | 1.6 | 0.7 |
| $1956^4$ | 1,512 | 290 | 20,380 |
| % Change, 2nd period (1900-1956) | 3.6 | 0.6 | 1.3 |
| $1976^5$ | 4,496 | 598 | 33,590 |
| % Change, 3rd period (1956-1976) | 5.2 | 3.6 | 2.5 |

Sources:
1. Issawi (1971: 26-27).
2. Issawi (1971: 27-29).
3 and 4. Bharier (1977: 333-34).
5. Kazemi (1980: 230).
6. Rough estimates.

The British occupation of Egypt and imposition of colonial administration had its indelible effects on spatial development in Egypt as well, making spatial development of Tehran and Cairo during the second period substantially different compared to that of the first period. For one thing, selection of Cairo as the political capital and a desired urban location for the British colonial administration revived the city and provided a new impetus for urban growth. In particular, Cairo owed its unusually rapid growth during the second period to the influx of foreign immigrants of all sorts, who, following the British occupation came to Egypt in order to take advantage of a fertile new ground for speculation and profiteering.

**Table 11.3: Population Changes and Average Annual Growth Rates for Cairo and Alexandria during the Three Historical Periods, 1800-1976**

| Year | Population (000s) | | |
|------|-------|------------|------------------|
|      | Cairo | Alexandria | Total population |
| 1821[1] | 219 | 12 | 4,423 |
| 1882[2] | 375 | 231 | 7,840 |
| % Change, 1st period (1821-1882) | 0.9 | 4.8 | 0.9 |
| 1947[3] | 2,100 | 919 | 18,967 |
| % Change, 2nd period (1882-1947) | 2.6 | 2.1 | 1.4 |
| 1976[4] | 5,077 | 2,319 | 36,626 |
| % Change, 3rd period (1947-1976) | 3.0 | 3.1 | 2.3 |

Sources:
1 and 2: from Table 6.1.
3: from Abu-Lughod (1965: 334-36).
4: from Mohie-el-Din (1982: 398).

By the turn of the 20th century about 70 percent of Cairo's population increase was due to in-migration, of which about two-thirds were foreigners. The European immigrants' immediate needs for provision of services by the natives, from house maids to gardeners and repair crew, was accompanied by an unprecedented number of rural migrants who came to Cairo in search of employment due to a stagnating agricultural economy in the countryside. As a result, Cairo developed a dual spatial characteristic: a pre-capitalist Cairo accommodating the old residents and new rural-urban immigrants; and a colonial Cairo with modern urban facilities accommodating the British colonialists and army officers, foreign residents and the Egyptian ruling elite.

On the other hand, things were quite different in Iran, as an undisturbed pre-capitalist economy with a predominantly rural population was not yet conducive to an accelerated urban growth process. For example, compared with its status in the early 19th century, Tehran at the turn of the 20th century had not significantly changed in terms of acquiring urban facilities and functional importance. Two significant social and political events during the early decades of the 20th century however set the tone for Tehran's future urban growth. First, the 1906 Constitutional Revolution contributed to Tehran's urban development, as it became the center of social and political change in Iran. But unlike Cairo, foreign residents were not instrumental in contributing to Tehran's numerical and spatial growth. Second, political events culminating in the 1921 military coup d'état in Iran which reinforced the British influence through her indirect control of the Iranian political economy were also a turning point for Tehran's spatial development. Initiation of measures for economic development and the need for a centralized bureaucracy in the 1920s turned Tehran into a political and economic capital of an emerging dependent capitalist economy. In fact, short of the influx of foreign immigrants, Tehran's post-1921 sociospatial development is comparable to that of Cairo after 1882. Related to other urban centers, unlike Alexandria in Egypt which sustained a steady rate of growth during the second period; once the most important Iranian urban center for trade the city of Tabriz lost its prominence and consequently experienced a period of decay and population decline. Thus dependent urbanization in Iran after the 1920s was synonymous with Tehran and its unusual growth as the only significant center of urban development (see table 11.2).

## Petty Commodity Production and Urban Employment in Iran and Egypt: The Case of Tehran and Cairo

As an endemic phenomenon in many post-colonial countries with a continued dependency to the West, the petty commodity production sector's economic contribution in Iran and Egypt has been substantial. Again, while acknowledging the scanty nature of data on this issue, in the following pages I will sketch out the overall picture of employment conditions within various branches of the petty commodity production sector.[6]

## a. Small-Scale Industries

Employing less than ten workers, small-scale industries (SSI) in Iran and Egypt slightly differed in terms of their share of the labor force and the extent of their concentration in urban localities. For example, in 1967 about 30 percent of all small-scale industries in Egypt were concentrated in Cairo and Alexandria, employing 35 percent of total labor force for the SSI. On the other hand, Tehran remained the main urban center and by 1968 about 33 percent of Iran's small-scale industries were located in the Capital employing 33.4 percent of the labor force. This was an even higher degree of concentration of the SSI for Cairo and Alexandria combined. But despite this strong presence employment within the SSI sector in both countries declined during the third period. For instance, the share of SSI in total employment during the 1956–1966 period declined from 91 percent to 85 percent in Iran. Similarly, between 1960 and 1964 the small-scale industries' share of employment in Egypt also dropped from 62 percent to 51.2 percent. With 85 percent share of total industrial employment, it is clear that the small-scale industries were dominating industrial production in Iran, compared with only 51.2 percent in Egypt.

Another major difference is the average size of workshops within the SSI sectors in Iran and Egypt. In 1963 more than 93 percent of small-scale industries in Greater Tehran employed between 1 and 4 workers, and the average SSI firm size was 2.1.[7] There are no comparable data available for Cairo, but the share of employment for the 1-4 size class in Egypt dropped from 55 percent in 1957 to 35 percent in 1972.[8] In general, while in 1966 the SSI generated 31 percent of total industrial value added in Iran, the comparable figure for Egypt in 1967 was about 16 percent. The disparity may suggest that large-scale industries employing 10 or more workers were far more developed in Egypt as compared to Iran. Further-more, the apparent vitality of the SSI for Iran's industrial production is an indication of Iran's industrial-capitalist sector's relatively lower level of development versus that of Egypt.

## b. Service and Distribution Activities

In comparing the data for this category in Iran and Egypt two patterns stand out. First, in both countries petty traders, street hawkers, peddlers and news vendors increased in numbers and importance during the third period. For instance, the number of people engaged in the above activities increased by 154.6 percent between 1966 and 1976 in Iran and 129.3 percent between 1947 and 1960 in Egypt. This increase was conducive to capitalist growth, as it provided a cheap and efficient means for distribution of commodities produced by the capitalist sector. For example, petty traders and street peddlers offered a wide spectrum of consumer-goods items to urban residents, such as cigarettes, candies, plastic wares, textiles, shoes, toys, audio equipments, etc. Had the petty traders not provided this service, the capitalist producers would have been forced to provide market outlets and distribution centers with considerably higher operational costs leading to a lower rate of return. In addition, the extreme mobility of petty traders enabled the capitalist producers to penetrate in small towns and villages which were not yet fully integrated into a national market economy. The second pattern concerns the difference in employment conditions for housekeeping and related service activities in Iran and Egypt. For example, while the development of dependent capitalism and emergence of a new capitalist class provided a fertile ground and increasing need for such services in Iran, the aftermath of the 1952 revolution in Egypt disrupted the lifestyle of the well-to-do families and hence caused a decline in numbers of paid domestic workers (see table 11.4).

**Table 11.4: Changes in the Structure of Employment of the Service and Distribution Activities within the Petty Commodity Sectors in Iran and Egypt during the Third Period**

Numbers Employed (000s)

| Occupational Category | Iran | | | Egypt | | |
|---|---|---|---|---|---|---|
| | 1966 | 1976 | Change (%) | 1947 | 1960 | Change (%) |
| Petty traders, street Hawkers and Peddlers | 24 | 60 | 154.6 | 82 | 188 | 129.3 |
| Paid domestic Servants | 36 | 58 | 63.1 | 235 | 192 | -18.3 |

Source: Table constructed based on Tables 10.12 and 11.12

### c. Self-Employed Petty Commodity Producers

In this category, available data for Egypt do not provide an itemized breakdown of self-employment within different occupations for the 1950-1970 period. But even the scanty data indicate that self-employment declined in Egypt as large-scale industries filled in the employment gap (see table 10.7). In Iran's case, the only available itemized data are for 1956, whereby over 44 percent of male workers in Iran were self-employed and 37 percent were wage-earners.[9] The situation in Tehran was quite the opposite, where 59 percent of male workers were wage-earners and only 20 percent were self-employed.[10] This occupational disparity clearly corresponds to a high degree of concentration of industrial activities in the Capital which necessitated the presence of a larger pool of wage-earning workers.

## Conclusion

Dependent urbanization in Iran and Egypt during the third period (1950–1970) was the result of two major factors: 1) land reform in the countryside as a planned strategy for a complete disintegration of a pre-capitalist rural economy; and 2) a well-planned (if not well-executed) strategy for industrialization based on capitalist relations in the cities. Thus, along with most of the provincial urban centers but with more intensity Tehran and Cairo were expanded beyond their capacity in order to provide facilities and employment for a new wave of rural-urban migrants. Uneven urban growth in the form of concentration of capital investment and commercial and industrial activities in few urban localities also reached its peak during the third period. In the aftermath of land reforms in both countries the intensity of uneven urban growth was exacerbated by a new wave of rural-urban migrants who came to cities in search of employment. In Egypt's case this was continuation of a pattern which was laid out during the 19th century albeit with a new direction: unlike the second period, Cairo's rural immigrants between 1954 and 1960 came mostly from the Upper Egypt rural areas. The intensity of rural-urban migration in Iran is also clearly noticeable during the third period, as rural-urban migration to Tehran increased from 39 percent during the 1900–1956 period to 65 percent during the 1956–1966 period.

A comparison of available data indicate that Iran and Egypt experienced two divergent processes of uneven urban growth—while Alexandria and Cairo developed as dual poles for urban growth in Egypt, Tehran retained its status as the only major urban center in Iran (see table 11.5). Clearly, the three urban centers represented the "urban core" of a growing dependent capitalist economy in Iran and Egypt in terms of the number of factories, the magnitude of capital investment, number of workers employed and location of the headquarters for major companies.

The third period in this study is a historically significant era both in terms of the nature of political and economic developments and spatial manifestation of such development in Iran and Egypt. First, during this period the United States emerged as the leading capitalist power within the world capitalist system. Second, the emergence of the multinational corporations and their consolidation of political power and financial might signaled a new phase of monopoly capital at the global level. Third, the post-WWII years also witnessed the intensification of class struggles and nationalist independence movements in the peripheries, with the middle class emerging as the champions of nationalist movements. It was during this period that final obstacles to the development of a dependent capitalist economy in Iran and Egypt were removed.

**Table 11.5: A Comparison of Concentration of Factories, Work Force, Capital Investment and Firm Headquarters in Cairo, Alexandria and Tehran during the Third Period (1950–1970)**
(Percentage)

| City | Factories | Labor Force | Capital Investment | Firm Head-quarters |
|---|---|---|---|---|
| Cairo | 48.9 | 27.9 | 15.4 | 75 |
| Alexandria[1] | 17.9 | 23.6 | 18.7 | 14 |
| Tehran | 46.0[2] | 36.2[2] | 35.0[3] | 97 |

1: Figures are for the 1957–1963 period.
2: 1967 data.
3: 1964 data.

Sources: Table constructed based on Tables 8.2, 9.3, 9.5; and chapter 6.

The spatial outcomes of the dominance of capitalism in Iran and Egypt can be summarized as: 1) massive rural-urban migration especially after the implementation of land reform laws; 2) concentration of economic and political activities in few urban localities, leading to uneven urban development; and 3) the growth and increasing importance of petty commodity production for a nascent dependent capitalist economy. A combination of the above factors resulted in the continuous growth of Tehran and Cairo as the manifestation of hyper-urbanization in the two countries. Finally, a comparative analysis of data for Iran and Egypt indicates the growing importance of petty traders, street hawkers and peddlers in the urban economy which I relate to the importance of this sector of petty commodity production as an efficient and cheap means of distribution of commodities produced by the capitalist economic sector.

## Notes

1. See Chapters 3 and 4.
2. See Chapter 3.
3. See Chapters 5 and 8.
4. See my discussion of David Harvey's two phases of globalization, namely *Fordism* and *flexible accumulation* in the Introduction chapter.
5. For a detailed analysis of the events leading to the Egyptian Revolution in 1952 see Abdel-Malek (1968) and Hussein (1973).
6. The following discussion should only be considered as a brief introduction for further research, and the reader is cautioned about differences in data collection methods and conceptualization of variables by census enumerators in Iran and Egypt.
7. See Table 6.7, Chapter 6.
8. See Chapter 10.
9. See Chapter 6.
10. See Table 6.9., Chapter 6.

# Epilogue

# Globalization, the "New World Order," and Prospects for Iran and Egypt in the Region

In the aftermath of the Soviet Union's disintegration and culmination of the Cold War Kenichi Ohmae (1995: 2–5) characterized this new phase of globalization as the end of national boundaries and beginning of regional economic power houses. Globalization, according to him, is comprised of four "Is"— emergence of capital markets and trans-border capital movement and *investment*; new types of *industry* that rely on the mobility of knowledge, labor and capital controlled by multinational corporations; development of *information technology* that has made the need for the proximity of management and labor (planning/decision making and execution) almost obsolete; and emergence of global *individual consumers* whose consumption habits are shaped by finding better quality products with the lowest possible costs in a global market.

In similar fashion Saskia Sassen (1996) acknowledges the importance of labor and capital mobility for a globalized economy which in turn contribute to the emergence of a "new geography of power": actual territories where "much globalization materializes," the "ascendance of a new legal regime" that oversees the cross-border/cross-national economic transactions, and emergence of the "electronic space" that has effectively made national territorial boundaries obsolete for the new globalized capitalist economy. Stiglitz (2002: 10-13) adds yet another dimension, the new assigned role of the World Bank and the International Monetary Fund (IMF) in the 1980s as "the new missionary institutions for globalization" whose directives force poor countries to assume responsibility for their economic failures in order to maintain their eligibility for monetary loans and assistance. As a political footnote, it was also at this historical junction that in addressing the joint session of Congress on September 11, 1990 the former U.S. President George Bush Sr. declared the dawn of the *New World Order*, which was followed by the first Gulf War in Iraq.

201

In the preceding chapters I have tried to provide a critical historical analysis of sociospatial manifestations of dependent urbanization in Iran and Egypt related to each nation's incorporation into the world capitalist economy during the first phase of globalization. This period was what David Harvey (1990) calls *Fordist-Keynsian*; with its rigid system of mass production with large inventories, vertical corporate structures, and an increasingly deskilled labor force that was trained to suit the demands of the economically inefficient Fordist assembly lines. I would like to end the book by briefly sketching the two nations' divergent and distinctly unique entry into the second phase of globalization in the late 1970s that is dubbed by Harvey as the era of *flexible production*. In particular I will focus on the two countries' relations with the United States as the main global powerhouse that has shaped the course of events during the second phase.

While the Iranian Revolution in the late 1970s removed the U.S.-supported Shah and severed the U.S.-Iranian dependency links; amidst riots and mass public protests in Egypt, Anwar Sadat's pro-American government managed to survive by promulgating its so-called "Open Door" policy that provided unrestricted access to the Egyptian labor, industries, and natural resources by foreign capital. Thus while the post-revolution government in Iran launched an anti-American political, and ideological campaign to rid Iran from "toxic cultural influences" of the West in general and the United States in particular, Egypt remained in the American orbit and continued to receive massive American aid and political/ideological support. In the following sections I will briefly compare and contrast Iran and Egypt's status within the second phase of globalization by examining several indicators that are identified by Ohmae, Sassen and Stiglitz.

## Mobility and Availability of Labor and Knowledge

The constantly changing needs of *flexible* production in the current phase of globalization require availability of a highly mobile work force, both skilled and unskilled, that can be utilized either within their home country or moved with little or no hindrance across political borders. Related to international labor migration, one common assumption made by the conventional wisdom is that extreme poverty and high rates of unemployment in developing (peripheral) countries is the major force driving out unskilled migrants to developed (core) nations. While this may be true for temporary migrant workers, many studies have documented that the poor comprise the majority of rural-to-urban migrants *within* the periphery but not emigrants to core countries. One social factor that triggers emigration is the outbreak of a social revolution, which is rooted in inequality, political repression and social class conflict. Almost all the successful revolutions in Africa, Asia and Latin America have produced major International population movements. The first wave of emigrants are usually the political refugees, as the "prospect of a successful revolution often triggers the exodus of the old ruling class and their associates, threatened with or afraid of retribution" (Zolberg, 1989: 419-420). The first wave is often followed by a second and larger outflow which encompasses a "variety of social groups and strata negatively affected by the exigencies of revolutionary reconstruction" such as the educated/professional middle class and highly skilled workers (op. cit.). In addition, while the advanced capitalist countries allow specified types of labor and a limited number of asylum seekers to cross their borders, they tend to bend the rules concerning immigrants from former colonies and/or countries in crisis whose economy is dependent on theirs (ibid., 406).

Similar emigration patterns seem to apply to Iran ad Egypt that have had a history of dependency relations with the United States. For example, the data presented for the 1951–1970 period in Table 12.1 clearly support the above argument, as Egyptian immigration to the United States was much higher than that for Iran during the turbulent years of *Arab Socialism* under Gamal Abdol-Nasser, while reinstatement of the pro-American Shah in Iran temporarily created a more stable environment for Iranian intelligentsia, the middle-class, and the elite *comprador* class. In contrast, with the global economic recession creeping in during the mid-1970s and the outbreak of the Iranian Revolution in 1979 we see a sharp reversal of immigration trend, with the number of Iranian immigrants far surpassing that for Egyptian counterparts. Similar to Iran's safe pro-American and pro-West environment in the 1950–1970 period, Anwar Sadat's initiation of *open door* policy in Egypt in the 1970s provided a social environment that was instrumental in keeping the aforementioned social classes in Egypt (see table 12.1).[1]

**Table 12.1. Immigrants to the United States by Country of Birth, 1951–1995 (in Thousands)**

| Country | 1951–1960[1] | 1961–1970[1] | 1971–1980[2] | 1981–1990[3] | 1991–1995[4] | Total 1951–1995 |
|---|---|---|---|---|---|---|
| Egypt | 3.7 | 17.2 | 25.5 | 31.4 | 21.6 | 99.4 |
| Iran | 2.5 | 10.4 | 46.2 | 154.8 | 115.8 | 329.7 |

Sources:
1. U.S. Bureau of the Census (1980) *Statistical Abstracts of the U.S.: 1980 (101st edition)*.
2. U.S. Bureau of the Census (1990) *Statistical Abstracts of the U.S.: 1990 (110th edition)*.
3. U.S. Bureau of the Census (1995) *Statistical Abstracts of the U.S.: 1995 (115th edition)*.
4. U.S. Bureau of the Census (1997) *Statistical Abstracts of the U.S.: 1997 (117th edition)*.

Socioeconomic and cultural ties between the colonized and the colonizers appear to significantly influence the direction of migration. For instance, Portes and Borocz (1989: 609) consider migration from former colonies to Western Europe during the post-WWII period as one of the major forms of migration:

> Algerians, Moroccans and Tunisians have immigrated to France in large numbers while virtually ignoring the "comparative advantages" of other Western European countries. A similar case is that of nationals of African, Asian and Caribbean members of the British Commonwealth or of those from the Netherlands's former colonies. In each instance, labor outflows have been directed to the former colonial power.

If we exclude political refugees and illegal immigrants from our discussion, individuals emigrating from a given country for social, economic and cultural reasons are usually "self-selected" citizens. In fact, a person's conscious decision to migrate is an implication that they are characteristically different from the rest of the population and in a better position to emigrate. As is shown in table 12.2, naturalized Egyptian and Iranian immigrants have much higher median family income compared with that of average American citizens.

**Table 12.2. Income and Poverty Status of Naturalized Immigrant Families in the United States, 1980–1990 (1990 Data)**

|                              | Egypt[1] | Iran[2] | U.S. Average[3] |
|------------------------------|----------|---------|-----------------|
| Median family income ($):    | 44,514   | 41,658  | 36,812          |
| % Families below poverty:    | 9.6      | 11.5    | 13.5            |

Sources:
1. U.S. Department of Commerce (1993) *1990 Census of Population: Ancestry of Population in the U.S.* (1990 CP-3-2), pp. 415 & 455, August.
2. U.S. Department of commerce (1993) *1990 Census of Population: Asians and Pacific Islanders* (CP-3-5), pp. 156 & 161, August.
3. U.S. Bureau of the Commerce (1992) *Current Population Reports*, p. 88; and U.S. Bureau of the Census (1993) *Money Income and Poverty Status of Families and Persons in the United States, Current Population Reports*, Series P-60, 1992 data.

Borjas (1990: 14) makes a special case for the United States by arguing that those who reach the American shores are "doubly self-selected," because they have "found it profitable to leave their home countries and who found it unprofitable (or were unable) to migrate elsewhere." This inevitably leads to a global process of *brain drain*, whereby a significant portion of immigrant populations are the highly educated and skilled individuals. Similarly, Iranian and Egyptian immigrants tend to be the better educated citizens; who in turn contribute to the host country's social, cultural and economic development (see table 12.3)

**Table 12.3. Educational Attainment and Occupational Status of Naturalized Individuals Immigrated to the United States, 1980-1990 (1990 Data)**

|                                                                 | Egypt | Iran |
|-----------------------------------------------------------------|-------|------|
| *Education (18 Yrs & Older)*                                    |       |      |
| % with bachelor's degree & higher:                             | 58.8  | 49.0 |
| % with high school diploma, some college or associate degrees: | 33.4  | 30.8 |
| *Occupation (16 yrs and Older)*                                 |       |      |
| % in managerial & professional:                                | 31.4  | 38.4 |
| % in technical, sales & administrative support occupations:    | 18.8  | 38.7 |

Source:    U.S. Department of Commerce (1993) *1990 Census of Population: Ancestry of Population in the U.S.* (1990 CP-3-2), pp. 211, 251, 313 and 353 (August).

## New Role of the World Bank and the IMF

Although in varying degrees, both Iran and Egypt have been incorporated into the new global financial network under the supervision of the corporate economic watchdogs, namely, the World Bank and the International Monetary Fund. In Egypt, Sadat's *Open Door* era's legal power came from Investment Law No. 43 in 1974 which legitimized foreign capital investment in virtually all fields, including industry, finance, mining, energy, housing and tourism (Waterbury, 1978: 222-223). In general, Sadat's liberalization policies have been evaluated as having negative consequences for Egypt by helping the growth of parasitic economic activities; increasing the income distribution gap;

exploiting Egyptian resources for the benefit of foreign capital; and allowing interference by international capitalist institutions such as the world Bank and the International Monetary Fund (IMF) to determine price and subsidy policies (Kandil, cf. Baker, 1990: 98).

Backed by the United States and the IMF, Sadat's decision to reduce subsidies on basic food items such as rice, sugar and cooking gas in 1977 touched off a massive protest by students, workers and the urban poor all over Egypt who attacked and destroyed "symbols of state power, conspicuous consumption, and Western influence" (Baker, 1990: 118).[2] The American economic assistance to Egypt, mostly administered by the U.S. Agency for International Development (USAID) passed $8 billion mark for the 1974–1983 period, only second to Israel to receive the highest amount of financial aid in the region. In order to manage USAID-sponsored development projects, by late 1980s the U.S. government stationed more than 2,000 diplomatic personnel in Egypt (Metz, 1990: 109). USAID funds were predominantly allocated for economic development and infrastructure, with only $330 million set aside for social services including education.

On the other hand, although the Iranian Revolution disrupted the cozy political and economic relations between Iran and the United States, the former continues to be dependent on Western (and recently Asian) technology and know-how as well as the global capitalist markets, on both of which she has limited leverage. This includes Iran's limited ability to build machines that build machines, and the effect of sustained international sanctions and financial constraints that keep Iran's currency far below a fair and realistic exchange rate in international markets. In addition, Iran's intransigence in opposing the American policies and interests in the Middle East has led to imposition of economic and political sanctions by the United States. Since Iran has no formal diplomatic relations with the United States, American aid agencies are not directly involved in Iran. But the U.S. policy objectives can still be conveyed through other channels such as the World Bank, the International Monetary Fund, and the UNDP in particular. For instance, when in 2000 the World Bank approved a $234 million loan to support two civil projects in Iran, the United States was the only country that fiercely opposed its approval (the World Bank, 2000). The donor countries and agencies also send often contradictory messages to the borrowing nations. For example, in the aforementioned case the World Bank at that time made it clear that "it will only consider a broader resumption of lending after the current efforts under the leadership of President Khatami [at the time] to strengthen governance and economic reforms begin to show concrete results" (op. cit.). In general, Post-Revolution Iran's path to reduce dependency seems to have yielded some positive results vis-à-vis those for Egypt and her continued dependency on the international financial regulatory agencies. This is evident in the World Bank's Millennium Report on development indicators for the two countries (see table 12.4).

**Table 12.4. Selected Indicators of Millennium Development Goals for Iran and Egypt, 2005**

| | Iran | Egypt |
|---|---|---|
| *General indicators* | | |
| Population (million) | 68.3 | 74.0 |
| GNI per capita ($) | 2,600 | 1,250 |
| Adult literacy rate | | |
|     (% of people ages 15 and over) | 82.4 | 71.4 |
| Total fertility rate (births/woman) | 2.1 | 3.1 |
| Life expectancy at birth | 71.1 | 70.5 |
| External debt (% of GNI) | 11.4 | 38.3 |
| | | |
| *Achieving universal primary education* | | |
| Net primary enrollment ratio | | |
|     (% of relevant age group) | 95.2 | 93.7 |
| Youth literacy rate (% ages 15-24) | 97.4 | 84.9 |
| | | |
| *Promoting gender equality* | | |
| Ratio of girls to boys in primary & | | |
|     secondary education (%) | 105.0 | 93.1 |
| Ratio of young literate females to | | |
|     males (% ages 15-24) | 98.6 | 87.6 |
| Share of women employed in the | | |
|     nonagricultural sector (%)[1] | 13.7 | 20.6 |
| Proportion of seats held by women | | |
|     in national Parliament (%) | 4.1 | 2.9 |
| | | |
| *Reducing child mortality* | | |
| Under 5 mortality rate (per 1,000) | 36.0 | 33.0 |
| Infant mortality rate | | |
|     (per 1,000 live births) | 31.0 | 28.0 |
| | | |
| *Developing a global partnership for* | | |
|     *development* | | |
| Fixed line and mobile telephones | | |
|     (per 1,000 people) | 384.0 | 324.5 |
| Personal computers | | |
|     (per 1,000 population) | 109.1[2] | 37.8 |

Note: (1) & (2) are 2004 data.
Sources: The World Bank Millennium Development Goals Reports.[5]

## Emergence of Capital Markets and Trans-Border Capital Movements and Investment

Unlike the rest of Asia, economies of most countries in southwest Asia (the Middle East) have not been substantively affected by the trans-border flow of capital and labor of the new global economy. In fact, there are indications that the objectives of joint American-British invasion and occupation of Iraq in 2003 went far beyond "regime change" and toppling of Saddam Hussein's government—that the ulterior motive was (and still is) to implement a plan similar to NAFTA (North American Free Trade Agreement) to open up the yet untapped resources of the region for a new "post-Fordist" global economy that thrives on outsourcing and utilization of cheap, unregulated labor. This U.S.-sponsored plan is called MEFTA, which stands for Middle East Free Trade Areas, and promises to actively support membership of "peaceful countries" to the World Trade Organization (WTO); to expand the Generalized System of Preferences (GSP) with Middle Eastern countries that would facilitate duty-free entrance of the region's commodities into the U.S. markets; and to promote bilateral investment and free trade agreements. As a prelude to a more comprehensive free trade agreement by the end of 2006 the United States had signed Trade and Investment Framework Agreements (TIFAs) with Algeria, Egypt, Kuwait, Lebanon, Qatar, Saudi Arabia, Tunisia, United Arab Emirates, and Yemen.[3] According to MEFTA documents, "TIFAs promote the establishment of legal protections for investors, improvements in intellectual property protection, more transparent and efficient customs procedures, and greater transparency in government and commercial regulations."[4] As of this writing, the more comprehensive Free Trade Agreements (FTAs) are in place between the United States and Israel, Jordan, Morocco, Bahrain and Oman, with negotiations under way to bring the United Arab Emirates (UAE) into the loop. But the region's two most populated and technologically advanced nations, namely, Iran and Egypt have not yet fully tapped either for their substantial labor forces or markets for consumption goods.

### Notes

1. This policy has been continued and supported by Sadat's successor Hosni Mubarak to the present time.
2. To avoid an impending revolution, the government quickly canceled the subsidy cutbacks but also used the army and security forces to crush the mass protest. An estimated 160 were killed, hundreds more were wounded, and over a three month period some 3,000 Egyptians were arrested on charges of leftist subversive conspiracy. Furthermore, the United States quickly allocated $190 million to aid the Egyptian government,

so did the conservative Arab allies (Kuwait, Saudi Arabia and the United Arab Emirates) with their generous $1 billion financial aid package (Baker, 1978: 166).

3. For a summary of the Bush Administration's Middle East Fair Trade Initiative see the text of initial proposal: http://www.ustr.gov/Document_Library/Fact_Sheets/2003/ Middle_East_Free_Trade_ Initiative.html (accessed 10-20-2006).

4. For the latest TIFA initiative between the U.S. and Lebanon see the November, 2006 news release see:

http: //www.ustr.gov/Document_Library/Press_Releases/2006/November/United_States_ Lebanon_Sign_Trade_Investment_Framework_Agreement.html (accessed 12-19-2006).

5. See the following web sources for more information on Iran and Egypt, respectively:

http://devdata.worldbank.org/idg/IDGProfile.asp?CCODE=IRN&CNAME=Iran%2 C+Islamic+Rep.&SelectedCountry=IRN

http://devdata.worldbank.org/idg/IDGProfile.asp?CCODE=EGY&CNAME=Egypt %2C+Arab+Rep.&SelectedCountry=EGY (both sources accessed 10-21-2007).

12 sources    2000)
          900)
   17
18 page biblio

# References

Abdel–Fadil, M. (1975). *Development, Income Distribution and Social Change in Rural Egypt 1952–1970.* University of Cambridge, Department of Applied Economics Occasional Papers, No. 45. Cambridge: Cambridge University Press.

———. (1980). *The Political Economy of Nasserism: A Study in Employment and Income Distribution Policies in Urban Egypt, 1952–1972.* London: Cambridge University Press.

———. (1983). Informal Sector Employment in Egypt, *Cairo Papers in Social Science,* 6(2), 55–89.

Abdel–Malek, A. (1968). *Egypt: Military Society.* New York: Vintage Books.

Abrahamian, E. (1975). European Feudalism and Middle Eastern Despotism, *Science and Society,* 40, Summer.

———. (1979). The Causes of the Constitutional Revolution in Iran, *International Journal of Middle East Studies,* 10, 381–414.

———. (1980). *Iran between Two Revolutions.* Princeton: Princeton University Press.

Abu–Lughod, J. (1961). Migrant Adjustment to City Life: the Egyptian Case, *American Journal of Sociology,* 67(1): 22–32, July.

———. (1965a). Urbanization in Egypt: Present State and Future Prospects, *Economic Development and Cultural Change,* 13(3), 313–43, April.

———. (1965b). Tale of Two Cities: The Origins of Modern Cairo, *Comparative Studies in Society and History,* 7(4), 429–57.

———. (1971). *Cairo: 1,001 Years of the City Victorious.* Princeton: Princeton University Press.

———. (1989). *Before European Hegemony: The World System A.D. 1250–1350.* New York: Oxford University Press.

Acharya, S. (1983). The Informal Sector in Developing Countries: A Macro View Point, *Journal of Contemporary Asia,* 13(4), 432–45.

Afshari, M. R. (1983). The Pishivaran and Merchants in Pre–capitalist Iranian Society: An Essay on the Background and Causes of the Constitutional Revolution, *International Journal of Middle East Studies,* 15, 133–55.

Afzal al–Mulk, G., Ittihadiyah, M., and Sa`dvandiyan, S. 1982. *Afzal al–Tavarikh.* Tehran : Nashr–I Tarikh–i Iran Publishing.

Aiken, M. and Castells, M. (1977). New Trends in Urban Studies: Introduction,
*Comparative Urban Research*, 4(2– 3), 7–10.

Althusser, L. and Balibar, E. (1970). *Reading Capital.* London: New Left Books.

Amani, M. (1970). *Avvalin Sarshumari–yi Jamiyat–i Tehran* (The First Population Census of Tehran), Ulum–i Ijtima'i, 1. Tehran: Behnam Publishing Co. (Persian).

Amin, S. (1974). Modes of Production and Social Formations, *UFAHAMU*, 4(3), 57–85, Winter.

———. (1976). *Unequal Development: An Essay on the Social Formations of Peripheral Capitalism.* New York: Monthly Review Press.

———. (1978). *The Arab Nation.* Zed Press.

———. (1980) *Class and Nation, Historically and in the Current Crisis.* New York: Monthly Review Press.

Amuzegar, J. (1977). *Iran: An Economic profile.* Washington: The Middle East Institute.

Amuzegar, J. and Fekrat, M. A. (1971). *Iran: Economic Development Under Dualist Conditions.* Chicago: University of Chicago Press.

Anis, M.A. (1950). *A Study of the National Income of Egypt.* Cairo.

Ashraf, A. (1970). Historical Obstacles to the Development of a Bourgeoisie in Iran, in M. A. Cook (ed.), *Studies in the Economic History of the Middle East*, 308–332. London: Oxford University Press.

———. (1971). *Iran, Imperialism, Class, and Modernization from Above.* Doctoral dissertation, The New School for Social research.

———. (1974). Vizhegiha–ye Tarikhi–ye Shahr–neshini dar Iran–e' Dowreh–ye Eslami (Historical Traits of Urbanization During the Islamic Period in Iran). *Nameh–ye Olum–e Ejtemaie*, 1(4). Tehran (Persian).

Aspen Institute (1976). *Iran: Past, Present and Future.* New York.

Avery, P. (1965). *Modern Iran.* New York: Praeger.

Ayrout, H. H. (1963). *The Egyptian Peasant.* Boston: Beacon Press.

Baer, G. (1969). *Studies in the Social History of Modern Egypt.* Chicago: The University of Chicago Press.

Bahrambeygui, M. (1977). *Tehran: An Urban Analysis.* Tehran: Sahab Book Institute.

Baker, R. W. (1990) *Sadat and After: Struggles for Egypt's Political Soul.* Cambridge: Harvard University Press.

Bakhshi, M. (2006). *Tehran Has No More Pomegranates!* 35 mm documentary film. Farsi with English Subtitles.

Bakhtari, H. (1966). *As Shahr-e Tehran Che Midanim* (What do We Know about Tehran?). Tehran: Sahab Book Institute.

Baldwin, G. (1966). *Planning and Development in Iran*. Baltimore: the Johns Hopkins Press.

Balibar, E. (1970). The Basic Concepts of Historical Materialism, in Althusser, L. and Balibar, E, *Reading Capital*. London: New left Books.

Banaji, J. (1977). Modes of Production in a Materialist Conception of History, *Capital and Class*, 3.

Banani, A. (1961). *The Modernization of Iran 1921–1941*. Stanford: Stanford University Press.

Bank Melli Iran (1941–42). *Bulletin*. No. 55.

Barbour, K. M. (1972). *The Growth, Location, and Structure of Industry in Egypt*. New York: Praeger.

Barth, F. (1961). *Nomads of South Persia: The Basseri Tribe of the Khamseh Confederacy*. Boston.

Bartsch, W. H. (1971). Unemployment in Less Developed Countries: A Case Study of a Poor District of Tehran, *International Development Review*, 13–14(1), 19–22.

Bettelheim, C. (1972). Theoretical Comments by Charles Bettelheim, in Emmanuel, A, *Unequal Exchange: A Study in the Imperialism of Trade*. London: New Left Books.

Beckett, P. H. (1966). The City of Kerman, Iran, *Erdkunde*, 20(2), 119–25.

Behnam, J. and Rasekh, S. (1969). *Mugaddameh bar Jame-eh- Shenasi-e Iran* (An introduction to Iran's Sociology). Tehran: Kharazmi Publishing Co. (Perian).

Berque, J. (1972). *Egypt: Imperialism and Revolution*. London: Faber & Faber.

Bharier, J. (1968). A Note on the Population of Iran, 1900–1966, *Population Studies*, 22(2), 273–79.

———. (1971). *Economic Development in Iran, 1900–1970*. London: Oxford University Press.

———. (1977). The Growth of Towns and Villages in Iran, 1900–1966, in J. Momeni (ed.), *The Population of Iran*, 331–41. Honolulu: The East–West Population Institute.

Bienefeld, M. (1975). The Informal Sector and Peripheral Capitalism: The Case of Tanzania, *Institute of Development Studies Bulletin* 6, 53–73.

Bill, J. A. (1963). The Social and Economic Foundations of Power in Contemporary Iran, *The Middle East Journal*, 17(4).

Bluestone, B. and Harrison, B. (1984). *The Deindustrialization of America: Plant Closings, Community Abandonment, and the Dismantling of Basic Industry*. Basic Books.

Bonnine. M. E. (1979). Morphogenesis of Iranian Cities, *Association of Ameri-*

can *Geographers*, Annals, 208–244.

———. (1997). *Population, Poverty, and Politics in Middle East Cities.* Gaines-ville: University Press of Florida.

Borjas, G. (1990). *Friends or Strangers: The Impact of Immigrants on the U.S. Economy.* New York: Basic books.

Bradby, B. (1975). Destruction of Natural Economy, *Economy and Society*, 4(2), 127–61.

Breman, J. (1976). A Dualistic labor System? A Critique of the "Informal Sector" Concept, *Economic and Political Weekly*, 11, 1870–1876 and 1939–1944.

Brenner, R. (1977). The Origins of Capitalist Development : A Critique of Neo-Smithian Marxism, *New Left Review*, 104, 25–92.

Bricault, G. (1975). *Major Companies of the Arab World and Iran.* London; Graham & Trotman.

Brookfield, H. C. (1973). On one Geography and A Third World, *Transactions of the Institute of British Geographers*, 58, 1–20.

Burja, A. S. (1973). The Social Imperialism of Developmental Policies: A Case Study from Egypt, in Nelson, D. (ed.), *The Desert and the Sown: Nomads in the Wider Society*, 143–57. Research Series No. 21, Institute of International Studies, Berkeley; University of California.

Capper, A. (1909). *View of Cairo, Egypt.* Original postcard, from Dr. Paula Sanders' collection, Rice University.

Cairo Postcard Trust. (n.d.). *Port Said: Panoramic View.* Original postcard, from Dr. Paula Sanders' collection, Rice University.

Castells, M. (1978). Collective Consumption and Urban Contradiction in Advanced Capitalism, in Castells, M. (ed.), *City, Class and Power.* London; McMillan.

———. (1980). *The Urban Question.* Cambridge, Mass.: The MIT Press.

Central Bank of Iran (1970). *Bulletin.* No. 8, June.

Chaichian, M. A. (1988). The Effects of World Capitalist Economy on Urbanization in Egypt: 1800–1970, *International Journal of Middle East Studies*, 20(1): 23–43.

———. (1997). "Dependent Urbanization in Iran: Tehran's Uneven Development," *Mehregan*, 6(3), 139–149 (in Persian).

Chayanov, A. V. (1966). *The Theory of Peasant Economy.* Homewood, Ill.: Dersey Press.

Childe, G. (1964). *What Happened in History?* Baltimore: Penguine Books.

Chinchilla, N. S. (1980). *Articulation of Modes of Production and the Latin American Debate.* School of Social Sciences, University of California Research paper.

Chinchilla, N. S. and Dietz, L. (1981). Toward a New Understanding of

Develop-ment and Underdevelopment, *Latin American Perspectives*, 1(3–4), 138–47.

Clarke, B. D. (1973). *The Iranian City of Shiraz*. Durham: University of Durham, Department of Geography, Research Paper No. 7.

Clarke, B. D. and Costello, V. (1973). The Urban Systems and Social Patterns in Iranian Cities, *Transactions of British Geographers*, 59, 99–128.

Clawson, P. (1977–1978). Egypt's Industrializtion: A Critique of Dependency Theory, *MERIP Reports*, 7–8(72), 17–23.

Cohen, R.B. (1981). The New International Division of Labor, Multinational Corporations and Urban Hierarchy, in Dear, M. and Scotth, A. J. (eds.), *Urbanization and Urban Planning in Capitalist Society*, 287–315. New York: Methuen.

Cooper, M. N. (1983). State Capitalism, Class Structure, and Social Transforma-tion in the Third World: The Case of Egypt, *International Journal of Middle East Studies*, 15, 451–69.

Corliss, W. R. (1999). *Ancient Infrastructures*. Glen Arm, MD: The Source Book Project.

Costello, V. (1976). *Kashan: A City and Region of Iran*. London: Center for the Middle Eastern and Islamic Studies of the University of Durham.

Crinson, M. (1997). Abadan: Planning and Architecture under the Anglo–Iranian Oil Company, *Planning Perspectives*, 12, 341–359.

Critchley, J. S. (1978). *Feudalism*. London: George Allen & Unwin.

Crouchley, A. E. (1936). *The Investment of Foreign Capital in Egyptian Companies and Public Debt*. Technical Paper No. 12. Egypt: Ministry of Finance.

———. (1938). *The Economic Development of Modern Egypt*. London; Longman Greens.

———. (1939). A Century of Economic Development, *L'Egypte Contemporaine*, 30, 133–55.

Curzon, G. N. (1966). *Persia and the Persian Question* (Two Volumes). London: Frank Cass.

Davis, K. and Golden, H. H. (1954). Urbanization and Devlopment of Pre-industrial Areas, *Economic Develpment and Cultural Change*, 3(1), 6–26.

de Gobineau, A. (1971). Merchants and Craftsmen, in Issawi, C. (ed.), *The Economic History of Iran 1800–1914*, 36–40. Chicago: The University of Chicago Press.

de Janvry, A. (1981). *The Agrarian Question and Reformism in Latin America*. Baltimore: The Johns Hopkins University Press.

de Planhol, X. (1968). Geography of Settlements, in Fisher, W. B. (ed.), *The Cambridge History of Iran*, Vol. I. London: Cambridge University Press.

de Silva, S. B. D. (1982). *The Political Economy of Underdevelopment*. Boston: Routledge & Kegan Paul.

Denoeux, G. (1993). *Urban Unrest in the Middle East: A Comparative Study of Informal Networks in Egypt, Iran, and Lebanon*. Albany, NY: State University of New York Press.

Dhamija, J. (1976). *Non–Farm Activities in Rural Areas and Towns: The Lessons and Experiences of Iran*. Studies in Employment and Rural Development # 31. International Bank for Reconstruction and Development (IBRD). Washington, D.C.

Dos Santos, T. (1970). The Structure of Dependence, *American Economic Review*, LX (May), 231–36.

Dupree, G. and Rey, P. P. (1973). Reflections on the Pertinence of a Theory of the History of Exchange, *Economy and Society*, 2 (May).

Eckstein, S. (1975). The Political Economy of Lower–Class Areas in Mexico City: Societal Constraints on Local Business Opportunities, in Cornelius, W. and Trueblood, F. (eds.), *Latin American Urban Research*, 4. Beverley Hills: Sage.

Egypt. CAPMAS (1967). *Census of Industrial Production.*

Egypt. Governmental Printing Office (1956). *The Master plan of Cairo*. Cairo.

Ehsani, K. (2003). "Social Engineering and the Contradictions of Modernization in Khuzestan's Company Towns: A Look at Abadan and Masjed–Soleyman," *International Instituut voor Sociale Geschiedenis*, 48, 361–399.

El–Shakhs, S. and Shoshkes, E. 1998. "Cairo as a World City: the Impact of Cairo's Orientation Towards Globalization," in Lo, F. and Yeung, Y. (editors). 1998. *Globalization and the World of Large Cities*. New York: United Nations University Press.

Elwell–Sutton, L. P. (1955). *Persian Oil, A Study in Power Politics*. London.

English, P. W. (1966). *City and Village in Iran: Settlement and Economy in the Kirman Basin*. Milwaukee: The University of Wisconsin Press.

Evans, P. (1979). *Dependent Development: The Alliance of Multinational, State and Local Capital in Brazil*. Princeton: Princeton University Press.

Fahmy, M. (1954). *La Revolution de L'industrie en Egypte et Ses Consequences Sociales au XIXe Siecle (1800–1850)*. Leyden.

Fas'a'i, H. (1972). *History of Persia Under Qajar Rule*. Translated from Persian by H. Busse. New York: Columbia University Press.

Fesharaki, F. (1976). *Development of the Iranian Oil Industry*. New York: Praeger Publishing.

Firoozi, F. (1977a). Tehran: A Demographic and Economic Analysis, in J. Momeni (ed.), *The Population of Iran*, 342–58. Honolulu: East–West Population Institute.

————. (1977). Demographic Review, Iranian Censuses 1956 and 1966: A Comparative Analysis, in J. Momeni (ed.), *The Population of Iran*, 74–82. Honolulu: East–West Population Institute.

Fisher, W. B. (1968). Physical Geography, in Fisher, W. B. (ed.), *The Cambridge History of Iran*, Vol. I, 3–111. London: Cambridge University Press.

Flandin, E. (1945). *Safarname-ye Eugene Flandin dar Iran, 1840–1841* (Eugene Flandin's Journey in Iran). Tehran; 2nd edition.

Forbes, D. (1981). Petty Commodity Production and Underdevelopment: The Case of Peddlers and Trishaw Riders in Ujung Pandang, Indonesia, *Progress in Planning*, 6(2), 105–178.

Foster–Carter, A. (1973). Neo–Marxist Approaches to Development and Underdevelopment, *Journal of Contemporary Asia*, 3(1), 7–33.

————. (1978). The Modes of Production Controversy, *New Left Review*, 107, 47–77.

Franklin, S. H. (1965). Systems of Production, Systems of Appropriation, *Pacific Viewpoint*, 1(2), 145–66.

————. (1969). *The European Peasantry: The Final Phase*. London: Methuen.

Freund, B. (2007). *The African City: A History*. New York: Cambridge University Press.

Friedman, J. and Sullivan, F. (1972). *The Absorption of Labor in the Urban Economy: The Case of Developing Countries*. Los Angeles: University of California, School of Architecture and Urban Planning. Mimeo.

Garzuel, M. and Skolka, J. (1976). *World Employment Research: Working Papers*. Geneva: International Labor Office.

Gaube, H. (1979). *Iranian Cities*, New York: New York University Press.

Geertz, G. (1963). *Peddlers and Princes: Social Change and Economic Modernization in Two Indonesian Towns*. Chicago: University of Chicago Press.

Gerry, C. (1975). *Petty Production and Capitalist Production in Dakar: The Crisis of the Self-employed*. Unpublished working paper, British Sociological Association, Development Group.

————. (1979). Small–Scale Manufacturing and Repairs in Dakar: A Survey of Market Relations Within the Urban Economy, in Bromley, R. and Gerry, C. (eds.), *Casual Work and Poverty in Third World Cities*, 229–50. Chichester: Wiley.

Ghannam, F. (2002). *Remaking the modern: Space, Relocation, and the Politics of Identity in a Global Cairo*. Berkeley, CA: University of California Press.

Gibb, H. A. R. and Bowen, H. (1950). *Islamic Society and the West*. 1(1).

London: Oxford University Press.

Gibb, J. P. and Martin, W. T. (1959). Toward A Theoretical System of Human Ecology, *Pacific Sociological Review*, 2, 29–36.

Gilbert, A. and Gugler, J. (1982). *Cities, Poverty and Development: Urbanization in the Third World*. New York: Oxford University Press.

Girvan, N. (1976). *Corporate Imperialism, Transnational Corporations and Economic Nationalism in the Third World*. New York: Monthly Review Press.

Glamann, K. (1958). *Dutch–Asiatic Trade, 1620–1740*. Copenhagen; Danish Science Press.

Godelier, M. (1974). On the Definition of a Social Formation, *Critique of Anthropology*, 1, 63–73.

———. (1977). *Perspectives in Marxist Anthropology*. London: Cambridge University Press.

———. (1978). The Concept of the Asiatic Mode of Production and Marxist Models of Social Evolution, in Seddon, D. (ed.), *Relations of Production: Marxist Approaches to Economic Anthropology*. London: Frank Cass.

Goldscheider, C. (1983). The Tehran, Iran Migration Study: Background, in Goldscheider, C. (ed.), *Urban Migrants in Developing Nations*, 185–88. Boulder: Westview Press.

G. O. P. F. (the Guerilla Organization of the People's Fedaee). (1976). *Land Reform and Its Direct Effects in Iran*. London: Iran Committee.

Gordon, D. (1971). *Problems in Political Economy: An Urban Perspective*. Lexington: D.C. Heath.

Graham, R. (1979). *Iran: The Illusion of Power*. New York: St. Martin's Press.

Gugler, J. (1982). Over–urbanization Reconsidered, *Economic Development and Cultural Change*, 31(1), 173–189.

———. (Editor). 1988. *The Urbanization of the World*. Oxford University Press.

———. (Editor). (2004). *World Cities beyond the West: Globalization, Development and Inequality*. Cambridge, MA: Cambridge University Press.

Gugler, J. and Flanagan, W. G. (1978). *Urbanization and Social Change in West Africa*. Cambridge: Cambridge University Press.

Habibi, S. M. 1996. *Az Shaar ta Shahr (de la Cite' a la Ville)*. Tehran: Tehran University Press (in Persian).

Hadwin, M. (n.d.). *Cairo—A Case Study of an LEDC Megacity*. http://home.barton.ac.uk/curriculum/sc_env/geology/Geography%202/CA–IRO.htm. Accessed 10–18–2007.

Halliday, F. (1979). *Iran: Dictatorship and Development*. Penguin Books.

Hakamy, M. (1964). Tarikhche-ye Jamee' Shenasi-ye Shahr-e Tehran (A History of Tehran's Sociology), in *Sukhanraniha va Guzarishha dar*

*Nukhustin Siminar–i Barrasi–i Masail–i Ijtima–i Shahr–i Tehran* (in Persian). Tehran: Institute of Social Research.

Harloe, M. (1977). *Captive Cities*. London: John Wiley and Sons.

Hart, K. (1973). Informal Income Opportunities and Urban Employment in Ghana, *Journal of Modern African Studies*, 11(1), 61–89.

Hauser, P. and Schnore, L. F. (1965). *The Study of Urbanization*. New York: John Wiley.

Harvey, D. (1973). *Social Justice and the City*. Baltimore: Johns Hopkins University Press.

———. (1991). *The Conditions of Postmodernity*. Cambridge, MA: Blackwell.

———. (2005). *The New Imperialism (Clarendon Lectures in Geography and Environmental Studies)*. Oxford University Press.

Hemmasi, M. (1974). *Migration in Iran*. Shiraz: Pahlavi University Publications.

Heyworth–Dunne, J. (1938). *An Introduction to the History of Modern Education In Egypt*.

Hill, R. C. (1977). Capital Accumulation and Urbanization in the United States, *Comparative Urban Research*, 4(2–3).

Hindess, B. and Hirst, P. (1975). *Pre–capitalist Modes of Production*. London: Routledge Kegan & Paul.

———. (1977). *Modes of Production and Social Formation*. London: McMillan Press.

Hirsch, E. (1973). *Employment and Income Policies in Iran*. Geneva: International Labor Office (ILO).

Hirschman, A. O. (1958). *The Strategy of Economic Development*. New York: Yale University Press.

Holfgott, L. (1976). Iran: Capitalist Formation on the Periphery, *The Review of Iranian Political Economy and History*, 1(1).

Hooglund, E. (1982). *Land and Revolution in Iran 1962–1980*. Austin: University of Texas Press.

Hoselitz, B. F. (1955). Generative and Parasitic Cities, *Economic Development and Cultural Change*, 3, 278–94.

Hurewitz, J. C. (ed.). (1975). *The Middle East and North Africa in World Politics: A Documentary Record* (two volumes). London: Yale University Press.

Hussein, M. (1973). *Class Conflict in Egypt 1945–1970*. New York: Monthly Review Press.

Hymers, S. (1971). The Multinational Corporations and the Law of Uneven Development, in Bhagvatti, J. S. (ed.), *Economics and the World Order*, 113–40. New York: World Law Fund.

Ibrahim, S. E. M. (1975). Over–urbanization and Under–urbanism, the Case of the Arab World, *International Journal of Middle East Studies*, 6, 29–45.

———. (1987). Cairo: a Sociological Profile, in *Urban Crisis and Social Movements,* edited by Salim Nasr and Theodor Hanf. Beirut: Euro–Arab Social Research Group, 88–99.

Ikram, K. (1980). *Egypt: Economic Management in a Period of Transition.* London: Johns Hopkins University.

International Labor Office (ILO). (1956). *Labor Conditions in the Oil Industry in Iran.*

———. (1970). *Problems of Employment Creation in Iran.* Geneva.

———. (1974). *Iran: Rural Employment and Income Research.* Technical Report No. 1, IRA/72/009. Geneva.

INP/ILO. (1968). *Final Report on Employment  Problems in Rural Areas.* Cairo.

Iran. Ministry of Interior (1956). *Census Districts Statistics of the First National Census of Iran: Tehran Census District.* Tehran (Aban 1335).

———. (1962). *National and Province Statistics of the First National Census of Iran, November 1956.* Tehran: Public Statistics Division.

———. (1964). *Industrial Census of Iran, 1963: Tehran District.* Tehran.

Iran. Ministry of Labor (1964). *bar–Rasi–ye Masael–e Nirouye Ensanni–ye Iran* (A Survey of Iran's Manpower), No. 35, Tehran.

Iran. Plan and Budget Organization (1966a). *Statistical Yearbook.* Tehran: Statistical Center of Iran.

———. (1966b). *Population and Housing Census, Tehran District, Vol. 10.* Tehran; Staistical Center of Iran.

———. (1972). *Pazhouheshi dar Mohajerat haye Dakheli–ye Keshvar* (A Survey on Internal Migration in Iran), Vol. 1. Tehran: Statistical Center of Iran.

———. (1973). *Amar–i Muntakhab.* Iranian Statistical Center.

———. (1975). *5th Development Plan of Iran* (revised). Tehran.

———. (1976). *National Census of Population and Housing (based on 5% Sample): Tehran Shahrestan.* Tehran: Statistical Center of Iran.

———. (1980). *Population and Housing Census for 1976, Central Province, Tehran District, No. 3.* Tehran: Statistical Center of Iran.

Iranian Statistical Center (1966). *National Census of Population and Housing, Vol. 10,* Tehran District.

Iranian–American Economic Survey (1967). New York: Manhattan Printing Co.

Issawi, C. (1961). Egypt Since 1800, a Study of Lopsided Development, *Journal of Economic History*, 21(1), 1–25, March.

———. (1963). *Egypt in Revolution: An Economic Analysis.* New York: Oxford University Press.

————. (1966). *The Economic History of the Middle East: 1800–1914.* Chicago: University of Chicago Press.

————. (1968). Assymetrical Development and Transport in Egypt, in W. R. Polk and R. L. Chambers (eds.). *Beginnings of Modernization in the Middle East,* 394. Chicago; University of Chicago Press.

————. (1969). Economic Change and Urbanization in the Middle East, in Lapidus, I. M. (ed.), *Middle Eastern Cities,* 102–21. Berkeley: University of California Press.

————. (1971). *The Economic History of Iran 1800–1914.* Chicago: The University of Chicago Press.

Jamalzadeh, M. A. (1956). *Ganj–i Shaigan.* Berlin.

Jazani, B. (1978). *Vaghaye–e si Saleh dar Iran* (Thirty Years of Historical Events in Iran). Tehran: Nouzdahe' Bahman.

————. (1980). *Capitalism and Revolution in Iran.* London; Zed Press.

Jefferson, M. (1939). The Law of Primate City, *Geographical Review,* 19, 226–232.

Katouzian, H. (1981). *The Political Economy of Modern Iran: Despotism & Pseudo–Modernism, 1926–1979.* London: McMillan Press.

Katouzian, S. (1996). Tehran, Capital City: 1786–1997. The Re–invention of a Metropolis, in Environmental Research, *Journal of Islamic Environmental Design Research Center,* 1: 34–45.

Kay, G. (1975). *Development and Underdevelopment: A Marxist Analysis.* New York: St. Martin's Press.

Kazembeyki, M. A. (2003). *Society, Politics and Economics in Mazandaran, Iran, 1848–1914.* London: Routledge–Curzon.

Kazemi, F. (1980). *Poverty and Revolution in Iran: The Migrant Poor, Urban Marginality and Politics.* New York: New York University Press.

Kazemi, F. and Abrahamian, E. (1978). The Nonrevolutionary Peasantry of Modern Iran, *Iranian Studies,* 11, 259–304.

Keddie, N.R. (1960). *Historical Obstacles to Agrarian Change in Iran.* Claremont.

————. (1966). *Religion and Rebellion in Iran; The Tobacco Protest of 1891–1892.* London: Frank Cass & Co.

————. (1968). The Iranian Village Before and After Land Reform, *Journal of Contemporary History,* 3(3), 69–91.

————. (1972). The Economic History of Iran, 1800–1914 and Its Political Impact: An overview, *Iranian Studies,* 5(2–3), Summer.

————. (1972). Stratification, Social Control and Capitalism in Iranian Villages Befor and After Land Reform, in Richard, A. and Harik, I. (eds.), *Rural Politics and Social Change in the Middle East.* Indiana University Press.

————. (1981). *Roots of Revolution: an Interpretive History of Modern Iran*. New Haven: Yale University Press.

Kennett, A. (1968). *Bedouin Justice*. London: Frank Cass & Co.

Kheirabadi, M. (2000). *Iranian Cities: Formation and Development*. Syracuse, NY: Syracuse University Press.

Khosrovi, K. (1973). Les Paysans san Terre en Iran: Les Khochnechin, *Journal of the European Society for Rural Sociology*, 23.

Kinneir, J. M. (1813). *Geographical Memoir of the Persian Empire*. London.

Laclau, E. (1977). Feudalism and Capitalism in Latin America, in *Politics and Ideology in Marxist Theory*. London: New Left Books.

Lacauture, J. and Lacauture, S. (1958). *Egypt in Transition*. New York: Criterion Books.

Lahsaeizadeh, A. (1984). *The Effect of the 1962 Land Reform on Rural Social Class Structure*. Michigan State University: Doctoral Dissertation.

————. (2006). *Sociology of Abadan.* Tehran: Kianmehr Publishing (in Persian).

Lambton, A. K. S. (1963). Rural Development and Land Reform in Iran, in *Symposium on Rural Development*. Central Treaty Organization (CENTO).

————. (1965). Some Reflections on the Question of Rural Development and Land Reform in Iran, *Tahqiqat-e Eqtesadi*, 3(9–10), 3–9, Tehran (in Persian).

————. (1969). *The Persian Land Reform 1962–1966* Oxford: Clarendon Press.

————. (1970). Islamic Society in Persia, in Sweet, L. E. (ed.), *Peoples and Cultures of the Middle East*, Vol. 1. New York: The National History Press.

Lapidus, I. M. (1969). Muslim Cities and Islamic Societies, in Lapidus, I. M. (ed.), *Middle Eastern Cities*, 49–79. Berkeley: University of California Press.

Lebrun, O. and Gerry, C. (1975). Petty Producers and Capitalism, *Review of African Political Economy*, 3.

Leeds, A. (1971). The Culture of Poverty Concept: Conceptual, Logical and Empirical Problems, With Perspectives from Brazil and Peru, in Leacock, E. (ed.), *The Culture of Poverty: A Critique*. New York: Simon and Schuster.

Lefebvre, H. (1970). *La Revolution Urbanine*. Paris; Gallimard.

Lenin, V. I. (1964). *Collected Works*, Vol. 22. Moscow: Progress Publishers.

————. (1968). *Imperialism: The Highest Stage of Capitalism*. Moscow: Progress Publishers.

Lewis, N. N. (1955). The Frontiers of Settlement in Syria 1800–1950, *International Affairs*, 31(1).

Leys, C. (1975). *Underdevelpment in Kenya: The Political Economy of Neo–*

*Colonialism*. Berkeley: University of California Press.

————. (1977). Underdevelopment and Dependency: Critical Notes, *Journal of Contemporary Asia*, 7(1), 92–107.

Little, T. (1958). *Egypt*. New York: Praeger.

Lockhart, L. (1960). *Persian Cities*. London.

Lojkine, J. (1976). Contribution to a Marxist Theory of Capitalist Urbanization, in Pickvance, C. G. (ed.), *Urban Sociology: Critical Essays*. London: Tavistock.

Looney, R. (1973). *The Economic Development of Iran: A Recent Survey with Projections to 1981*. New York: Praeger.

————. (1977). *Iran at the End of the Century: A Hegelian Forecast*. London: D.C. & Co.

Lubeck, P. and Walton, J. (1979). Urban Class Conflict in Africa and Latin America: Comparative Analyses from a World Systems Perspective, *International Journal of Urban and Regional Research*, 3(1), 3–28.

Luxemburg, R. (1963). *The Accumulation of Capital*. London.

McGee, T. G. (1971). *The Urbanization Process in the Third World: Explorations in the Search of a Theory*. Bell.

————. (1978). *Doubts about Dualism: Implications for Development Planning*. Working Paper 78–03, United Nations Center for Regional Development. Nagoya.

McLachlan, K. S. (1968). Land Reform in Iran, in Fisher, W. B. (ed.), *The Cambridge History of Iran*, Vol. 1, 684–716. Cambridge: The University Publishing House.

McLoan, J. C. (1882). *Egypt As It Is*. New York: Dodd, Mead & Co.

Mabogunje, A. L. (1981). *The Development Process: A Spatial Perspective*. New York: Holmes and Meier.

Mabro, R. and Radwan, S. (1976). *The Industrialization of Egypt 1939–1973: Policy and Performance*. Oxford: Clarendon Press.

Madanipour, A. (1998). *Tehran: The Making of a Metropolis*. New York: Wiley.

Magdoff, H. (1972). Imperialism without Colonies, in Owen, E. J. R. and Sutcliffe, R. B. (eds.), *Studies in the Theory of Imperialism*, 144–71. London: Longman.

Mahdi, A. A. (1983). *The Iranian Social Formation: Pre–Capitalism, Dependent Capitalism, and the World System*. Unpublished doctoral dssertation, Michigan State University.

Malcolm, J. (1971). The Melville Papers, in Issawi, C. (ed.), *The Economic History of Iran 1800–1914*, 262–67. Chicago: The University of Chicago Press.

Mandel, E. (1968). *Marxist Economic Theory* (Vol. 1). New York: Monthly Review Press.

———. (1970). The Laws of Uneven Development, *New Left Review*, 59, 19–39.

———. (1978). *Late Capitalism*. London: Verso.

———. (1979). *Revolutionary Marxism Today*. New Left Books.

Mansfield, P. (1971). *The British in Egypt*. London: Weidenfeld and Nicolson.

Mao Tse–Tung (1965). *Selected Works of Mao Tse–Tung* (vol. 1). Peking: Foreign Language Press.

Marlowe, J. (1965). *A History of Modern Egypt and Anglo–Egyptian Relations 1800–1956*. Connecticut: Archon Books.

Marx, K. (1971a). *On Colonialism*. New York: International Publishers.

———.(1971b). *A Contribution to the Critique of Political Economy*. Lawrence and Wishart.

———. (1977). *Capital* (Vol. 1). New York: International Publishers.

———. (1980). *Pre–capitalist Economic Formations*. New York: International Publishers.

Mehrain, F. (1979). *Emergence of Capitalist Authoritarian States in Periphery Formations*. Unpublished Doctoral Dissertation. Madison: University of Wisconsin.

Meillasoux, C. (1964). *L'Anthropologie Economique des Gouro de Cote d'Ivoire*. Paris: Mouton.

———. (1980). From Reproduction to Production: A Marxist Approach to Economic Anthropology, in Wolpe, H. (ed.), *The Articulation of Modes of Production*, 189–201. Boston: Routledge & Kegan Paul.

———. (1988). *The Communist Manifesto*, edited by Frederick L. Bender. New York: W. W. Norton and Company.

Melamid, A. (1968). Communications, Transport, Retail Trade and Services, in Fisher, W. B. (ed.), *The Cambridge History of Iran* (Vol. 1), 552–564. Cambridge: The University Printing House.

Metz, H. C. (1990). *Egypt: A Case Study*. Federal Research Division, Library of Congress. Washington, D.C.: Government Printing Office.

Mills, C.W. (1959). *The Sociological Imagination*. New York: Oxford University Press.

Mingione, E. (1981). *Social Conflict in the City*. Oxford: Basil and Blackwell.

Missen, G. J. aand Logan, M. I. (1977). National and Local Distribution Systems and Regional Development: The Case of Kelantan in West Malaysia, *Antipode*, 9, 60–73.

Montagne, R. (1947). *La Civilisation du Desert*. Paris.

Moser, C. (1978). Informal Sector or Petty Commodity Production: Dualism or Dependence in Urban Development? *World Development*, 6, 1040–1064.

Mosto'fi, H. (1957). *Nez–hat al–Gholoub.* translated from Arabic to Persian by M. D. Siaghi. Tehran: Tahouri Publishers.

Mouzelis, N. (1980). Modernization, Underdevelopment, Uneven Development: Prospects for a Theory of Third World Formations, *The Journal of Peasant Studies*, 7(3), 352–74.

Mubarak, A. (1888). *Khitat al–Tawfiqiyah al–Jadidah* (Arabic). Cairo: Bulaq Press.

Munck, R. (1981). Imperialism and Dependency: Recent Debates and Old Dead ends, *Latin American Perspectives,* 8(3–4), 162–179.

Murray, G. W. (1950). *Sons of Ismael: A Study of the Egyptian Bedouin.* New York: The Humanities Press.

Nafisi, S. (1966). *Tarikh–e Siaai va Ejtemai–e Iran* (Iran's Political and Social History), Vol. 1 (Persian).

Nashat, G. (1981). From Bazaar to Market: Foreign Trade and Economic Development in Nineteenth Century Iran, *Iranian Studies*, 14(1–2), 53–85.

Nassef, A. F. (1970). *The Egyptian Labor Force: Its dimensions and Changing Structure, 1907–1960.* Philadelphia.

Niroumand, B. (1969). *Iran; The New Imperialism in Action.* New York: The Monthly Review Press.

Nomani, F. (1972). The Origin and Development of Feudalism in Iran, 1300–1600 A. D, Part 1, *Tahqiqat–e Eqtesadi*, 9(27– 28), summer & fall (in Persian).

Ohmae, Konichi. (1995). *The End of the Nation State: The Rise of Regional Economies. New York: The Free Press.*

Omran, A. R. (ed.). (1973). *Egypt: Population and Prospects.* Chapel Hill: University of North Carolina Population Center.

Palloix, C. (1975). The Internationalization of Capital and the Circuits of social Capital, in Radice, H. (ed.), *International Firms and Modern Imperialism*, 63–88. Baltimore; Penguin Books.

Paydarfar, A. (1967). Modernization Process and Demographic Change, *Sociological Review*, 15(2), 141–53.

———. (1968). *Social Change in a Southern Province of Iran.* Chapel Hill: University of Carolina Press.

Peatti, L. (1968). *The View from the Barrio.* Ann Arbor: The University of Michigan Press.

Peet, R. (1980). Historical Materialism and Mode of Production: A Note on Marx's Perspective and Method, in Peet, R. (ed.), *An Introduction to Marxist Theories of Underdevelopment*, 9–25. Research School of Pacific Studies, Department of Human Geography. Canberra: The Australian National University.

Petruchevsky, I. P. et al. (1967). *Tarikh–i Iran as Dawre–yi Bastan ta payan–i Sade–yi Hezdahum* (Iranian history from Ancient Times to the End of 18th Century). Translated by K. Kishavarz. Tehran (Persian).

Pickvance, C. G. (1976). *Urban Sociology: Critical Essays.* London: Tavistock.

Portes, A. and J. Borocz. (1989). Contemporary Immigration: Theoretical Perspectives on Its Determinants and Modes of Incorporation, *International Migration Review*, 23(3): 606–630.

Portes, A. and Walton, J. (1976). *Urban Latin America: The Political Condition from Above and Below.* Austin: University of Texas Press.

Portez, A., Castells, M. and Benton, L. (1989). *The Informal Economy: Studies in Advanced and Less Developed Countries.* Baltimore, MD: Johns Hopkins University Press.

Poulantzas, N. (1973). *Political Power and Social Class.* London: New Left Books.

Przeworski, A. and Teune, H. (1970). *The Logic of Comparative Social Inquiry.* New York; John Wiley.

Quijano. A. (1974). The Marginal Pole of the Economy and the Marginalized Labor Force, *Economy and Society*, 3, 393– 428.

Raafat, Samir. (1999). "The Baehler Skyline," *Cairo Times,* October 28.

Razavi, H. and Vakil, F. (1984). *The Political Environment of Economic Planning in Iran, 1971–1983: From Monarchy to Islamic Republic.* London: West View Press.

Razi, A. (1968). *Tarikh–I Kamel–I Iran.* Tehran: Eqbal Publishing Co.

Research Group (1970). An Analysis of the Law Governing the First Stage of Land Reform in Iran, *Tahqiqiat–e eqtesadi*, 7(17), Winter (in Persian).

———. (1984). A Review of the Statistics of the First Stage of Land Reform, *Tahqiqat–e Eqtesadi*, 2(7–8) (in Persian).

Rey, P. P. (1973). *Les Alliances Des Classes.* Paris: Maspero.

Richards, A. (1981). *Egypt's Agricultural Development: Technical and Social Change, 1800–1980.* Boulder: Westview Press.

Riyahi, F. (1976). *Bar–Rasi–e Elal–e Muhajerat–e Roostayian be Shahr* (An Investigation of the Causes for Rural–Urban Migration). A Summary of Discussion in the Bou Ali University. Hamadan (in Persian).

Roberts, B. (1978). *Cities of Peasants: The Political Economy of Urbanization in the Third World.* London: Edward Arnold.

Rodenbeck, M. (1998). *Cairo: The City Victorious.* Cairo: American University in Cairo Press.

Ronall, J. O. (1976). Foreign Investment in Iran, in *Iranian–American Survey 1976*, 36–39. New York: Manhattan Publishing Co.

Roxborough, I. (1976). Dependency Theory in the Sociology of Development: Some Theoretical Problems, *West African Journal of Sociology and*

*Political Science*, 1(2), 116–23.

Saab, G. S. (1967). *The Egyptian Agrarian Reform, 1952–1962*. London: Oxford University Press.

Safa, H. I. (1982). *Towards a Political Economy of Urbanization in Third World Countries*. Delhi: Oxford University Press.

Santos, M. (1976). Articulation of Modes of Production and the Two Circuits of Urban Economy, *Pacific Viewpoint*, 17, 23–26.

Santos, M. (1977). Spatial Dialectics: The Two Circuits of Urban Economy in Underdeveloped Countries, *Antipode*, 9(3), 49–59.

———. (1979). *The Shared Space: The Two Circuits of the Urban Economy in Underdeveloped Countries*. Methuen.

Sassen, Saskia. 1996. *Losing Control? Sovereignty in an Age of Globalization.* New York: Columbia University Press.

Scott, A. M. (1978). Who are the Self–employed? in Gerry, C. and Broomley, R. (eds.), *The Casual Poor in Third World Cities*. London: John Wiley.

Schroeder, P. (2007). *Memories of an American Boy.* Accessed 10-17-2007: http://www.iranian.com/Abadan/2007/April/1958/index.html.

Seale, J. et al. (1982). *Small–Scale Enterprises in Egypt: Fayoum and Kalyubiya Governorates Phase I Survey Results*. Michigan state University Rural Development Series, Working Paper No. 23, Department of Agricultural Economics.

Shaji'i, Z. (1965). *Nemayandegan–i Majlis–i Shawra–yi Melli dar Bistu Yek Dawreh–i Qanunguzari* (The Members of the National Assembly during Twenty–One Legislative Sessions). Tehran (in Persian).

Shamim, A. A. (1963). *Iran Dar Doreh–i saltanat–i Qajar* (Iran during the Qajar Reign). Tehran (in Persian).

Shearman, J. (1961). A View of Tehran, *the Geographical Magazine*, 33(10), 569–78.

Slater, D. (1975). Colonialism and the Spatial Structure of Underdevelopment: Outline of an Alternative Approach, with Special Reference to Tanzania, *Progress in Planning*, 5(4), 163–67.

———. (1977). Geography and Underdevelopment—Part I, *Antipode*, 9(3), 1–31.

———. (1978). Towards a Political Economy of Urbanization in Peripheral Capitalist Societies: Problems of Theory and Method With Illustration from Latin America, *International Journal of Urban and Regional Research*, 5, 26–52.

Smith, J. M. (1978). Turanian Nomadism and Iranian Politics, *Iranian Studies*, 11, 57–83.

Soja, E. W. (1980). The Socio–spatial Dialectic, *Annals of the Association of*

*American Geographers*, 70(2), 207–225.

Souza, R. and Tokman, V. (1976). The Informal Sector in Latin America, *International Labor Review*, 114(3), 355—366.

Sovani, N.V. (1964). The Analysis of Over–Urbanization, *Economic Development and Cultural Change*, 129 (2), 113–22.

Stiglitz, Joseph E. (2002). *Globalization and Its Discontents*. New York: W. W. Norton & Co.

Sunderland, E. (1968). Pastoralism, Nomadism and the Social Anthropology of Iran, in Fisher, W. B. (ed.), *The Cambridge History of Iran* (Vol. 1). Cambridge: The University Publishing House.

Szentes, T. (1971). *The Political Economy of Underdevelopment*. Budapest: Akademiai Kiads.

Tabb, W. and Sawers, L. (eds.). (1978). *Marxism and the Metropolis: New Perspectives in Urban Political Economy*. New York: Oxford University Press.

Taylor, J. (1979). *From Modernization to Modes of Production: A Critique of Development and Underdevelopment*. London: McMillan.

Terray, E. (1972). *Marxism and Primitive Societies*. New York: Monthly Review Press.

Tignor, R. (1982). Equity in Egypt's Recent Past: 1945–1952, in Abdel–Khalek, G. and Tignor, R. (eds.), *The Political Economy of Income Distribution in Egypt*, 20–54. New York: Holmes & Meier.

Turk, A. T. (1973). The Sociological Relevance of History: A Footnote to Research on Legal Control in South Africa, in Armer, M. and Grimshaw, A. D. (eds.), *Comparative Social Research: Methodological Problems and Strategies*, 285–299. New York: John Wiley & Sons.

UN–Habitat. (2004). *State of the World's Cities: Trends in Middle East & North Africa*: http://ww2.unhabitat.org/mediacentre/documents/sowc/NorthAfrica.pdf, accessed 2/9/2008.

United Nations (1980). *Patterns of Urban and Rural Population Growth*. Population Studies No. 68, Department of International Economic and Social Affairs.

UN/UNESCO (1957). *Urbanization in Asia and Far East*. Proceedings of the Joint UN/UNESCO Seminar, Bangkok, 1956. Calcutta: UNESCO Research Center for Social Implications of Industrialization in Southern Asia.

Vali, A. (1980). The Character of the Organization of Production in Iranian Agriculture, 1891–1925, in Slauth, G. (ed.), *Iran, Pre–Capitalism Capitalism and Revolution*. Saarbrucken, Germany: Verlag Breitenbach Publishers.

Vardasbi, A. (1976). *Elal–i Kondi va na–payvastagi–ye Takamol–i Jamee'–ye*

*Feodali–ye Iran* (The Causes of Slowness and Discontinuity in the Evolution of Feudalism in Iran). Tehran: Chapar Publications (in Persian).

Wallerstein, I. (1974). The Rise and Future Demise of the World Capitalist System: Concepts for Comparative Analysis, *Comparative Studies in Society and History*, 16(4).

———. (1979). *The Capitalist World Economy*. Cambridge: Cambridge Univer–sity Press.

Walters, P. et al. (1980). *Conceptualization of the Urbanization Process in the Core and the Periphery*. Paper presented at the Society for the Study of Social Problems. New York.

Walton, J. (1976). Political Economy of World Urban System: Directions for Comparative Urban Research, in Walton, J. and Masotti, L. (eds.), *The City in Comparative Perspective*. New York: Sage Publications.

———. (1981). The New Urban Sociology, *International Social Science Journal*, 33(2), 374–390.

Warren, B. (1973). Imperialism and Capitalist Industrialization, *New Left Review*, 81, 3–44.

Waterbury, J. (1978). *Egypt: Burden of the Past, Options for the Future*. Bloomington: Indiana University Press.

———. (1983). *The Egypt of Nasser and Sadat: The Political Economy of Two Regimes*. Princeton: Princeton University Press.

Watkins. M. H. (1963). A Staple Theory of Economic Growth, *the Canadian Journal of Economics and Political Science*, 29 (2), 141–58.

Weulersse, J. (1946). *Paysans de Syrie et du Proche Orient*. Paris.

Wolpe, H. (1975). The Theory of Internal Colonialism: The South African Case, in Oxaal et al. (eds.), *Beyond the Sociology of Development*. London: Routledge & Kegan Paul.

———. (1980). Introduction, in Wolpe, H. (ed.), *The Articulation of Modes of Production*, 1–43. Boston: Routledge & Kegan Paul.

World Bank. (1977). *Arab Republic of Egypt: Survey of Small–Scale Industry*. Report No. 1818–EGT, Dec.

———. (2000). *World Bank Approves Loans to Iran for Primary Health and Seweragre*. News Release No. 2000/352/S (May 18).

Wright, E. O. (1976). Contradictory Class Locations, *New Left Review*, 98 (July/August).

Zolberg, A. (1989). The Next Waves: Migration Theory for a Changing World, *International Migration Review*, 23(3): 403–430.

Zonis, M. (1968). *Iran: The Politics of Insecurity*. Unpublished doctoral dissertation. MIT.

# Index

Abadan, 54, 74, 87, 89–92, 103, 189; as
   a dual city, 90
Abdel Nasser, Jamal, 147, 150
Abrahamian, E., 4, 36, 42, 49, 61–62,
   70, 75n1, 79, 82, 86, 98
Abu-Lughod, J., 28, 29, 132n3, 144–
   45, 154, 156–57, 159–63, 165,
   169, 175n1, 194
Ahwaz, 74, 87, 103, 189
AIOC. See Anglo-Iranian Oil company
Agrarian economy: mono-culture, 141,
   145; pre-capitalist, 2, 105;
   subsistence, 26
al Afghani, Jamal ed-Din, 134
Alexandria, 29, 124, 126, 127–29, 131,
   135, 137, 183–84, 188, 192–96,
   198–99; infrastructure, 138;
   location of factories, 139, 143–45,
   159, 160, 163, 165–68, 172, 174
American Civil War, 56, 124, 182
Anglo-Iranian Oil Company (AIOC),
   75n4, 76–77, 90, 92
Anzali, 54, 183
Aqa Mohammad Khan, 54
Arab Socialism, 152–53, 157n4, 191,
   203
Arabi, Colonel Ahmed, 134–35, 161,
   184–85, 190
Arak, 73, 96
Ashraf, Ahmad, 28, 35–36, 40–42, 48,
   59n2, 65–66, 92, 93n1
Astarabad, 51, 53, 75n4, 96

Babol, vii, 54
backward linkage effects, 5n1, 22, 27
Bank Melli, 66, 73
Bank Misr, 142
banking, 29, 40, 49, 56, 66, 86, 125–

26, 186; modern, 66
Barfroosh, 50–51, 53–54, 183
bazaar, 18, 48–49, 61–63, 73, 86, 97,
   105
brain drain, 205
Britain, 62, 64, 147, 182
British colonial policy, 64, 140–41,
   185–86, 188
British colonial rule, 137, 160
British colonialism, 133–45, 174
British Petroleum, 77–78
British colonization of Egypt, 4, 149
Bushehr, 53–56, 183

Cairo, 2–4, 29–30, 32, 90, 114, 121–22,
   124, 126, 128–29, 131, 133–34,
   137–40, 143–45, 154–63, 165–69,
   172, 174–75, 184, 188–89, 192–
   96, 198–99; colonial, 139, 160,
   162, 174, 195; pre-capitalist, 139,
   162, 194
capital: centralization of, 9; Concentration of, 101, 174, 186, 198
capital accumulation, 2, 9, 11–12, 18,
   23, 70, 97, 137, 141, 163, 186
capital markets, 201, 208
capitalism: commercial, 61–75;
   dependent, 18, 23, 150, 166, 197;
   peripheral, 3, 12, 23n3
capitalist class, 73, 101, 152, 197
capitalist development, 2, 13–14, 23n3,
   65–66, 70, 78, 97, 100–01, 104,
   187–88; dependent, 3, 98, 110,
   152, 189–90; nascent, 153; state-
   controlled, 11, 68; unrestricted,
   153
Caspian Sea, vii, 51, 543, 56, 183
Castells, M. 5n3, 9–11, 14, 16, 21, 28

*Index*

# About the Author

Mohammad Ali Chaichian is Professor of Sociology at Mount Mercy College. Before entering academics, he was a practicing architect in Tehran, Iran, in the 1970s and later studied urban planning at the University of Michigan and sociology at Michigan State University. He has published numerous articles on contemporary Iran, Egypt, China, urban political economy, immigration issues, and race relations. His book, *White Racism on the Western Urban Frontier: Dynamics of Race and Class in Dubuque, Iowa* was published in 2006 (Africa World Press).